BORDEAUX

ROUGH
GUIDES

Written by
Stuart But

Contents

Introduction to
Bordeaux

Bordeaux, the world's largest urban UNESCO World Heritage Site, cuts
a fine figure. A blend of Neoclassical grandeur and modern innovation,
its multitude of historic and elegant buildings tower above the
buzzing quays that line the River Garonne. Bordeaux, the sixth largest
city in France, has always had a reputation for its first-rate museums,
excellent shopping, fine restaurants and lively student-led nightlife,
but in the past few years the city has upped its game. Ambitious
regeneration projects of the former docklands and the opening of a
flurry of spectacular new museums and galleries, including the futuristic
Cité du Vin, an incredible decanter shaped work of modern art that
houses one of the best wine museums in Europe, have all helped to
turn Bordeaux into one of the most happening cities in France.

At the heart of the old town centre is place de la Bourse. Smart streets radiate out from
here: the city's main shopping streets, rue Ste-Catherine and the cours de l'Intendance
to the south and west, and the sandy, tree-lined allées de Tourny to the northwest.
The narrow streets around place du Parlement and place St-Pierre – lined with ancient
townhouses doubling up as bistros, boutiques and vintage shops – make for a pleasant
stroll.

Crossing the river just south of the fifteenth-century Porte Cailhau is the
impressive Pont de Pierre – "Stone Bridge". It was built on Napoleon's orders during
the Spanish campaigns, with seventeen arches in honour of his victories. The views of
the river and quays from here are stunning, especially at dusk.

Bordeaux's best museums are scattered in the streets around the cathedral. Directly
behind the classical hôtel de ville is the Musée des Beaux-Arts. It has a small star-studded
European art collection, featuring Titian and Rubens, and good temporary exhibitions.

To the northwest of the city centre is the beautiful formal park, the Jardin Public,
containing the city's botanical gardens. To the east of the Jardin Public, close to

BORDEAUX

Bassins des Lumières
RUE DE NEW YORK
RUE LUCIE AUBRAC
BACALAN
RUE ROPRE ST-MAUR
RUE HENRI BRUNET
Bassins à Flot n° 2
Musée Mer Marine
RUE DELBOS
RUE DES ÉTRANGERS
BASSINS À FLOT
Les Vivres de l'Art
PL. PIERRE CÉTOIS
QUAI DE GIRONDE
Bassins à Flot n° 1
Les Halles de Bacalan
QUAI ARMAND LALANDE
QUAI DU MARNE
Cité du Vin
La Cité du Vin
CAP Sciences
PONT JACQUES CHABAN DELMAS

RUE RIGAL
R. ABEL ANTOUNE
RUE ABEL
ALLÉE DE BOUTAUT
BOULEVARD ALFRED DANEY
RUE JEAN HAMEAU
RUE LUCIEN FAURE
COURS LOUIS TARGUE
RUE LUCIEN FAURE

Le Bouscat
AVENUE ARISTIDE BRIAND
PL. RAVEZIES
AVENUE JULES GUESDE
ROND-POINT DE FUKUOKA
ALLÉE HAUSSMANN
COURS DU RACCORDEMENT
COURS BOURON
RUE BOURON
Musée de l'Histoire Maritime de Bordeaux
RUE ÉDOUARD VAILLANT
RUE ORLOFF
RUE CHANTECRIT
RUE DE LA PALINGENIE

AVENUE MARCELIN BERTHELOT
BOULEVARD GODARD
R. CALIXTE CAMILLE
CHARTRONS
COURS SAINT-LOUIS
RUE SAINT-LOUIS
CITÉ CHANTECRIT
PL. LEWIS BROWN
PL. JOSÉPHINE
RUE DUPATY

BOULEVARD GODARD
RUE DU DR ALBERT SCHWEITZER
GRAND PARC
RUE DES TRÈBES PORTMANN
AVENUE ÉMILE COUNORD
COURS DU MÉDOC
COURS JOURNU AUBER
RUE PRUNIER
RUE BALGUERIE STUTTENBERG
Saint-Martial
QUAI DE BACALAN

RUE ROBERT-SCHUMAN
COURS DE LUZE
RUE MARSAN
COURS SAINT-LOUIS
RUE DE LEYBARDIE
COURS DU MÉDOC
RUE POYENNE
COURS BALGUERIE

RUE MANDRON
RUE ALBERT
RUE CONDORCET
RUE BIMUD
RUE DU JARDIN PUBLIC
RUE FONDAUGE
Le M.U.R

Parc Rivière
RUE CAMILLE GODARD
RUE CAMILLE GODARD
RUE PAUL VERLAINE
RUE PORTAL
RUE BARREYRE
Musée du Vin et du Négoce
Les Hangars (Médoc)
Fabrique Pola

SAINT SEURIN FONDAUDÈGE
RUE MANDRON
RUE FRÈRE
RUE FRÈRE
RUE DUCAU
R. MINVIELLE
RUE DE LA MARTINIQUE
RUE BORIE
Saint-Louis-des-Chartrons
Bastide Darwin
QUAI DE BRAZZA
R. DU COMMANDANT COUSTEAU

RUE LAGRANGE
RUE ALBERT PITRES
RUE MANDRON
R. RAZE
Bastide Darwin
Grand Moulins de Paris
QUAI DES QUEYRIES
R. DU MARECHAL NIEL

RUE DAVID JOHNSTON
RUE LAROCHE
RUE LE CARPENTIER
R. DE LA COURSE
P. DOUMER
PL. MITCHELL
QUAI DES CHARTRONS
BASTIDE-BRAZZA
RUE BOUTHIER

RUE FONDAUDÈGE
RUE D'AVIAU
R. CONSTANTIN
Darwin Eco-Système
RUE HORTENSE

Saint-Ferdinand
RUE NAUJAC
Jardin Botanique
Palais du Capitole
CR XAVIER ARNOZAN
Parc aux Angéliques
RUE REIGNIER

R. DE LA CROIX DE SEGUEY
Jardin Public
Musée d'Art Contemporain
Jardin Botanique de Bordeaux
BASTIDE-NIEL

PL. DE LA LILE
Museum Bordeaux Sciences et Nature
ALLÉES DE CHARTRES
ALLÉE JEAN GIONO
AVENUE THIERS

Palais Gallien
RUE FONDAUDÈGE
Monument aux Girondins
ALLÉES DE BRISTOL
QUAI DES QUEYRIES
RUE NUYENS
AVENUE ABADIE
COURS LE ROUGE

RUE TURENNE
RUE TURENNE
QUINCONCES
ALLÉES DES QUINCONCES
Cinéma Megarama
Sainte-Marie de la Bastide
COURS PAUL CAMELLE

Basilique St-Seurin
PL. DE CASTEJA
ALLÉES DE MUNICH
L'École du Vin de Bordeaux
Espace Vert des Quais
Quinconces (Jean-Jaurès)
LA BASTIDE
RUE DE CHÂTEAUNEUF

R.C. MARIONNEAU
RUE JUDAÏQUE
PL. DES GRANDS HOMMES
TRIANGLE D'OR
PL. DE LA COMÉDIE
Palais de la Bourse
Miroir d'eau
Stalingrad (Parlier)
RUE DE LA BENAUGE

MÉRIADECK
PLACE GAMBETTA
Notre Dame
Grand-Théâtre
PL. DE LA BOURSE
Musée National des Douanes
Embarcadère des Quincances
PLACE DE STALINGRAD
RUE HENRI DUNANT

Mériadeck Shopping Mall
Musée des Arts Décoratifs
HÔTEL DE VILLE
Saint-Pierre
SAINT-PIERRE
Jardins des Lumières
Parc des Berges

Bordeaux Métropole
Musée de l'Illusion
Hôtel de Ville de Bordeaux (Palais Rohan)
Porte Cailhau
Ponton d'honneur
QUAI DESCHAMPS

Patinoire de Mériadeck
Musée des Beaux-Arts
Château du Hâ
Cathédrale Saint-André
Musée d'Aquitaine
Porte de Bourgogne
PONT DE PIERRE
Benauge
BOULEVARD JOLIOT CURIE

SAINT-BRUNO SAINT-VICTOR
Sainte-Eulalie
Saint-Paul
Saint-Éloi
Grosse Cloche
SAINT-MICHEL
Basilique Saint-Michel

Great Synagogue
Porte d'Aquitaine
Musée d'Ethnographie
Théâtre National de Bordeaux en Aquitaine
Conservatoire de Bordeaux - Jacques Thibaud

SAINT-GENÈS
Saint-Nicolas
Marché des Capucins
CAPUCINS - VICTOIRE
Sainte-Croix
Saint-Jean Train Station
SAINT-JEAN
BELCIER

NANSOUTY

0   400
metres

the river, is the Musée d'Art Contemporain on rue Ferrère, occupying a converted nineteenth-century warehouse. The vast, arcaded hall is magnificent in its own right, and provides an ideal setting for the post-1960 sculpture and installations by artists like Richard Long and Sol LeWitt. Following the curve of the river north from the Musée d'Art Contemporain, you reach the down-at-heel but historic Chartrons, once the wine district. It's becoming increasingly cool, sprouting artists' studios, vintage shops and restaurants, as well as a Sunday farmers' market.

You only have to spend a few moments pacing the streets of Bordeaux's historic neighbourhoods, passing grand mansions and public buildings with imposing facades, to realise that this is a wealthy city. It's the wide and sluggish Garonne River that Bordeaux has to thank for that wealth. At one point in time Bordeaux was the second biggest port in the world. Trade (mainly sugar and slaves) with the West Indies brought some of the money to the city but the real wealth came from the grape. Bordeaux sits at the centre of the planet's best-known wine producing region.

Touring the local **vineyards** and sampling a few local wines is one of the great pleasures of Bordeaux. The wine regions lie in a great semicircle around the city, starting with the **Médoc** in the north, then skirting east through **St-Émilion**, before finishing south of the city among the vineyards of the **Sauternes**. In between, the less prestigious districts are also worth investigating, especially **Blaye**, to the north of Bordeaux, and **Entre-Deux-Mers**, to the east.

You will quickly see that there's more to the region than wine though. Many of the Médoc's eighteenth-century châteaux are architectural treasures, while a vast fortress dominates the town of Blaye, and there's an older, ruined castle at Villandraut on the edge of the Sauternes. St-Émilion, eternally loved by tourists, is the prettiest of the wine towns, and has the unexpected bonus of a cavernous underground church. For scenic views you can't beat the green, gentle hills of Entre-Deux-Mers and its ruined abbey, **La Sauve-Majeur**.

The mighty Atlantic Ocean influences everything around this corner of France. The west winds carry with them the tang of salty air and head toward the coast and you'll discover long, wild and eternally beautiful golden sand beaches that fill with surfers and beach babes throughout the long, hot summer months. Gracious old Arcachon, set on the shores of a vast inland sea known as the Bassin d'Arcachon, is by far the most attractive of the coastal towns. Just to the south is the Saharan-like Dune du Pilat, the biggest sand dune in Europe.

Elsewhere in the region you can discover impregnable fortresses, reserves filled with ornithological wonders, medieval churches and huge lakes tailormade for waterborne fun.

When to go

Winters in and around Bordeaux can be very wet and cold snaps are not unusual, but far more common are long periods of dry, settled weather and pleasant temperatures.

AVERAGE MONTHLY TEMPERATURES AND RAINFALL

	Jan	Feb	Mar	Apr	May	Jun	Jul	Aug	Sep	Oct	Nov	Dec
Max/min (°C)	9/3	11/2	14/5	17/7	21/11	25/14	26/16	27/16	24/13	19/11	13/7	10/4
Max/min (°F)	49/37	51/37	58/41	63/45	69/51	76/58	89/61	80/61	75/57	67/52	56/44	51/39
Rainfall (days)	8	7	7	9	9	7	6	6	6	8	9	9

Spring is often wetter than winter, although some years see glorious weather. Temperatures begin to pick up around April and can reach the mid-30s by late-May. The height of **Summer** is almost always long and reliably hot. It's increasingly common for temperatures to creep above 40 degrees. At other times expect the temperature to hover in the high 20s. That said, early summer can see unpredictable rain, and heavy thunderstorms have become more commonplace; even violent at times. **Autumn** is longer and drier than spring, bringing sunny and pleasant weather until the end of October that can sometimes allow a t-shirt to be worn comfortably in the afternoon.

The most important factor in deciding when to visit is the **holiday seasons**. Bordeaux itself is rarely over-run with visitors, but the wine towns and – even more so – the beaches are packed in July and August, peaking in the first two weeks of August, when hotels and campsites are bursting at the seams and top-rank sights are absolutely heaving. Conversely, from November to Easter many places close down completely. Overall, the **best time to visit** is September and early October, with May and June coming a close second.

VIEW OF THE CHARTRONS DISTRICT FROM THE GARONNE RIVER

Author picks

Our authors have explored every corner of Bordeaux and beyond in order to uncover the very best the city and neighbouring region has to offer. Here are some of their favourite things to see, do, and experience.

St-Émilion Yes, it can be overrun with visitors, but St-Emilion (see page 121) is pure poetry in stone and even if you don't visit any of the famous châteaux it's still one of the more charming villages in the southwest.

Blaye Often overlooked but fabulous in every way, the imposing battlements of riverside Blaye (see page 117) are an architectural wonder.

Bordeaux Métropole hiking trail See Bordeaux in a new way by hiking (see page 68) this multi-day, but otherwise easy, trail that encircles the city. It's the first official long distance urban trail in France.

Southern culture The people of Bordeaux and, indeed, the people of all of southwest France, are proud of their individuality from the rest of the French (by which they really mean the Parisians) and most people go to great pains to emphasize this. Whether it's a local *boulangerie* displaying a sign reading "*Ici on dit chocolatines*" ("Here, we say chocolatines") in reference to people in the north calling their chocolate croissants *pain au chocolat* to the locals easy disregard for basic time keeping; the southwest is in its essence very different.

Cycling Hundreds of kilometres of cycle paths (see page 25) lace across the countryside and one of the great joys of this part of France is a lazy peddle between wine villages, along the coast or even down the quays of central Bordeaux.

Our author recommendations don't end here. We've flagged up our favourite places – a perfectly sited hotel, an atmospheric café, a special restaurant – throughout the Guide, highlighted with the ★ symbol.

HISTORIC BLAYE

CYCLING IS A GREAT WAY TO SEE BORDEAUX CITY

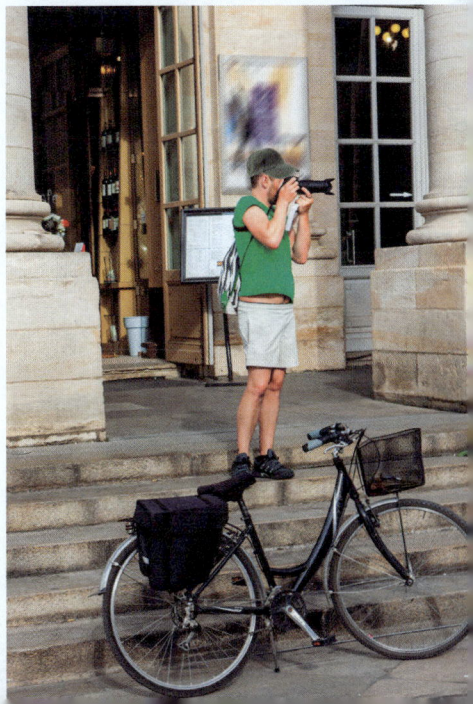

15

things not to miss

It's not possible to see everything that Bordeaux and the countryside around has to offer in one visit – and we don't suggest you try. What follows, in no particular order, is a selective taste of the city and region's highlights, from world-class museums to sublime beaches, delicious wine and historic monuments. All entries have a page reference to take you straight into the Guide, where you can find out more.

1 CITÉ DU VIN

See page 58

The centrepiece of the
ambitious regeneration of
the former docklands, the
Cité du Vin is Bordeaux's
unmissable sight. The
decanter-shaped building
is a modern architecture
masterpiece and inside you
will discover a futuristic
museum that explores
viniculture to its fullest.

2 HISTORIC BORDEAUX

See page 50

Such is the grandeur of
Bordeaux's superb ensemble
of eighteenth-century
architecture that it comes
as no surprise to anybody
that almost the entirety of
central Bordeaux has been
declared a UNESCO World
Heritage Site.

3 WINE TOURISM

See page 58

What would Bordeaux
be without the humble
grape? Devote your days to
answering this question by
signing up to a short course
at the famed École du Vin de
Bordeaux after which you can
head out into the countryside
to tour the vineyards and
enjoy some tastings in the
many stunning châteaux.

4 BORDEAUX BISTROS

See page 81

One of the delights of
visiting this city is its many
bistros. Some are solidly
old fashioned; others are
experimenting with fusion
trends, but all have a timeless
sense of place that makes
them an essential part of the
Bordeaux experience.

5 SURFING

See page 102

The coastline of Gironde
and Les Landes is home to
some of the world's finest
beach break waves. Close
to Bordeaux, Lacanau is the
big-name spot but the entire
coastline is one endless
surfer's playground. Sign up
for a lesson at any one of the
many summer surf schools.

6

7

8

6 BASSIN D'ARCACHON

See page 125

Like a calm, inland sea, the Bassin d'Arcachon is a place to savour. Sail to small islets where thousands of birds gather, drift past the white sand bar islands of the Banc d'Arguin and eat fresh oysters in the art-deco town of Arcachon.

7 DUNE DU PYLA

See page 127

Europe's largest dune is a mighty mountain of golden sand and the views from the top span the entire Côte d'Argent.

8 STREET ART

See page 58

While Bordeaux has some memorable art galleries, the streets themselves often serve as a giant canvas for creative street artists. Check out the Chartrons and Bacalan neighbourhoods as well as the Darwin Eco-Système for bold and interesting street art.

9 ISLAND HOPPING IN THE GARONNE

See page 116

The mighty Garonne is dotted with islands. Mostly uninhabited yet often still used for growing vines, taking a boat out to some of them is a wonderfully romantic way to spend an afternoon.

10 ST-ÉMILION

See page 121

The world's most famous wine town also happens to be one of the prettiest in the vicinity of Bordeaux. Spend your days exploring historic buildings, visiting legendary châteaux and taking in the pretty vine-clad countryside.

11 GRAND THÉÂTRE

See page 41

It's a tough call but the most beautiful of all of Bordeaux's many eighteenth century buildings just might be the Grand Théâtre. Snap a picture from outside or dress up for a memorable night of opera, ballet or classical music.

12 MARKETS

See page 97

From the buzzing daily markets of Bordeaux to weekly markets bringing life to otherwise quiet rural villages, visiting some of the region's markets is a great way to learn about regional delicacies.

13 BLAYE

See page 117

Awarded UNESCO World Heritage status, the small town of Blaye is utterly dominated by the imposing walls of its riverside citadel. Clamber around the ramparts, visit nearby vineyards, check out some Roman ruins and you'll quickly understand why Blaye is one of the best day trips you can make from Bordeaux.

14 SOULAC-SUR-MER

See page 129

Right at the northern tip of the coastline, where the Garonne spills into the Atlantic, the small town of Soulac-sur-Mer, which has attractive art-deco architecture, endless cycle trails, lighthouses to climb and a beach for everyone, is one of the unsung highlights of the Atlantic coast.

15 ABBAYE DE LA SAUVE-MAJEURE

See page 123

This ruined abbey was once an important stop for pilgrims en route to Santiago de Compostela in Spain. Listen out for their ghosts as you explore what remains of the Romanesque apse and chapels.

13

14

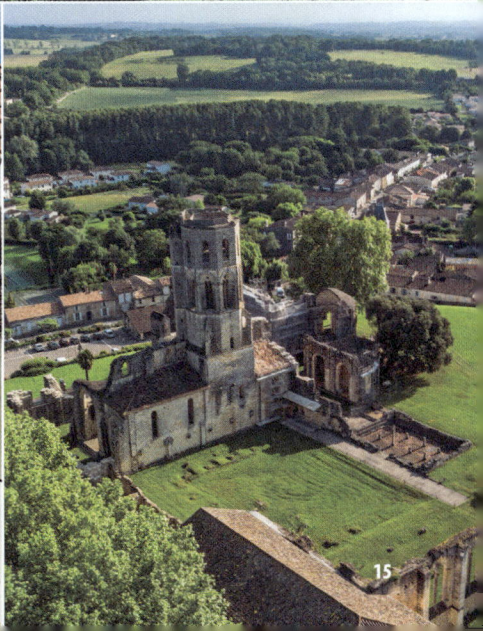

15

Itineraries

Bordeaux is perfect for exploring on foot or overground on its excellent tramway system, and makes for a perfect city break. Beyond the city limits, though, the area's renowned vineyards and beaches offer everything from wine and oyster tasting to lazy cycles and adrenalin-fuelled days in the surf. Combine the two itineraries or use each as a standalone trip.

A WEEKEND IN BORDEAUX

DAY 1

❶ **Tour Pey-Berland** On day one, get your bearings by clambering to the top of this tower which will afford sweeping views across the city. See page 39

❷ **Cathédrale Saint-André** Then it's across to the magnificent Cathédrale St-André, the seat of the archbishop and a thousand years of history in its nave and vaults. See page 39

❸ **Musée d'Aquitaine** Head down the street for a date with history at this impressive museum. See page 38

❹ **Bistro stop** Afterwards reward yourself with a leisurely lunch in one of the old town's many excellent bistros. Then walk north along the riverside quais to the Place de la Bourse, which is hemmed by stunning architecture. See page 81

❺ **Jardin Public** Head next toward this oasis of green in the city centre for a short pondside siesta, see page 42

❻ **Basilique St-Seurin** The afternoon can then be spent going back in time at the eleventh-century Basilique St-Seurin and wandering about the ruins of Palais Gallien — just a ten-minute stroll apart. See page 46

❼ **Grand Théâtre** Finish the day with an evening catching opera or classical music at this magnificent building. See page 41

DAY 2

❶ **Cité du Vin** After breakfast at your hotel, it's time to explore new Bordeaux. Begin at the unmissable Cité du Vin which will take up much of the morning. See page 58

❷ **CAP Sciences** Next stop is the family-friendly and fascinating for all science museum. CAP Sciences. There are plenty of nearby lunch options which will set you up for the afternoon. See page 63

❸ **Bassin des Lumières** Spend the afternoon at this state-of-the-art immersive gallery. See page 60

❹ **Darwin Eco-Système** For an evening *apéro*, cross the river to the where you can have a drink

---

Create your own itinerary with Rough Guides. Whether you're after adventure or a family-friendly holiday, we have a trip for you, with all the activities you enjoy doing and the sights you want to see. All our trips are devised by local experts who get the most out of the destination. Visit **www.roughguides.com/trips** to chat with one of our travel agents.

while being watched over by a giant gorilla as skateboarders flip and spin in front of you before dinner in and around Place de la Bourse. See page 68

WINE AND BEACHES

A week is the absolute minimum amount of time required to get a brief overview of the region surrounding Bordeaux. Stay longer and you can enjoy a few nights in each destination.

DAYS 1-2

Devote the first two days to the wine country east and south of the city. **St-Émilion** makes the most obvious base and there are dozens of châteaux in the area open to (pre-arranged) visits. For a change of scene, make sure you drop by the whimsical **Abbaye de La Sauve-Majeure**, a short drive south of St-Émilion. See pages 121 and 123

DAY 3

On day three head to the Médoc region north of Bordeaux. **Pauillac** makes a good base for more châteaux visits as well as boat trips to some of the islands in the Garonne River and the superb

riverside citadel of **Blaye**. See pages 113 and 117

DAY 4

Soulac-sur-Mer A 50-minute drive north of Pauillac will bring you to Soulac-sur-Mer. This charming resort town has bucketloads of character with its pretty Belle Époque villas, long, sandy shoreline and lively music events throughout the summer. Don't miss the UNESCO world heritage site of Basilica Notre-Dame-des-Terres, which was almost completely swallowed up by sand until the mid-nineteenth century. See page 129

DAY 5

Lacanau Winding back down the coast, this is a surf centre with gorgeous beaches. Spend a day here hitting the waves the region is so famous for. See page 128

DAY 6-7

Cap-Ferret This is the kind of Hamptons-esque place you'd be happy to dig your feet into the sand and settle down for an entire summer — at the very least, aim to spend at least two nights here. See page 127

Basics

Getting there

The quickest way to reach Bordeaux from most parts of the United Kingdom and Ireland is by air. From southern England, however, the Eurostar, with a change of station and train in Paris, makes for a more romantic way of reaching Bordeaux. It takes a little over two-hours from London to Paris and the new high-speed trains means it's less than two hours from Paris to Bordeaux. If you want to take your car to France though, cross-Channel ferries are usually cheaper. From the US and Canada a number of airlines fly direct to Paris, from where you can pick up onward connections to Bordeaux by plane or train. You can also fly direct to Paris from South Africa, while the best fares from Australia and New Zealand are generally via Asia.

Whether you are travelling by air, sea or rail, prices increasingly depend on how far in advance you book, but will also depend on the **season**. Fares are at their highest from around early June to the end of August, when the weather is best, drop during the "shoulder" seasons – roughly September to October and April to May – and are at their cheapest during the low season, November to March (excluding Christmas and New Year when prices are hiked up and seats are at a premium). Note also that flying at weekends can be more expensive; price ranges quoted below assume midweek travel, and include all taxes and surcharges.

Flights from the UK and Ireland

There is a good range of flights between the UK, Ireland and Bordeaux. The main budget airline serving Bordeaux from the UK is EasyJet (https://easyjet.com) (Ryanair pulled out of Bordeaux in 2024), which links London, Manchester and Bristol with Bordeaux. Routes change frequently and with Ryanair quitting Bordeaux it's likely that other airlines will fill in the gaps. With southwest France being a summer holiday destination, some of the budget airline routes only

operate between Easter and late October. **Tickets** work on a quota system, and it's wise to book ahead for the cheapest fares. If you're prepared to be flexible about days that you fly and travel out of season then ticket prices can be very low but surcharges for checked-in baggage, seat allocation and priority boarding can all bump up the price considerably.

It's worth checking out the **traditional carriers**, such as Air France, British Airways and Aer Lingus, which have streamlined their schedules and lowered prices in response to competition from budget airlines, and these can sometimes be just as competitively priced with a better service.

There are no direct Bordeaux-UK/Ireland flights with **Air France** (http://airfrance.com) and you will need to change in Paris (check that your arrival airport in Paris is the same as the departure one or that there is at least enough time to travel between the airports). From Paris Air France operates several times daily to London Heathrow, Dublin and regional airports such as Birmingham and Manchester. **British Airways** (http://ba.com) has direct flights daily from Bordeaux to London Gatwick. In Ireland, **Aer Lingus** (https://aerlingus.ie) offers nonstop flights from Dublin to Bordeaux.

It's also worth looking at nearby airports as – despite being smaller - they sometimes have a better range of flights to the UK with budget airlines. La Rochelle, Biarritz and Bergerac are all within two hours' drive or train ride from Bordeaux. From La Rochelle EasyJet flies to Bristol, London-Gatwick and Manchester. Ryanair flies to Cork, Dublin and London Stansted. From Biarritz EasyJet flies to London Gatwick. Ryanair flies to Edinburgh, Dublin and London Stansted. From Bergerac, Ryanair flies to Bournemouth, Bristol, East Midlands, Liverpool, Edinburgh and London Stansted. BA flies to Southampton and London City and Jet2 flies to Leeds-Bradford and Manchester.

Flights from the US and Canada

There is only one direct flight from North America to Bordeaux with Air Transat (http://airtransat.com) flying between Montreal and Bordeaux. Otherwise,

---

A BETTER KIND OF TRAVEL

At Rough Guides we are passionately committed to travel. We believe it helps us understand the world we live in and the people we share it with – and of course tourism is vital to many developing economies. But the scale of modern tourism has also damaged some places irreparably, and climate change is accelerated by most forms of transport, especially flying. We encourage all our authors to consider the carbon footprint of the journeys they make in the course of researching our guides.

flying from the US and Canda to Bordeaux involves a transit in Paris or another European city. Air France has the most frequent services between Paris and North America; it also operates a codeshare with Delta. Other airlines offering **nonstop** services to Paris from a variety of US cities include: American Airlines from New York, Charlotte, Chicago, Dallas, Philadelphia and Miami; Delta from Boston, Washington, Los Angeles, Seattle, San Francisco and Cincinnati; and United from Chicago, New York, San Francisco and Washington DC. Air Canada offers nonstop services to Paris from Montréal and Toronto, while Air Transat offers good value scheduled and **charter flights** to Paris from a number of bases.

Flights from Australia, New Zealand and South Africa

There are no direct flights to Bordeaux from Australia, New Zealand or South Africa. Most travellers from **Australia** and **New Zealand** choose to fly to France via London, although some airlines can add a Bordeaux leg to an Australia/New Zealand–Europe ticket. Flights via Asia or the Gulf States, with a transfer or overnight stop at the airline's home port, are generally the cheapest option; those routed through the US tend to be slightly pricier.

From **South Africa**, Johannesburg is the best place to start, with Air France flying direct to Paris.

AIRLINES

Aer Lingus http://aerlingus.com.
Air France http://airfrance.com.
Air Transat http://airtransat.com.
British Airways http://britishairways.com.
easyJet http://easyjet.com.
Jet2 http://jet2.com.
KLM http://klm.com.
Lufthansa http://lufthansa.com.
Ryanair http://ryanair.com.

By train

Eurostar (http://eurostar.com) operates high-speed passenger trains daily from London's St Pancras International to France through the **Channel Tunnel**. There are 1–2 services an hour from around 5.40am to 8pm for Paris Gare du Nord; fast trains take 2hr15min. Once you arrive in Paris you will need to change trains – and stations – to get on your train to Bordeaux. Trains from Paris to Bordeaux go from **Gare Montparnasse**. Metro and RER trains link these two Paris stations but allow ample time to get across the city. Brussels-bound trains stop at Lille (1hr20), where you can connect with TGV trains heading south to Bordeaux.

Tickets can be bought online or by phone from Eurostar, as well as through travel agents and websites like http://lastminute.com. InterRail and Eurail **passes** entitle you to discounts on Eurostar trains. Under certain circumstances, you can also take your bike on Eurostar.

Rail passes

There is a variety of rail passes useful for travel within France, some of which need to be bought in your home country (for details of railcards that you can buy in France, see page 21). **Rail Europe** (http://rail europe.com) (see page 21), the umbrella company for all national and international rail purchases, is the most useful source of information on availability and cost.

InterRail Pass

InterRail Passes (https://interrail.eu) are only available to European residents (British citizens are still allowed to buy InterRail passes), or those who have lived in a European country for at least six months, and you will be asked to provide proof of residency (and long-stay visa if applicable) before being allowed to buy one. They come in first or second-class senior (over 60), first- or second-class over-27 or second-class under-27 versions, and cover thirty European countries. Children from 4–11 years can travel free as part of a family pass; those under 4 travel free, though they may not get a seat.

There are two types of passes available: **global** and **one-country**. The global pass covers all thirty countries with various options: five days travel in a fifteen-day period; ten days travel within a month; 15 days, 22 days; and one month continuous travel. The family pass is the same price as the over-27 pass per adult. Similarly, the one-country pass allows you to opt for various travel periods, ranging from three days to eight days travel in one month with prices varying between countries (see http://interrail.eu). In each case, first-class passes are also available at an additional cost.

InterRail Passes do not include travel within your country of residence, though pass-holders are eligible for discounts on Eurostar and on ferries from Rosslare in Ireland.

Eurail Pass

Eurail Passes are not available to European residents but once ordered can be delivered to a European address (http://eurail.com). Again, there are various options. The Saverpass offers a 15 percent discount on Eurail passes for between two and five people travelling together, and children named on the pass go free.

RAIL, CHANNEL TUNNEL AND BUS CONTACTS

Eurail http://eurail.com.
Eurostar http://eurostar.com.
Eurotunnel http://eurotunnel.com.
International Rail http://internationalrail.com.
Rail Europe http://raileurope.com.
Rail Plus http://railplus.com.au.
SNCF http://sncf.com. For regional train tickets and timetables.
Trainseurope http://trainseurope.co.uk.

Ferries

Though slower than travelling by plane or via the Channel Tunnel, the ferries plying between Dover and Calais offer the cheapest means of travelling to France **from the UK** and are particularly convenient if you live in southeast England although again it leaves the problem of an 8-9hr-drive from Calais to Bordeaux. It's also worth bearing in mind that if you live west of London, the ferry services to Roscoff, St-Malo, Cherbourg, Caen, Dieppe and Le Havre can save some driving time and, once you arrive in France, the drive down to Bordeaux is shorter than from Calais. **From Ireland**, putting the car on the ferry from Cork (14hr) or Rosslare (17hr 30min) to Roscoff in Brittany, or Rosslare to Cherbourg (19hr) in Normandy cuts out the drive across Britain to the Channel.

Ferry **prices** are seasonal and, for motorists, depend on the type of vehicle. In general, the further you book ahead, the cheaper the fare and it's well worth playing around with dates and times to find the best deals: midweek and very early or late sailings are usually cheapest.

Some ferry companies also offer fares for **foot passengers** on cross-Channel routes; accompanying **bicycles** can usually be carried free.

FERRY CONTACTS

Brittany Ferries UK http://brittany-ferries.co.uk; Republic of Ireland http://brittanyferries.ie.
Condor Ferries http://condorferries.co.uk.
DFDS http://dfdsseaways.co.uk.
Direct Ferries http://directferries.co.uk.
Ferry Savers http://ferrysavers.com.
Irish Ferries http://irishferries.com.
P&O Ferries http://poferries.com.

By car

Driving through France can be a real pleasure, with its magnificent (but pricey) network of *autoroutes* providing sweeping views of the countryside. If you're in a hurry, it's worth paying motorway tolls to avoid the often-congested toll-free *routes nationales* (marked, for example, RN116 or N116 on signs and maps), many of which have been reclassified as *routes départementales* in recent years. Many of the more minor *routes départementales* (marked with a D) are uncongested and make for a more scenic – if slow – drive.

There are times when it's wiser not to drive at all: around major seaside resorts in high season; and at peak holiday migrations such as the beginning and end of the month-long August holiday, and the notoriously congested weekends nearest July 14 and August 15.

Licences, petrol and tolls

US, UK, Canadian, Australian, New Zealand, South African and all EU **driving licences** are valid in France for up to twelve months, though an International Driver's Licence makes life easier. The minimum driving age is 18 and you must hold a full licence. Drivers are required to carry their licence with them when driving, and you should also have the insurance and registration documents with you in the car.

All the major car manufacturers have garages and service stations in France, which can help if you run into mechanical difficulties. You'll find them listed in the Yellow Pages of the phone book under "*Garages automobiles*"; for breakdowns, look under "*Dépannages*". If you have an accident or theft, contact the local police – and keep a copy of their report in order to file an insurance claim. Within Europe, most car **insurance policies** cover taking your car to France;

TRAVELLING WITH PETS FROM THE UK

If you wish to take your dog or cat to France, the **Pet Travel Scheme (PETS)** enables you to avoid putting it in quarantine when re-entering the UK as long as certain conditions are met. Current regulations are available on the Department for Environment, Food and Rural Affairs (DEFRA) website at http://gov.uk/taking-your-pet-abroad. Note that since Brexit, taking a pet from the UK to anywhere in the EU requires more paperwork than it did previously and a UK issued Pet Passport is no longer sufficient.

ROAD INFORMATION

Up-to-the-minute information regarding traffic jams and road works in Bordeaux and throughout France can be obtained from the Bison Futé free-dial recorded information service (0800 100 200; French only) or their website www.bison-fute. gouv.fr. For information regarding *autoroutes*, you can also consult the bilingual website http://autoroutes.fr. Once on the *autoroute*, tune in to the national 107.7FM information station for 24-hour music and updates on traffic conditions.

check with your insurer. However, you're advised to take out extra cover for motoring assistance in case your car breaks down.

Rules of the road

Since the French **drive on the right**, drivers of right-hand-drive cars must adjust their **headlights** to dip to the right. This is most easily done by sticking on glare deflectors, which can be bought at most motor accessory shops, at the Channel ferry ports or the Eurostar terminal and on the ferries. It's more complicated if your car is fitted with High-Intensity Discharge (HID) or halogen-type lights; check with your dealer about how to adjust these well in advance. Dipped headlights must be used in poor daytime visibility.

All non-French vehicles must display their **national identification letters** (UK, etc) either on the number plate or by means of a sticker, and all vehicles must carry a red warning triangle, a reflective safety jacket and a single-use breathalyser. Since 2021, if driving in mountain areas between November and the end of March it's compulsory to have chains or winter tyres

in the vehicle (though chains only need to be fitted to the tyres when required). You are also strongly advised to carry a spare set of bulbs, a fire extinguisher and a first-aid kit. **Seat belts** are compulsory and children under 10 years must travel in an approved child seat, harness or booster appropriate to their age and size.

In built-up areas the law of *priorité à droite* – **giving way** to traffic coming from your right, even when it is coming from a minor road – still sometimes applies, including at some roundabouts. A sign showing a yellow diamond on a white background indicates that you have right of way, while the same sign with a diagonal black slash across it warns you that vehicles emerging from the right have priority. *Cédez le passage* means "Give way"; *vous n'avez pas la priorité* means "You do not have right of way".

If you have an **accident** while driving, you must fill in and sign a *constat d'accident* (declaration form) or, if another car is also involved, a *constat à l'amiable* (jointly agreed declaration); in the case of a hire car, these forms should be provided with the car's insurance documents.

Unless otherwise indicated **speed limits** are: 130kph (80mph) on *autoroutes*; 110kph (68mph) on dual carriageways; 80kph (50mph) on other roads; and 50kph (31mph) in towns. In wet weather, and for drivers with less than two years' experience, these limits are 110kph (68mph), 100kph (62mph) and 80kph (50mph) respectively, while the town limit remains constant. Many towns and villages have introduced traffic-calming measures and 30kph limits particularly in town centres where there are lots of pedestrians. Fixed and mobile radars are now widely used. The **alcohol limit** is 0.05 percent (0.5 grams per litre of blood), and random breath tests and saliva tests for drugs are common. There are stiff **penalties** for driving violations, ranging from on-the-spot **fines** for minor infringements to the immediate confiscation of

BY CAR VIA THE CHANNEL TUNNEL

The simplest way to take your car to France from the UK is on one of the drive-on drive-off shuttle trains operated by **Eurotunnel**. The service runs continuously between Folkestone and Coquelles, near Calais, with up to four departures per hour (one every 1hr 30min from midnight–6am) and takes 35 minutes. It is possible to turn up and buy your ticket at the check-in booths, though you'll pay a premium and at busy times booking is strongly recommended; if you have a booking, you must arrive at least thirty minutes before departure. Note that Eurotunnel does not transport cars fitted with LPG or CNG tanks.

There's room for only six **bicycles** on any departure, so book ahead in high season.

Although this will get you to France quickly and easily, Calais is 870km from Bordeaux which takes approximately nine hours to drive. If you're only intending to visit Bordeaux and a few nearby places then it may be easier to leave your car at home and travel by plane or train.

your licence and/or your car for more serious offences. Note that radar detectors and SatNav systems that identify the location of speed traps are illegal in France.

Agents and operators

There are a vast number of travel agents and tour operators offering holidays in and around Bordeaux, with options varying from luxury, château-based wine breaks to family-fun on the gorgeous nearby beaches. The following is a list of the most useful contacts.

AGENTS AND OPERATORS

Arblaster & Clarke http://arblasterandclarke.com. Wine-themed tours to all the great wine regions including, of course, Bordeaux.
Canvas Holidays http://canvasholidays.co.uk. Tailor-made caravan and camping holidays at four locations on the Gironde coastline.
Cycling for Softies http://cycling-for-softies.co.uk. Easy-going cycle holidays in the vicinity of Bordeaux.
Discover France http://discoverfrance.com. Self-guided cycling and walking holidays.
Eurocamp http://eurocamp.co.uk. Camping holidays with kids' activities and single-parent deals.
European Waterways http://europeanwaterways.com. River cruise in lovely canal boats down the Garonne River.
France Afloat http://franceafloat.com. France-based UK operator offering canal and river cruises down the Garonne.
Headwater http://headwater.com. UK-based operator offering walking tourism the countryside around Bordeaux.
Holiday France Direct http://holidayfrancedirect.co.uk. Website offering thousands of properties throughout the country, from cottages and villas to châteaux and mobile homes.
Inntravel http://inntravel.co.uk. Cycling holidays through the Bordeaux wine regions.

Visas and red tape

EU citizens need only a valid national identity card or passport to enter France. Other Europeans – including British citizens – as well as citizens of the United States, Canada, Australia and New Zealand, require a passport but no visa and can stay as a tourist for up to ninety days, but from May 2025 will need an ETIAS visa waiver (see http://schengenvisainfo.com). Other nationalities (including South Africans) must get a visa from a French embassy or consulate before departure. Visa requirements do change, so check the current situation before you leave home.

Non-EU citizens wishing to stay longer than 90 days need to apply for a long stay visa (valid for 12 months). This must be done through a French embassy before you leave home and they are generally only granted if you are working, studying or investing in France or are a part of an internship or training programe.

Embassies and consulates

Most countries have their embassies in Paris, but a couple maintain a consulate in Bordeaux including most European countries (but not Ireland). You'll need to contact them if you lose your passport or need other assistance. Most consulates are open for enquiries Monday to Friday, usually 9am–12.30pm and 2.30–5.30pm, though the morning shift is the most reliable.

FOREIGN CONSULATES IN BORDEAUX

UK 14 Rue Montesquieu, www.gov.uk/contact-consulate-bordeaux
USA 89 Quai Des Chartrons, https://fr.usembassy.gov/embassy-consulates/bordeaux/

Getting around

Bordeaux is a compact city and everything within the city centre is within easy walking distance of each other. What's more the fabulous architecture, numerous parks and green spaces and generally pedestrian friendly streets make Bordeaux a real pleasure to stroll in. For sites further out of the centre there's a comprehensive public transport network with trams and buses serving most parts of the city.

Exploring the wine areas and coastal resorts by public transport is possible but with many of the more appealing places being just small villages, services can be very limited. Unless you join an organised tour then it's best to have your own wheels for this – either car or bicycle.

Most Bordeaux city transport is controlled by TBM (http://infotbm.com). Tickets for buses and trams can be bought through their website.

Arriving in Bordeaux

To/from the airport

Bordeaux-Mérignac airport is 12km west of the city. The airport is fairly small and relaxed although Terminal Billi, which is the dedicated budget airline terminal, leaves quite a lot to be desired! To travel between the airport and the city centre there is a choice of shuttle buses, normal buses, tram or taxi.

Shuttle Bus

Bio-fuel powered **shuttle buses** (navette; http://30direct.com; roughly hourly; charge) travel from outside Hall B, Gate 7 at the airport to the city's main train station, Gare Saint-Jean. The journey is supposed to take 30 minutes though at busy times of day it can be delayed. From the train station the buses depart from the forecourt opposite Hall 2. Tickets can be bought on the bus or, with a 10% discount, online. There's rarely any need to book them in advance.

Bus

Public bus number #1 runs every 20min between 5.50am and 8.30pm Mon-Fri and every 30min on Saturday from 7am to 8.30pm between the airport and the main Saint-Jean train station. Bus Corol 39 runs on the same schedule between the airport and Pessac train station where you can either catch a train into the city or hop on another bus. Tickets can be bought from the machines by the bus stops. Buses don't operate on Sundays.

Tram

Ligne A of Bordeaux's tram network now extends out to the airport from the very heart of the city. If you're heading into the city centre the tram is the quickest and easiest method. City centre stops include: Palais de Justice, Hôtel de Ville, Sainte Catherine, Jardin Botanique and others. Frustratingly though it doesn't go to the train station. To reach that change at Porte de Bourgogne and take Ligne C four southbound for four stops. Buy tickets online (http://infotbm.com) or from one of the ticket machines by tram stops. Trams generally operate from 5am to 12.30am.

Taxi

There's a **taxi rank** right outside the airport terminal entrance. Taxis to the train station cost around €50 (more at night or on Sundays and holidays). To the city centre the price averages €30 in the day and €45 at night. Taxis can be paid for with Visa cards.

To/from the train station

Bordeaux Saint Jean train station is 3km south of the city centre; bus #16 and tramline C run into town every few minutes from 5am to 12.30am. Walking takes a little over half-an-hour depending where in the city centre you're headed for. Bordeaux marks the southern extension of the new high-speed lines that now connect many major French cities. Using these trains it takes just under two hours to reach Paris. Heading south though and you're on the older style lines and it takes two hours to reach Bayonne, which is just 185km away compared to Paris which is nearly 600km away.

Destinations Angoulême (16–22 daily; 1hr–1hr 30min); Arcachon (15–25 daily; 50–55min); Bayonne (9 daily; 1hr 40min–2hr 10min); Bergerac (7–14 daily; 1hr 15–1hr 30min); Biarritz (9 daily; 2hr–2hr 45min); Brive (2–3 daily; 2hr 35min); Hendaye (6–9 daily; 2hr 30min); La Rochelle (6–8 daily; 2hr–2hr 20min); Lourdes (6–10 daily; 2hr 20min–3hr); Marseille (6 daily; 4hr); Mont de Marsan (5–6 daily; 1hr 30min); Nice (3–8 daily; 9–10hr); Paris-Montparnasse (1–2 hourly; 4hr); Périgueux (8–14 daily; 1hr–1hr 25min); Pointe de Grave (7–9 daily to Lesparre; 1hr 20min; then bus #713 to Pointe de Grave 1–5 daily Mon–Sat; 1hr); Poitiers (11–14 daily; 1hr 45min–2hr 30min); Saintes (6–9 daily; 1hr 40min); St-Émilion (7–14 daily; 40min); St-Jean-de-Luz (8–10 daily; 2hr–2hr 40min); Toulouse (10–16 daily; 2hr–2hr 40min).

Arriving by bus

There's no central bus station, but bus stops congregate on the south side of the esplanade des Quinconces, on allées de Munich (where you'll also find the information centre – http://infotbc.com). Exceptions are the bus to Blaye, which leaves from "Buttinière" (take tramline A) and buses to Margaux and Pauillac, which leave from "place Ravezies" (tramline C).

Destinations Blaye (4–7 daily; 1hr 45min); Cap Ferret (6–12 daily; 1hr 30min); Lacanau (5 daily; 2hr 15min); Pauillac (3–7 daily; 45min–1hr 10min).

City Transport

The main forms of city transport are the trams and buses. There are also boats linking different parts of the city as well as a bike rental scheme and taxis. Trams, buses and boats are all operated by TBM (Transports Bordeaux Métropole.; http://infotbm.com).

Tickets

Various types of ticket and transport pass are available including a single ticket, two-journey ticket, ten-journey ticket, evening travel pass and a 7-day travel pass. The tourist office CityPass also includes public transport.

You can either purchase single tickets or packs of ten from machines at tram, bus and boat stops, from the driver on the transport itself or online via the website or app of the city public transport system TBM (http://infotbm.com). You can also buy an unlimited-use pass, available for between one and seven days. For short journeys (no more than 3-4 stops) it's cheapest to buy a single ticket. They are valid for 1 hour. You must validate your ticket at the machines next to the doors on the trams, buses and boats.

By tram

Tram services (http://infotbc.com) operate on the four lines – A, B, C and D - regularly between 5am and 12.30am, and extend several kilometres into Bordeaux's suburbs.

Trams run from 5am to 12.30am Monday to Wednesday and until 1am on Thursday, Friday and Saturday. They come at 4 to 7 min intervals during the day and 8 to 15 min at night. On Sundays and public holidays, the schedule is very limited.

Ligne A, the longest of the lot, connects the airport, Mérignac, Bordeaux city centre, Cénon, Floriac Dravemont and La Gardette Bassens Carbonblanc. It passes some of the city's key areas, such as Place de la Victoire and Place des Quinconces. Crossing the Garonne River, it comes to the left bank suburb of Cénon. From there, it continues through Floirac Dravemont to end at La Gardette Bassens Carbonblanc.

Ligne B links the city centre with the student areas of Talence and Pessac to the southwest of the city. It starts at Place des Quinconces and passes the Pont de Pierre and Place de la Victoire.

Ligne C runs from Villenave d'Ornon, to the south of Bordeaux centre and heads north through Bègles, the city centre and, after crossing the River Garonne, it passes through Bruges before ending in Blanquefort.

Ligne D connects central Bordeaux with Le Bouscat and Eysines. It passes some of the Jardin Public and the Cathedral.

By bus

With sixty different lines, Bordeaux has a very comprehensive bus network, which provides easy access to the parts of the city that are not covered by trams. Bus stops are prominently marked, and timetables are available both at most bus stops as well as online. However, most short stay visitors concentrating on city centre attractions are unlikely to need to bother with using buses as the tram is sufficient. As with the trams, timetables can be viewed and tickets bought on the TBM site and app (http://infotbc.com). Tickets can also be bought from machines at main bus stops and on the bus itself.

By river shuttle

By far the most enjoyable way of moving up and down the river front quays of Bordeaux is by boat. The Batcub, Bordeaux's river shuttle, stops in five different places. The most useful for tourists is the central Quinconces and La Cité du Vin. Boats operate between 7am and 7.30pm Mon-Fri and 9am to 7.30pm (8.30pm in July and August) at weekends and holidays. As with the buses and trams the boats are operated by TBM and can be purchased online, from machines at tram stops or onboard, though note that there's a slight additional charge if buying onboard. In 2025 a new boat line is expected to be launched.

By bicycle

Le Vélo is the free-service **bike rental** scheme in Bordeaux. Again, it's operated by TBM (http://infotbc. com). There are 180 different bike pick up and drop off locations throughout the city and over 2000 bikes are available – both classic bikes and electric bikes. You will need to download the dedicated app from the TBM website and there's a hefty deposit to be paid. The service is only available to those over 15 years of age.

Taxi

There are **taxis** throughout the city. The city website (https://www.bordeaux.fr/p1247/en-taxi) has a list of all taxi stations and contact details of taxi companies. In general taxis are an expensive way to get around and aren't much quicker – and often slower – than taking the tram or bus. The only exception might be if you need to get to or from the airport or train station in a hurry.

By car

If you will only be visiting Bordeaux then having your own vehicle will be more of a hassle than a benefit. If though you're planning on touring the areas around the city for several days then it can be worth considering bringing your own car or renting on arrival at the airport or train station.

Parking

There are numerous underground **car parks** in the centre, though it's cheaper to use the ones next to the tram stations on the east bank of the Garonne: buy a round-trip park-and-ride ticket and hop on a tram to the centre. For more information see http://infotbm.com.

Car rental

Numerous rental firms are located in and around the train station, including Europcar http://europcar. fr; Hertz http://hertz.fr; and National/Citer http://national.fr. They all have outlets at the airport as well.

Travel essentials

Accessible travel

The French authorities have been making a concerted effort to improve facilities for travellers with disabilities. Though haphazard parking habits and stepped village streets remain serious obstacles for anyone with mobility problems. Ramps and other forms of access are gradually being added to hotels, museums and other public buildings. All but the oldest hotels are required to adapt at least one room to be wheelchair accessible, and a growing number of *chambres d'hôtes* are doing likewise. Accessible hotels, sights and other facilities are gradually being inspected and, if they fulfil certain criteria, issued with a **Tourisme & Handicap** certificate. Listings produced by Logis (see page 76) and Gîtes de France (see page 76) indicate places with specially adapted rooms. It's essential to double-check when booking that the facilities meet your needs.

Most **train stations** now make provision for travellers with reduced mobility. Spaces for **wheelchairs** are available in first-class carriages of all **TGVs** for the price of the regular, second-class fare; note that these must be booked in advance. For other trains, a wheelchair symbol in the timetable indicates services offering special on-board facilities, though it's best to double-check when booking. SNCF also runs a scheme called **Accès Plus**, through which they assist travellers with disabilities, including ticket reservations, baggage assistance and a full reception service. You must, though, get in contact with them 48 hours in advance. Full details are on the website http://accessibilite.sncf.com, which also includes a downloadable guide.

Taxi drivers are legally obliged to help passengers in and out of the vehicle and to carry guide dogs. Ask at the local tourist office or *mairie* for further information on specially adapted taxis. All the big **car rental** agencies can provide automatic cars if you reserve sufficiently far in advance, while most agencies should also be able to able to offer cars with hand controls on request – again, make sure you give them plenty of notice.

If you can read French, there are some other excellent guides to make use of. The association **Vacances Accessibles** (http://vacances-accessibles. apf.asso.fr) produces the *Handi-plus Aquitaine* (http:// handiplusaquitaine.fr) booklet, which outlines suitable itineraries across the whole region. *Handi-tourisme* published annually by Petit Futé (http:// petitfute.com) covers the whole of France.

For general **information** about accessibility, special programmes and discounts contact one of the organizations listed below before you leave home.

CONTACTS FOR TRAVELLERS WITH DISABILITIES

Access Tourisme Service http://access-tourisme.com. Organized and customized holidays for people with special needs, including adapted vehicle rental, accessible hotels and even travel companions if required.

APF (Association des Paralysés de France) http://apf.asso.fr. National association that can answer general enquiries and put you in touch with their departmental offices.

Costs

Prices have been rising steadily in recent years, and the Bordeaux region, like most of France, is a fairly pricey part of Europe to visit. That said, there are ways of keeping costs under control. When and where you go will make a big difference: Arcachon and other beach towns in July and August will see accommodation costs rise hugely compared to out of season prices. The most popular wine villages, such as Saint-Émilion, will always cost more than if you stick to less celebrated wine villages. In Bordeaux itself, prices remain fairly steady year-round.

For a reasonably comfortable existence, including a double room in a mid-range hotel, lunch and dinner in a restaurant, plus moving around, café stops and museum visits, you need to allow around €120/£100/US$130 a day per person based on two people sharing. But by counting the pennies, staying at youth hostels or camping, and being strong-willed about extra cups of coffee and doses of culture, you could manage on around €70/£60/US$80 a day each, to include a cheap restaurant meal.

Youth and student discounts

Once obtained, various official and quasi-official youth/student ID cards soon pay for themselves in savings. Full-time students are eligible for the **International Student ID Card** (ISIC; http://isic.org in the UK), which entitles you to special air, rail and bus fares, and discounts at museums, theatres and other attractions. It also gives you access to a free 24-hour helpline to call in the event of a medical or legal emergency. You have to be 25 or under to qualify for the **International Youth Travel Card**, while teachers are eligible for the **International Teacher Card**, offering similar discounts. They are available through universities and student travel specialists such as STA Travel, USIT and Travel CUTS.

Taxes

The majority of goods and services in France are subject to **value-added tax** (*taxe sur la valeur ajoutée* or *TVA* in French), usually at a rate of 20 percent, which is included in the price. Most local authorities also levy a **tourism tax** on hotel and *chambre d'hôte* accommodation – called a *taxe de séjour* – generally not more than €1 per person per night depending on the category; in some areas this tax only applies in peak season. While the tax is not included in room rates, it must be clearly indicated as a separate item.

Crime and personal safety

With a population of around a quarter of a million, Bordeaux is one of the ten largest cities in France and, like all large cities, there are areas where crime can be an issue. However, the city centre and almost any other part of the city a tourist might visit, are generally problem-free, but be aware of the risk of **pick-pocketing** and **petty theft**. Petty theft can also be an issue in beach resorts in summer – though this mainly takes place in campsites rather than actually on the beach. In rural areas any kind of crime aimed at tourists is rare. Overall though, this is a very **safe** part of the world.

Even so, it obviously makes sense to take the normal **precautions**: don't flash wads of notes around; carry your bag or wallet securely; never leave cameras, mobile phones or other valuables lying around; and park your car overnight in a monitored parking, garage or, at the very least, on a busy and well-lit street. It's wise to keep a separate record of credit card numbers, and the phone numbers for cancelling them. Finally, make sure you have a good insurance policy.

There are two main types of **police** in France – the Police Nationale and the Gendarmerie Nationale. The former deals with all crime, parking and traffic affairs within large and mid-sized towns, where you will find them in the Commissariat de Police. The Gendarmerie Nationale covers the rural areas.

If you need to **report a theft**, go to the local Gendarmerie or Commissariat de Police (addresses of commissariats are given in the Guide for the major towns), where they will fill out a *constat de vol*. The first thing they'll ask for is your passport, and vehicle documents if relevant. Although the police are not always as cooperative as they might be, it is their duty to assist you if you've lost your passport or all your money. As in most European countries the police generally won't bother to do more than a cursory investigation into car break-ins.

If you have an **accident** while driving, you must fill in and sign a *constat d'accident* (declaration form) or, if another car is also involved, a *constat aimable* (jointly agreed declaration); these forms should be provided with the car's insurance documents. The police can impose on-the-spot fines for minor **driving offences** and take away your licence for anything more serious.

POLICE

Commissariat Central 23 rue François-de-Sourdis (05 57 85 77 77 or 17 in emergencies).

Drugs

Drug use is just as prevalent in France as anywhere else in Europe – and just as risky. People caught smuggling or possessing drugs, even just a few grams of marijuana, are liable to find themselves in jail. Should you be **arrested** on any charge, you have the right to contact your consulate, though don't expect much sympathy.

> ## EMERGENCY NUMBERS
> **Police** 17
> **Ambulance** 15
> **Fire** 18
> **All emergencies** 112

Racism

Though the self-proclaimed home of "*liberté, égalité, fraternité*", France has its share of **racist-related** issues. The majority of racist incidents are focused against the Arab community, although black and Asian visitors may also encounter an unwelcome degree of curiosity or suspicion from shopkeepers, hoteliers and the like. Anti-Semitic violence has had a high profile in France since the torture and murder of a young Jewish man, Ilan Halimi, in a Paris *banlieue* in 1996. In 2018, the antisemitic murder of 85-year-old Mireille Knoll shook the whole of France to the core. If you suffer a **racial assault**, contact the police, your consulate or one of the local anti-racism organizations (though they may not have English-speakers); SOS Racisme (http://sos-racisme.org) and Mouvement contre le Racisme et pour l'Amitié entre les Peuples (MRAP; http://mrap.fr) have offices in most regions of France. Alternatively, you could contact the **English-speaking helpline** SOS Help (01 46 21 46 46, daily 3–11pm; http://soshelpline.org). The service is staffed by trained volunteers who not only provide a confidential listening service, but also offer practical information for foreigners facing problems in France.

Electricity

The **electricity** supply in France is almost always 220V, using plugs with two round pins. If you need a transformer, it's a good idea to buy one before leaving home, though you can find them in big department stores.

Health

Visitors to Bordeaux have little to worry about as far as health is concerned. No vaccinations are required, there are no nasty diseases to be wary of and tap water is safe to drink. The worst that's likely to happen is a case of sunburn or an upset stomach from eating too much rich food – or a hangover from all that wonderful wine. If you do need treatment, however, you should be in good hands: the French healthcare system is rated one of the best in the world.

Under the French health system, all services, including doctor's consultations, prescribed medicines, hospital stays and ambulance call-outs, incur a charge which you have to pay upfront. **EU citizens** are entitled to a refund (usually between 70 and 80 percent), providing the doctor is government registered (*un médecin conventionné*) and provided you have a European Health Insurance Card (EHIC; *Carte Européenne d'Assurance Maladie*). Note that everyone in the family, including children, must have their own cards, which are free. Since Brexit, UK citizens are no longer entitled to the **EHIC card** and instead must apply for a **UK GHIC** card before leaving home. This card gives you much the same rights as the EHIC card did and if you require medical treatment while in France you will receive the same state healthcare as a French resident (in other words; you will get very good health care!). However, the French system doesn't cover 100 percent of medical expenses. Most French people have a top-up medical insurance plan to cover the excess. To avoid a potentially huge bill, make sure that you also have a general travel insurance policy.

In the UK you can apply for them online through the Department of Health website (http://dh.gov.uk) or by post – forms are available from post offices.

For minor complaints go to a **pharmacie**, signalled by an illuminated green cross. You'll find at least one in every small town and even some villages. They keep normal shop hours (roughly Mon–Sat 9am–noon and 3–6/7pm), though some stay open late and, in larger towns, at least one (known as the *pharmacie de garde*) is open 24 hours according to a rota; details are displayed in all pharmacy windows (although you might actually have to phone the pharmacy to get someone to come and open up).

For anything more serious you can get the name of a **doctor** from a pharmacy, local police station,

tourist office or your hotel. Alternatively, look under "Médecins" in the Yellow Pages (*Pages Jaunes*) phone directory. The consultation fee is in the region of €25. You'll be given a statement of treatment (*Feuille de Soins*) for later insurance claims. Any prescriptions will be fulfilled by a pharmacy and must be paid for; little price stickers (*vignettes*) from each medicine will be stuck on the *Feuille de Soins*.

In serious **emergencies** you will always be admitted to the nearest general hospital (*centre hospitalier*). Phone numbers and addresses are given in the Guide for all the main cities. The national number for calling an ambulance is 15.

HOSPITAL

Centre Hospitalier Pellegrin-Tripode place Amélie-Raba-Léon (05 56 79 56 79), to the west of central Bordeaux.

Insurance

It's advisable to take out an insurance policy before travelling to cover against theft, loss and illness or injury. Before paying for a new policy, however, it's worth checking whether you are already covered: some all-risks home insurance policies may cover your possessions when overseas, and many private medical schemes include cover when abroad. In Canada, provincial health plans usually provide partial cover for medical mishaps overseas. Students will often find that their student health coverage extends during the vacations and for one term beyond the date of last enrolment.

A typical **travel insurance policy** usually provides cover for the cost of medical treatment and damage caused by accidents, as well as cancellation or curtailment of your journey. Cover for lost or stolen cash, cheques and possessions usually costs a little extra. Most policies exclude so-called dangerous sports unless an extra premium is paid. Many policies can be chopped and changed to exclude coverage you don't need.

ROUGH GUIDES TRAVEL INSURANCE

Looking for travel insurance? Rough Guides partners with top providers worldwide to offer you the best coverage. Policies are available to residents of anywhere in the world, with a range of options whether you are looking for single-trip, multi-country or long-stay insurance. There's coverage for a wide range of adventure sports, 24-hour emergency assistance, high levels of medical and evacuation cover and a stream of travel safety information. Even better, roughguides.com users can take advantage of these policies online 24/7, from anywhere in the world – even if you're already travelling. To make the most of your travels and ensure a smoother experience, it's always good to be prepared for when things don't go according to plan. For more information go to http://roughguides.com/bookings/insurance.

If you need to **make a claim**, you should keep receipts for medicines and medical treatment, and in the event you have anything stolen, you must obtain an official statement from the police (called *un constat de vol*).

Internet

Wi-fi is the norm in even the cheapest French hotels and even the majority of campsites (less so with very basic farm campsites), and is almost always free and fast. Internet cafés are now about as common as a dodo, though most cafés will have wi-fi available – you'll just be obliged to buy a drink. Unless specified otherwise, all accommodation establishments listed in this guide have wi-fi.

Laundry

Laundries are still reasonably common in French towns – just ask in your hotel, or the tourist office, or look in the phone book under "*Laveries automatiques*" or "*Laveries en libre-service*". They are usually unattended, and while some have machines for changing notes, it's prudent to come armed with small change. Washing powder (*la lessive*) is always available on site. Machines are graded in different wash sizes. Most hotels forbid doing any laundry in your room, though you should get away with just one or two small items.

Mail

French **post offices**, known as **La Poste** and identified by bright yellow-and-blue signs, are generally open from around 9am to 5pm or 6pm Monday to Friday, and 9am to noon on Saturday. Although those in smaller towns and villages have far more erratic hours (perhaps only a morning or two a week) or have closed down completely.

Stamps (*timbres*) are sold at *tabacs* and newsagents as well as post offices. For information on postal rates, among other things, log on to the post office website http://laposte.fr.

To post your letter on the street, look for the bright yellow **post boxes** – make sure, where necessary, to put your letter in the box marked "étranger" (abroad).

Maps

In addition to the **maps** in this guide and the various free town plans you'll be offered along the way, the one extra map you might want is a good, up-to-date road map of the region. The best are the regional maps produced by Michelin and IGN (http://ign.fr). To cover the area encompassed by this guide, Michelin's Aquitaine map (1:200,000) is worth seeking out. Alternatively, both companies issue large spiral-bound road atlases covering the whole of France at around the same scale.

If you're planning to walk or cycle, it's well worth investing in the more detailed IGN maps. The Carte de Randonnée (1:25,000) series is specifically designed for walkers, while the Carte de Promenade (1:100,000) is ideal for cyclists. IGN's Bordeaux map and Gironde map are the ones you need for hiking and cycling routes in the region.

Money

France's currency is the **euro** (€), which is divided into 100 cents (also called *centimes*). There are seven notes – in denominations of 5, 10, 20, 50, 100, 200 and 500 euros – and eight different coins: 1, 2, 5, 10, 20 and 50 cents, and 1 and 2 euros. It's very rare that you will ever see a note larger than fifty euros and most shops will raise their eyebrows in concern if presented with a larger note.

For the most up-to-date **exchange rates** for these and other currencies, consult http://xe.com.

The best way to access money in France is to use your **credit** or **debit card** to withdraw cash from an **ATM** (known as *un distributeur de billets* or *un point argent*); most machines give instructions in several European languages. Note that there is often a transaction fee, so it's more efficient to take out a sizeable sum each time rather than making lots of small withdrawals.

Credit and debit cards are widely accepted in shops, hotels and restaurants, though some smaller establishments don't accept cards, or only for sums above a certain threshold. Visa – called Carte Bleue in France – is almost universally recognized, followed by MasterCard (also known as EuroCard). American Express ranks a lot lower.

You can **change cash** at most banks and main post offices. There are money-exchange counters (*bureaux de change*) at French airports, major train stations and usually one or two in city centres as well, though they don't always offer the best exchange rates.

As in much of the world travellers cheques are now next to useless and to change one can involve a special journey to the main branch of a bank or post office in a major city and a significant commission charge so don't bother with them.

Newspapers and radio

The large number of Brits living in France has also led to an active **English-language press** in the country.

The main monthly newspaper in English is *The Connexion* (http://connexionfrance.com). It's available from newsagents (*maisons de la presse*) and, in larger towns, from street-side kiosks.

As for **radio**, **Radio Liberté** (http://radioliberte. fr) broadcasts an English-language show with news during the week.

Opening hours and public holidays

Basic **hours of business** are 9am to noon and 2 to 6pm. Small food shops often don't reopen till halfway through the afternoon, closing around 7.30 or 8pm, just before the evening meal. Supermarkets also tend to stay open to at least 7.30pm and bigger ones in Bordeaux remain open until much later.

The standard **closing day** is Sunday, though some food shops, particularly bakeries (*boulangeries*), and newsagents are open in the morning. Many independent shops and businesses, particularly in the rural areas, also close on one other day a week. Frequently this is a Monday.

Core **banking hours** are Monday to Friday 9am to noon and 2 to 6pm. Some branches close on Monday, while others stay open at midday and may also open on Saturday morning. All are closed on Sunday and public holidays.

Most tourist offices are open all day every day throughout July and August, but hours outside these months vary considerably. **Museums** tend to open around 9.30 or 10am, close for lunch from noon until 1 or 2pm, and then run through to 5 or 6pm. In summer some stay open all day and close later, while in winter, many open only in the afternoon. Museum closing days are usually Monday or Tuesday, sometimes both. Many state-owned museums have one day of the week or month when they're free or half price.

PUBLIC HOLIDAYS

January 1 New Year's Day
March/April Easter Monday
Ascension Day (forty days after Easter)
Pentecost or Whitsun (seventh Sunday after Easter)
May 1 Labour Day
May 8 Victory in Europe (VE) Day 1945
July 14 Bastille Day
August 15 Assumption of the Virgin Mary
November 1 All Saints' Day
November 11 Armistice Day 1918
December 25 Christmas Day

Churches are generally open from around 8am to dusk but may close at lunchtime and are reserved for worshippers during services (times of which will usually be posted on the door). Country churches are increasingly kept locked; there may be a note on the door saying where to get the key, usually from the priest's house (*le presbytère*) or someone else living nearby, or from the *mairie*.

France celebrates eleven **public holidays** (*jours fériés*), when banks and most shops and businesses (though not necessarily restaurants), and some museums, are closed.

Phones

Payphones (*cabines*) essentially no longer exist and where you do see one it has probably been converted into a book swap.

French **telephone numbers** have ten digits. Numbers beginning 0800 or 0805 are free-dial numbers; those beginning 081 and 086 are charged as a local call; anything else beginning 08 is premium-rated. Numbers starting 06 and 07 are mobile numbers.

Mobile phones

If you have a non-European (including UK) mobile phone and want to use it in France, contact your phone provider before leaving home to check whether it will work locally, and what the call charges are.

French mobile phones operate on the European GSM standard, so many **US cell phones** won't work in France unless they are "tri-band". The quickest and cheapest option is probably to change your phone and/or service provider.

There are no roaming charges between EU countries. The situation with British mobile phones has changed since Brexit and whether you are charged or not for using your phone in France depends upon your operator and contract. Check with your service provider.

Smoking

Smoking is banned in all enclosed public spaces, including museums, hotels, restaurants, bars and nightclubs.

Time

France lies in the **Central European Time Zone** (GMT+1). This means it is one hour ahead of the UK, six hours ahead of Eastern Standard Time, and nine hours ahead of Pacific Standard Time. Between April and

CALLING HOME FROM ABROAD

Note that the initial zero is omitted from the area code when dialling the UK, Ireland, Australia and New Zealand from abroad.

Australia international access code + 61
New Zealand international access code + 64
UK international access code + 44
US and Canada international access code + 1
Republic of Ireland international access code + 353
South Africa international access code + 27

October France is eight hours behind eastern Australia and ten hours behind New Zealand; from November to March it is ten hours behind southeastern Australia and twelve hours behind New Zealand. Daylight Saving Time (GMT+2) in France lasts from the last Sunday of March to the last Sunday of October.

Tipping

Hotels and almost all restaurants include a **service charge** of fifteen percent in their prices (*service compris*). It's therefore not necessary to leave an additional cash **tip** at restaurants unless you feel you have received service out of the ordinary; if so, an extra two or three percent is plenty. It's customary to tip porters, tour guides and taxi drivers one or two euros, and to leave the small change at cafés.

Tourist information

The French government tourist office, **Maison de la France** (http://france.fr) has a very comprehensive website covering the whole country. Each region, department and city in France then has its own tourism authorities all of which invariably have their own website.

Tourist offices

Bordeaux's main tourist office is on the southern edge of the very central Quinconces. In addition, there are several smaller offices in the city. Outside of Bordeaux you'll find a tourist office – usually an **Office du Tourisme** (OT) but sometimes a **Syndicat d'Initiative** (SI) – in practically every town and many villages (details in the Guide). For the practical purposes

of visitors, there is little difference between them; sometimes they share premises and call themselves an OTSI. In small villages where there is no OT or SI, the *mairie* (town hall) will offer a similar service.

All these offices are well stocked with information, both locally and regionally, including hotels and restaurants, leisure activities, bike rental, markets and festivals, while those in the wine regions will provide information on local vineyards, and in peak season may also conduct vineyard tours; many can also book accommodation for you.

Most offices can provide a town/village plan and/or walking leaflets, while an increasing number now provide audio-guides (with English language) for self-guided town or village walks, though there will be a charge for this. Most, too, have maps and local walking guides on sale.

Information

Bordeaux's extremely helpful main tourist office, near the Grand Théâtre is on 12 cours du 30-juillet (http://bordeaux-tourisme.com). Visitors can book accommodation, city and vineyard tours. If you're planning on visiting multiple museums, the Bordeaux City Pass represents great value. It offers free museum entry, public transport, walking and bus tours, and various discounts: simply visiting the **Cité du Vin** and the Bassins des Lumières makes it worth the purchase, with anything else a bonus. One, two or three-day passes are available, and they can be bought either at the tourist office or online at www.visiter-bordeaux.com/en/bordeaux-citypass.html.

REGIONAL AND DEPARTMENTAL TOURIST OFFICES

Nouvelle Aquitaine http://nouvelle-aquitaine-tourisme.com.
Bordeaux https://bordeaux-tourisme.com.
Gironde http://gironde-tourisme.com.
Les Landes http://tourismelandes.com.

Work and study in Bordeaux

EU citizens are free to work in France on the same basis as a French citizen. This means you don't have to apply for a residence or work permit. Most **non-EU citizens – including UK nationals –** will need a work permit (*autorisation de travail*) and a residence permit along with a whole host of other papers; contact your nearest French consulate or, if already in France, your local *mairie* or *préfecture* to check what rules apply in your particular situation. Generally, it's not an easy process organising all of this paperwork and when possible the job will always go to a French or EU citizen. Whatever your nationality, once you have a work permit, you are entitled to exactly the same conditions as French workers, including the national **minimum wage** (SMIC), currently set at €11.65 per hour.

When **looking for a job**, a good starting point is to read one of the books on working abroad published by Vacation Work (http://vacationwork. co.uk). You could also try the websites http://monster. fr and http://jobs-ete.com, which focuses on summer jobs for students. Once in France, you'll find "Offres d'Emploi" (Job Offers) in the national and regional papers, or there's the national employment agency, **pôle emploi** (www.francetravail.fr), with offices all over France and which advertises temporary jobs in all fields. Non-EU citizens will have to show a work permit to apply for any of their jobs.

A degree and a **TEFL** (Teaching English as a Foreign Language) or similar qualifications are normally required for **English-language teaching** posts. The online *EL Gazette* newsletter (https://www.elgazette. com) is a useful source of information, as is the annual *Teaching English Abroad* published by Vacation Work. The TEFL website (www.tefl.com) has a good database of English-teaching vacancies.

Foreign students pay the same as French nationals to enrol for a course and you'll be eligible for subsidized accommodation, meals and all the student reductions. French **universities** are fairly informal, but there are strict entry requirements, including an exam in French, for undergraduate degrees, but not for postgraduate courses. For full details and prospectuses, contact the Cultural Service of any French embassy or consulate.

FURTHER CONTACTS

AFS Intercultural Programs http://afs.org. Opportunities for high-school students to study in France for a term or full academic year, living with host families.

Campus France www.campusfrance.org. Government-run agency set up to promote French higher education abroad.

Erasmus http://british-council.org or contact their university's international office. EU-run student exchange programme enabling students at participating universities in Britain and Ireland to study in one of 31 European countries.

Language Courses Abroad http://languagesabroad.co.uk.

World Wide Opportunities on Organic Farms (WWOOF) http://wwoof.fr. Volunteer to work on an organic farm in return for board and lodging.

Vieux Bordeaux

The best place to begin exploring Bordeaux is in its old town (Vieux Bordeaux), starting with the ostentatious place de la Bourse, which was created in the eighteenth century when city planners cleared the old medieval walls to expand the town to the riverside. From here, work your way into the narrow streets around place du Parlement and place St-Pierre, dotted with pretty townhouses, many of which now host attractive pavement cafés or boutique shops.

1 Place de la Bourse

 Place de la Bourse

Hemmed on three sides by grand buildings and facing out across the Garonne River on the fourth, the eighteenth-century **place de la Bourse** is a vast and elegant plaza that for all intents and purposes, marks the very heart of the city. Impressive by day it's at its best when lit up at night. By standing in the middle of the square and taking in the buildings around you will get a fast-track overview of all the Neoclassical decorative elements that are so characteristic of Bordeaux. There are sculpted mascarons on the keystones of some of the windows (human figures sculpted in stone), wrought iron balustrades, as well as arresting semicircular arcades and columns, while in the very centre of the square is the bronze and marble fountain of the Three Graces (Aglaea, Euphrosyne and Thalia, the three daughters of Greek god Zeus). Taken together, this ensemble is pretty heady stuff and you'll immediately understand why UNESCO chose to make Bordeaux the world's largest urban World Heritage Site.

Inaugurated in 1749, the square, which was originally called the Place Royale in honour of the king, was built over a twenty-year period (it was renamed after the French Revolution in 1848 and the establishment of the Second Republic). It was designed by Ange-Jacques Gabriel, the favoured architect of Louis XV, but when he died before the square was completed his son took on the project. By constructing it right on the

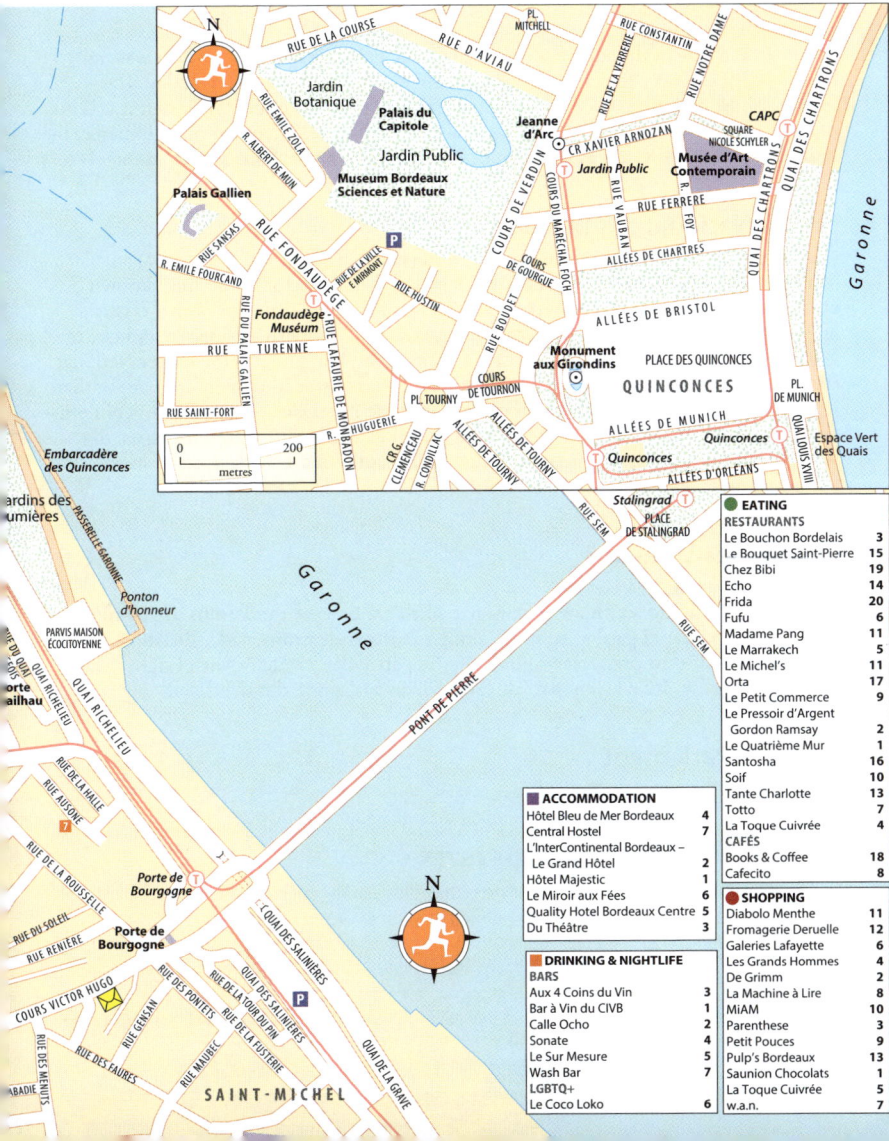

EATING

RESTAURANTS

Le Bouchon Bordelais	3
Le Bouquet Saint-Pierre	15
Chez Bibi	19
Echo	14
Frida	20
Fufu	6
Madame Pang	11
Le Marrakech	5
Le Michel's	11
Orta	17
Le Petit Commerce	9
Le Pressoir d'Argent Gordon Ramsay	2
Le Quatrième Mur	1
Santosha	16
Soif	10
Tante Charlotte	13
Totto	7
La Toque Cuivrée	4

CAFÉS

Books & Coffee	18
Cafecito	8

SHOPPING

Diabolo Menthe	11
Fromagerie Deruelle	12
Galeries Lafayette	6
Les Grands Hommes	4
De Grimm	2
La Machine à Lire	8
MiAM	10
Parenthese	3
Petit Pouces	9
Pulp's Bordeaux	13
Saunion Chocolats	1
La Toque Cuivrée	5
w.a.n.	7

ACCOMMODATION

Hôtel Bleu de Mer Bordeaux	4
Central Hostel	7
L'InterContinental Bordeaux – Le Grand Hôtel	2
Hôtel Majestic	1
Le Miroir aux Fées	6
Quality Hotel Bordeaux Centre	5
Du Théâtre	3

DRINKING & NIGHTLIFE

BARS

Aux 4 Coins du Vin	3
Bar à Vin du CIVB	1
Calle Ocho	2
Sonate	4
Le Sur Mesure	5
Wash Bar	7

LGBTQ+

Le Coco Loko	6

1

riverfront, the intention was to open the medieval city onto the river and, in turn, the nearby Atlantic Ocean. To do so involved demolishing parts of the old city walls as well as a number of riverfront buildings.

Although the square is an historical and architectural masterpiece, for most of today's visitors the real attraction is the 2006 addition of a summer-only Miroir d'Eau (water mirror) that beautifully reflects the buildings around it. At 137m long and 40m wide, this 2cm film of water is the largest water mirror in the world. Every 23 minutes jets shoot a fine mist of water up into the air – to the great delight of passing children.

Palais de la Bourse
🛈 Place de la Bourse

The northern side of the square is taken up by the **Palais de la Bourse**, which was built from 1742-9 to house the chamber of commerce, a function it still fills today. The interior of the structure was damaged by fire in 1925 and again in 1940 when it was hit during a World War II English bombing raid. As well as the Chamber of Commerce, the building is also used today as a conference centre and is normally closed to casual visitors.

Musée National des Douanes
Place de la Bourse • Charge, included with City Pass • http://musee-douanes.fr • 🛈 Place de la Bourse

The southern side of the square is taken up by the former customs building (known at the time as the Ferme Générale), which is one of the best examples of neo-classical architecture in the city. It was here that taxes were paid on items shipped in and out of Bordeaux from the seventeenth century. Today, the building houses the **Musée National des Douanes** (National Customs Museum), which is considerably more interesting than it sounds. Something of a cabinet of curiosities, much of the collection consists of items confiscated by customs officers. Items on display include furniture, opium pipes, maps, scale models, musical instruments and important works of art by the likes of Monet and Salvador Dali.

Jardins des Lumières
Place de la Bourse • Free • 🛈 Place de la Bourse

Stretching north and south away from the Miroir d'Eau are the **Jardins des Lumières**, a thin strip of park and garden running along the riverside promenade. Boasting 33,000 plants designed to impress year-round, they're particularly radiant with bright flowers in the springtime. It's a lovely part of town for a walk along the riverfront.

Place du Parlement
Place du Parlement • Free • 🛈 Place de la Bourse

A RIVER LEFT TO ITS OWN DEVÈZES

It goes without saying that the **Garonne** is the dominant river of Bordeaux, but unbeknownst to most people there is another river running through Bordeaux, the Devèze. Back when the city was first founded in Roman times, this river was equally as important as the Garonne and the original city was focused on the banks of this river. Due to silting in the Middle Ages the river is now a mere trickle of its former glory and for the most part runs through pipes hidden away under the city. A bronze statue of Hercules – now on display in the **Musée d'Aquitaine** – was discovered in the Place Saint-Pierre in 1832, and is thought to have stood at the point where the Devèze joined the Garonne.

THE PARLEMENT DE BORDEAUX

By the mid-1400s, in the face of the French king Charles VII's advances, the English were decisively losing the Hundred Years' War. In 1451, the French took Bordeaux, at which point a court of justice – known as a parliament – was established in the city. Occupying the Palace de l'Ombrière, it wielded considerable power in local and national politics, until it was abolished in the wake of the French Revolution.

From the Place de la Bourse, rue Fernard Philippart leads southwest to the attractive **Place du Parlement**. Surrounded by elegant eighteenth century houses, the square's centrepiece is a baroque fountain installed in the 1860s. Originally called the Place du Marché-Royal, the square was renamed Place de la Liberté after the Revolution, before assuming the current name, which commemorates the Parlement de Bordeaux. The square is lined by enticing open-air restaurants and cafés.

Église Saint-Pierre

Place Saint-Pierre • Free • 05 56 94 30 50 • ⊕ Place de la Bourse

In its earliest twelfth century incarnations, the **Église Saint-Pierre** (Saint-Pierre Church) overlooked the quays of the once important river Devèze just before it flowed into the Garonne. The current church, which is tucked just back from the modern waterfront and a block south of the place de la Bourse and appears squeezed between old town houses, was built in the fourteenth century and greatly remodelled five hundred years later. It's notable for its stained-glass windows, Gothic portal and choir. In front of it is a small square, the Place Saint-Pierre, perfect for a coffee or *vin* pit stop with cafés lining its cobbled surface and inviting outdoor tables covered in awnings and umbrellas.

Porte Cailhau

Place du Palais • Free • ⊕ Place de la Bourse

Back on the waterfront, and a couple of hundred metres south of the place de la Bourse is the extraordinary **Porte Cailhau**, a monumental 35m high gateway that leads into the old town. It derives its name from *calhau*, meaning 'stone' in the Gascon language. This remarkable fairytale-like gateway was built in 1494 to commemorate Charles VIII's victory at the Battle of Fornovo in Italy. A niche on the left on the riverside contains a likeness of the king: he's joined by St John the Baptist (in the centre) and Cardinal d'Epernay, the Archbishop of Bordeaux who fought by Charles VIII's side at Fornovo. On the town side, the gateway bears an elaborate carving of two figures holding a shield bearing the fleur-de-lis. As you walk through the gateway take note of the sign instructing you to be careful not to bang your head on the lintel: Charles VIII died after doing just that. The gateway contains a small exhibition room from which there is a stunning view over the river and displays detailing how the gateway itself was constructed.

Cinéma Utopia

5 place Camille Jullian • www.cinemas-utopia.org/bordeaux • Charge • ⊕ Place de la Bourse

No soulless multiplexes here: this is a cinema venue with a difference. **Cinéma Utopia** is housed in a converted church, making for a marvellously atmospheric place to catch a film. The programme concentrates largely on indies, but also takes in the occasional blockbuster. Films are almost always subtitled.

1

THE PALAIS DE L'OMBRIÈRE

There's no evidence of it now, but on the Place du Palais there once stood a medieval royal residence known as the **Palais de l'Ombrière**. Little is known of its design, but it seems to have been constructed piecemeal from the late eleventh century onwards. Well-known inhabitants include the famously unhappily married couple Louis VII and Eleanor of Aquitaine. Serving as the headquarters of the Parlement de Bordeaux from 1462 onwards, the palace was eventually demolished in the wake of the French Revolution.

Place Fernand Lafargue

Place Fernand Lafargue • Free • ⊙ Rue Sainte-Catherine

This small square was, in the medieval era, one of the principal points of the city, being an important marketplace and a site of public punishment for criminals. Its current name is in honour of Jean Fernand-Lafargue, a Bordeaux novelist of the late nineteenth century – a statue of him can be seen in the Jardin Public.

Grosse Cloche

Rue Saint-James • Charge (for guided visits) • ⊙ Rue Sainte-Catherine

The most charming of all the medieval gates into the old part of Bordeaux, the **Grosse Cloche** (Great Bell) is a thirteenth-century gateway topped by, you guessed it, a large bell. And by large bell, we mean giant. The bell, which is fondly known as Armande Louis, is 2m-high by 2m-wide and weighs more than seven tonnes. Despite – or perhaps because of – its weight, the bell seems to be rather delicate and has been replaced six times after breaking. The bell's original use was to alert citizens of fire and other disasters, as well as letting everyone know when the grape harvest was ready to be brought in.

The tower is crowned by a golden copper weathervane representing an English leopard (whatever that might be), given to the city during the period when the English ruled Aquitaine. Interestingly, the building served a double purpose and was once also used as a prison. You can still see some of the cells with their thick doors and huge clunky locks.

Musée d'Aquitaine

20 cours Pasteur • http://musee-aquitaine-bordeaux.fr • Charge, included with City Pass • ⊙ Musée d'Aquitaine

West of Grosse Cloche, on busy cours Pasteur, is the superb **Musée d'Aquitaine**, which traces the long history of this huge swathe of France, including a small section on wine. The two-storey museum starts way back in the hazy days of pre-history and includes the famed "Venus with Horn", a bas-relief discovered in the Dordogne in 1911, which is thought to be at least 20,000 years old. There is then a comprehensive outline of the region's little known Roman period, which includes some wonderful mosaics and statues and includes a recreation of Bordeaux's Roman Forum (see page 132). Upstairs focuses on the development of Bordeaux as a major European port. The displays don't try to hide the horrifying role the city played in the trans-Atlantic slave trade and the wealth it made from this human trade. One of the other major attractions for culture buffs is the tomb of Bordeaux-born, sixteenth century philosopher and writer, Michel de Montaigne.

In addition to the permanent collection, the museum also hosts interesting temporary exhibitions. Although the subject matter may not always be of interest to children, the museum has created a fun *parcours sensorial*: follow the orange stickers on the floor to discover interactive, child-friendly displays and activities. On the first Sunday of each month (except in July and August) the museum offers free entry.

Cathédrale Saint-André

1

Place Pey Berland • http://cathedrale-bordeaux.fr • Free • ⊕ Hôtel de Ville

Bordeaux's **cathedral** is a Gothic masterpiece and one of the undisputed highlights of the city. The original structure dates back to the eleventh century and was consecrated by Pope Urban II in 1096. However, little remains from that period and the majority of what you see today dates back to the fourteenth and fifteenth centuries, although the Royal Gate is from the thirteenth century. The cathedral was an important stop on the medieval pilgrimage to Santiago de Compostela in northwest Spain (and in recent decades, as interest in the pilgrimage has increased, the cathedral has again become an important stop for modern day pilgrims). In 1137 Eleanor of Aquitaine – the Princess Diana of the period – married the soon to be Louis VII inside this cathedral and her marriage was just as unhappy as that of her twentieth century British equivalent.

The interior of the cathedral is vast and impressive. Highlights include the choir, which provides one of the few complete examples of the late Gothic style known as Rayonnant. In the Chapelle Ste-Anne, which is behind the altar, you can just about make out some very faded medieval wall frescos. Another highlight is the stained-glass windows in the Chapelle du Mont Carmel and the mahogany pulpit and organ. The Portail Royal (Royal Gate) was once the main entrance to the cathedral, but today it's actually inside the building. The stunning stone masonry on it depicts the Last Judgement according to Matthew. All of the other original gates to the cathedral were destroyed during the Revolution.

Frequent music concerts are held inside the cathedral including the Baroque Music festival (June or July) and the Organ Festival (July). The tourist office can provide details. Most Tuesdays a delightful antiquarian book market takes place on neighbouring place Jean Moulin.

Tour Pey-Berland

Place Pey-Berland • http://pey-berland.fr • Charge • ⊕ Hôtel de Ville

The most striking thing about the cathedral isn't the cathedral itself but rather the fifty-metre-high bell tower, the **Tour Pey-Berland**, adjacent to the cathedral. The reason for the tower's construction (completed in 1466) was due to an engineering and mathematical miscalculation when it was discovered that the 11-tonne cathedral bell was too big and heavy for the cathedral spire and so a separate bell tower had to be built to house it. In 1863 the spire was topped with a gold statue of Notre Dame de l'Aquitaine (Our Lady of Aquitaine). Climb the 233 steep and narrow steps to the top for a superb view over the roof of the cathedral and nearby buildings. Be aware that only a very limited number of people are allowed to climb the tower at any one time and at busy times of the year it's wise to book a time slot online ahead of your visit.

Palais Rohan

Place Pey Berland • ⊕ Hôtel de Ville

Bordeaux's cathedral is so impressive that it's easy to overlook the **Palais Rohan**, which is found on the western edge of the square. It was built in 1771 when Ferdinand Maximilien Mériadec de Rohan, the Archbishop of Bordeaux, decided he needed a new palace to replace the existing medieval residence. The palace is typically grand, boasting huge pillars surrounding the monumental entranceway, and dramatic façades at both the front and back. Following the Revolution, the palace served as a residence for Napoleon and subsequently Louis XVIII, before becoming Bordeaux's town hall (Hôtel de Ville) in 1835. Entry is by guided tour (in French) only.

1

Musée des Beaux-Arts

20 cours d'Albret • http://musba-bordeaux.fr • Charge, included with City Pass • 🚇 Palais de Justice

Directly behind the Palais Rohan is the **Musée des Beaux-Arts**. Founded in 1801, it's the oldest museum in Bordeaux. The small but star-studded permanent collection covers French and West European art (Flemish artists are well represented) from the Renaissance period through to the middle of the twentieth century. International artists whose works are on display include Titian, Van Dyck and Rubens, among others, while Bordeaux and nouvelle Aquitaine are represented by neoclassical artists such as Lacour and Taillasson, art-deco painter Dupas and the cubist Lhote. The oldest piece on display (in the South Wing) is the 1469 piece, *Vièrge de pitié* (Virgin of Pity) by Flemish painter Hans Clot.

Other woks of interest include those by the Bordeaux artist Rosa Bonheur (died 1899) who shocked polite society by daring to wear trousers when she painted, which was more than simply not the done thing: it was also illegal. (The law introduced in 1800 banning French women from wearing trousers was, incredibly, not repealed until 2013.) Bonheur also undertook activities typically reserved for men, including smoking and hunting, and stated that the only men worthy of her attention were the bulls that were the subject of her artwork.

Like most Bordeaux museums, it also hosts good temporary exhibitions of contemporary works. The small **Jardin de la Mairie**, just outside the museum is a pleasant place to rest on a bench in the shade of a tree.

Fort du Hâ

10 rue des Frères Bonie • Free • 🚇 Palais de Justice

The **Fort du Hâ** was a castle built on the orders of Charles VII, following his victory in the Hundred Years' War which evicted the English from Bordeaux. The fortress was used as a prison during World War II, though the prison buildings were demolished in 1969. Two circular towers, linked by a large wall, still remain. The fort is not open to the public, but the towers, backed by the ultra-modern building of the Tribunal Judiciare de Bordeaux, make an impressive sight.

Musée des Arts Décoratifs

Rue Bouffard • http://madd-bordeaux.fr • Charge • 🚇 Gambetta

The **Musée des Arts Décoratifs** is housed in a handsome eighteenth-century mansion, once owned by the rich noble Pierre Raymond de Lalande: the building's beautifully restored period rooms evoke the grandeur of the Ancien Régime. Converted to a museum in 1924, the building holds an impressive collection of eighteenth- and nineteenth-century furnishings and porcelain, and also hosts temporary exhibitions usually devoted to Art Deco and contemporary design. The museum is due to reopen in January 2026 following major renovation works.

Galeries Lafayette

11-19 rue Sainte-Catherine • www.galerieslafayette.com/m/magasin-bordeaux • 🚇 Grand Théâtre

Even if you're not shopping, you might want to take a walk by Bordeaux's top department store, which occupies a splendid early twentieth century Art Nouveau building. Don't miss the outstanding decorative carvings above the entrance.

Place de la Comédie

Place de la Comédie • Free • 🚇 Grand Théâtre

Another of Bordeaux's impressive public squares, the **Place de la Comédie** is dominated by the neoclassical Grand Théâtre on the east side and the dramatic eighteenth century frontage of the opulent Grand Hotel. Until 1677, the square was home to a large Roman monument known as the Pillars of Tutelle, but this was destroyed by Louis XIV to make room for the construction of the Château Trompette fortress – which was demolished in its turn in 1818. On the southern edge of the square you'll spot an elegant cast iron sculpture of a face, almost flat when viewed from a corner but appearing to be a fully rounded head when seen front on. This is the sculpture Sanna by the Catalan artist Jaume Plensa, which was intended to be a temporary exhibit when it was installed in 2013 but proved so popular that it has remained on permanent display ever since.

Grand Théâtre

Place de la Comédie • http://opera-bordeaux.com • ❶ Grand Théâtre

Just back from the place de la Bourse is the magnificent **Grand Théâtre**. It was built by the architect Victor Louis in 1780, on the site of a Roman temple, the Pillars of Guardianship which was a part of the Roman forum. The Neoclassical exterior is adorned with twelve columns topped with statues representing the nine Muses and three Graces. Head inside to be greeted by flamboyant trompe l'oeil paintings and an eighteenth-century performance hall that is considered rivalled in its perfection only by the opera houses of Versailles and Turin. The auditorium has a huge circular dome, the ceiling of which is covered in frescos painted by Claude Robin in the eighteenth century. The frescos pay homage to the arts and the city of Bordeaux, with the city represented as a woman and the wealth being shown as wine, the sea and the slave trade. Also of note is the huge chandelier that weighs 1.2 tonnes, made with Bohemian crystals and containing four hundred individual lamps.

There are two ways of seeing the interior: you can either join one of the regular guided tours organised though the tourist office or, even better, attend an opera or ballet performance. Tickets can be bought online but demand is usually high so book as far ahead as you can.

Allées de Tourny

Les allées de Tourny • Free • ❶ Grand Théâtre

Stretching northwest from the Place de la Comédie is the wide avenue of **Les Allées de Tourny**. Named after Louis de Tourny, the eighteenth-century steward of Bordeaux who was responsible for much of the city's urban development at the time. Overlooked by elegant frontages on both sides, it's an attractive street which is particularly busy in December when it's used as the venue for the city's Christmas market.

L'École du Vin de Bordeaux

1-3 cours du 30 Juillet • http://ecoleduvindebordeaux.com • Charge • ❶ Grand Théâtre

On the southeast corner of Les Allees de Tourney, facing towards the Place de la Comédie, is the lovely Maison Gobineau, an impressive neoclassical building which vaguely resembles the front of a ship. As the headquarters of the winemaking organisation CIVB, its basement bar is an elegant, art-filled spot for sampling some of Bordeaux's vintages, and it is also home to the prestigious **L'École du Vin de Bordeaux**, (Bordeaux Wine School). With the Bordeaux wine world sometimes seeming a little intimidating and closed to those not in the know, the school demystifies the art of wine through short, two-hour tastings and blending workshops, as well as more advanced full-day workshops and longer term, high-level classes and courses. All classes are in French only and should be booked in advance through the website. There are no walk-in visits.

1

Salle Capitulaire

3 rue Mably • Free • ❶ Grand Théâtre

A block west from Les Allees de Tourny is the **Salle Capitulaire** and **Cour Malby** (chapter house and Malby courtyard). Built in 1684 over the ruins of a church and Jacobin convent that were destroyed during the Revolution, the complex was used as the headquarters of revolutionary groups, then as a military base before finally becoming a municipal library. In 1994, it had another re-birth, this time becoming an auditor office (perhaps better off as the former). Fortunately, the old chapter house and the Mably courtyard, named after Gabriel Bonnot de Mably, an eighteenth-century philosopher, has been turned into a cultural centre that hosts frequent art and cultural exhibitions. Ask at the tourist office for what's going on at the time of your visit. Outside stands a statue of Francisco Goya, the Spanish painter who was buried in Bordeaux's Chartreuse Cemetery.

Église Notre Dame

Place du Chapelet • Free • ❶ Grand Théâtre

Just next door to **Salle Capitulaire** and often overlooked by visitors to the city, the delightful **Église Notre Dame** (Church of Our Lady) was originally built as a Dominicain monastery. After being destroyed in 1678 it was rebuilt as a church in 1707. It has a richly ornamented façade with many bas-reliefs, statues and ornamental motifs. Above the entrance door, a bas-relief represents the Virgin giving the rosary to Saint Dominic framed by the full-length statues of the Doctors of the Church (Saints Ambrose, Gregory, Jerome and Augustinians). The interior is a sombre contrast to the exterior, but there are some notable murals above the Choir. The painter, Francisco Goya spent the last years of his life living just down the street from the church and his funeral was held here in April 1828.

Place des Quinconces

North of the Grand Théâtre and past Maison Gobineau, cours du 30-juillet lead to the bare, gravelly expanse of the **place des Quinconces**. Not a particularly attractive space, it's often enlivened by the presence of festivals or temporary fairgrounds. The square's chief feature is the **Monument aux Girondins**, on the west side: this glorious *fin-de-siècle* ensemble of statues and fountains was built in honour of the Girondin faction who – although in favour of the abolition of the monarchy – opposed the increasing extremism of the Revolution and ultimately fell victim to the mass executions of the Reign of Terror. The monument came under threat during World War II, when the occupying Nazis made plans to lower French morale by melting it down. Fortunately, the local Resistance got wind of the plot and, under cover of darkness, dismantled the monument piece by piece, hiding it in a barn in the Médoc until after the war.

Jardin Public

Cour de Verdun • Free • ❶ Jardin Public

Since 1746 the Bordelais have promenaded around the **Jardin Public**. Covering 11 hectares, this stately park is filled with century-old trees, expansive lawns and is hemmed in by magnificent mansions. Locals flock here for picnics, to sunbathe, to work up a sweat jogging or simply to feed the ducks and swans in the ponds. There are also children's playgrounds. Also here and not to be missed is the **Guignol Guérin** puppet theatre. Dating from 1853, this Punch and Judy style puppet theatre is the oldest in France and, remarkably, it's been owned by the same family throughout its existence.

The park also contains the **Jardin Botanique** which is home to over a thousand different plant species. There's a pleasant bar restaurant, **l'Orangerie** (https://www.lorangeriejardinpublic-bordeaux.fr) overlooking the water. Stop here to revive legs weary of walking on the terrace or indoors in cooler weather and indulge in savoury galettes or sweet crepes and ice cream. It has a nice selection of ciders and local wines, too. The park is classified as one of the 'Remarkable Gardens of France'.

Museum Bordeaux Sciences et Nature

Cour de Verdun • http://museum-bordeaux.fr • Charge, included with City Pass • ❂ Jardin Public or Fondaudège Muséum

Inside the Jardin Public is the **Museum Bordeaux Sciences et Nature** (Bordeaux Science and Nature Museum). First opened in 1791, this is one of the largest natural history museums in France, with over a million specimens.

Completely renovated in 2019, the museum has taken the rather Victorian displays of stuffed animals and attempted to bring them firmly into the twenty-first century. Alongside the extensive permanent collection are interesting temporary exhibitions, multimedia shows and regular workshops (in French-only).

The permanent exhibition is divided up to tell a specific story. These include, Nature seen by Man which gives a general overview of the wonderful richness of diversity found on our planet; The coastline of Aquitaine, which shows that there's more than just surfers off the beaches to the west of Bordeaux; and Eat me, if you can!, an exhibition which reveals the many diverse ways in which animals feed themselves and how their bodies work. Finally, there's an entire section devoted to the museum's youngest visitors in which children under six will learn all about baby animals.

Palais Gallien

126 rue du Dr Albert Barraud • Charge • ❂ Jardin Public

To the west and north of the Jardin Public lies a quiet, provincial quarter of two-storey stone houses that includes rue du Dr-Albert-Barraud, where you can see the **Palais Gallien**, a third-century arena – all that remains of Burdigala, Aquitaine's Roman capital. The arena could once host 15,000 spectators, but today there's nothing but a few walls and columns; tours can be arranged with the tourist office (charge). Nearby, on place Delerme, is the unusual round **market hall**.

Cours Xavier Arnozan

Cr Xavier Arnozan • Charge • ❂ Jardin Public

To the east of the Jardin Public, at the head of the wide avenue of **Cr Xavier Arnozan** is a statue of Joan of Arc, mounted on a horse and ready to do battle with the English. Following the avenue towards the river will take you past numerous grand merchants' houses dating from the eighteenth century. Maison Fenwick, found on

---

BORDEAUX AND THE AMERICAN REVOLUTIONARY WAR

The history of Bordeaux is linked in numerous ways to the **American Revolutionary War**: the first American consulate was established here due to Bordeaux's citizens having supplied the soldiers with weapons – and, perhaps more importantly, wine. One of the War's principal commanders, the Marquis de Lafayette, set sail from Bordeaux to join the American struggle, and the political thinker Montesquieu – famous for his development of the principle of separation of powers, which was subsequently built into the US Constitution – was a citizen of the city.

1

a small square where the avenue joins Quai des Chartrons, was the site of the first ever American consulate, which was established here in 1778 and remained in use until 1996.

Musée d'Art Contemporain

7 rue Ferrère • http://capc-bordeaux.fr • Charge, included with City Pass • ⓣ Capc

Close to the river, occupying a converted nineteenth-century warehouse, is the **Musée d'Art Contemporain**. The vast, arcaded hall is magnificent in its own right, and provides an ideal setting for the post-1960 sculpture and installations by artists such as Richard Long and Sol LeWitt. The main space is used for temporary exhibitions. There's a superb collection of art books in the library and a café-restaurant on the roof (lunch only). Occupying the same building is the **Arc en Rêve Centre d'Architecture**, a small gallery where you'll find temporary exhibitions primarily focussing on architecture, but dipping into other art forms as well.

Place Gambetta and Saint Seurin-Fondaudège

History goes back a long way in the Saint Seurin-Fondaudège neighbourhood. Here vestiges of a Roman past can be found nuzzled up against the mansions built by wealthy eighteenth- and nineteenth-century wine merchants. For visitors there are impressive religious buildings, Roman ruins and a museum in which nothing is quite what it seems.

Place Gambetta

🚇 Gambetta

One of the most emblematic squares in Bordeaux, **Place Gambetta** (formerly called Place Dauphine), is surrounded by impressive eighteenth-century buildings. It was once a busy transport crossroads but in recent years it's undergone significant renovation works which has seen the amount of green space increased and the addition of a small water mirror. Look out for the point zero sign outside number 10, from which all distances in Bordeaux are measured.

Porte Dijeaux

Rue de la Prte Dijeaux • Free • 🚇 Gambetta

Just off the southeast corner of Place Gambetta is the **Porte Dijeaux**, a neoclassical city gate built in 1746. This was at one point the western edge of the city, and the gate is the third city gate to stand on this spot, replacing a Roman gate which was destroyed in 1302 and the subsequent medieval gate, which was demolished to make way for this incarnation. Above the portal are carved images symbolising Bordeaux, including – fittingly – some grapes.

Basilique St-Seurin

Place des Martyrs de la Résistance • www.paroissebordeauxsauvetesaintseurin.fr • Free • 🚇 Mériadeck

The heart of the St-Seurin neighbourhood, parts of the current **Basilica of St-Seurin** date from the eleventh century. But a church has stood here since the sixth century, which in turn was built on top of a fourth-century necropolis containing symbols of Christian burials. Arguably, this makes the basilica the cradle of Christianity in Bordeaux, and it retained its prominence for centuries afterwards. During the Middle Ages, it was a particularly important stop on the pilgrimage trail to Santiago de Compostela in northwest Spain, when pilgrims called by to view relics associated with the legendary medieval knight Roland.

Of the original eleventh century structure, only the porch, the crypt and the base of the bell tower remain. Several side chapels were added throughout the fourteenth and fifteenth centuries, including the Chapelle Notre Dame de Bonne Bouvelle which contains an icon of the Virgin that rumour says can perform miracles. More architecturally pleasing is the Chapelle Notre Dame de la Rose, with a fifteenth century altarpiece with a dozen scenes depicting the life of the Virgin. The neo-Romanesque façade is a more modern addition designed in 1828 by the architect, Pierre-Alexandre Poitevin.

Deep down below the basilica is the crypt, one of the few surviving parts of the eleventh-century structure. One of the tombs here is that of St Fort, one of the first bishops of the city: from the seventeenth century onward, this tomb was the object of particular veneration on 16 May, when, if a mother was to bring her son here, then he would re-emerge as a man. The tourist office runs occasional guided tours into the crypt.

Site Archéologique de St-Seurin

Place des Martyrs de la Résistance • Charge • 🚇 Mériadeck

Right in front of the main entrance to the basilique is the entrance to the underground **Site Archéologique de St-Seurin** (St-Seurin Archaeological Site). This is a part of the fourth-century Christian necropolis upon which the church now stands. Down in its dark depths are numerous tombstones dating back to that period, which, after centuries under the soil and rock, were rediscovered in 1910 during archaeological excavations. Legend has it that Charlemagne had his men buried here, including his nephew Roland – though this should be taken with a pinch of salt, as Roland is also said to be buried in Blaye, 25 miles to Bordeaux's north. Many of the finest pieces discovered here are now on display in the Musée d'Aquitaine. Note that the site is only open in the summer and visits are by one-hour guided tours.

Musée de l'Illusion

4 rue Bonneaffé • http://museedelillusion.fr • Charge • Ⓣ Mériadeck

One of the quirkier museums in Bordeaux is the **Musée de l'illusion**. A great family-friendly day out, the museum of illusions has immersive exhibitions where you can snap a selfie of your head emerging out of a bathroom sink or of the kids clambering down the side of an historic Bordeaux town house. If anyone gets really annoying, you can also shrink them down to pint size.

Piscine Judaïque

164 rue Judaïque • 05 56 51 48 31 • Charge • Ⓣ Saint-Bruno

When the days heat up, head to the beautiful **Piscine Judaïque**, a swimming pool complex dating to 1936. Behind the fabulous Art Deco facade are a multitude of indoor and outdoor pools, water slides and a spa. Swimming caps are obligatory, as are speedos for men. Both can be bought onsite. Closed every second Monday and on bank holidays.

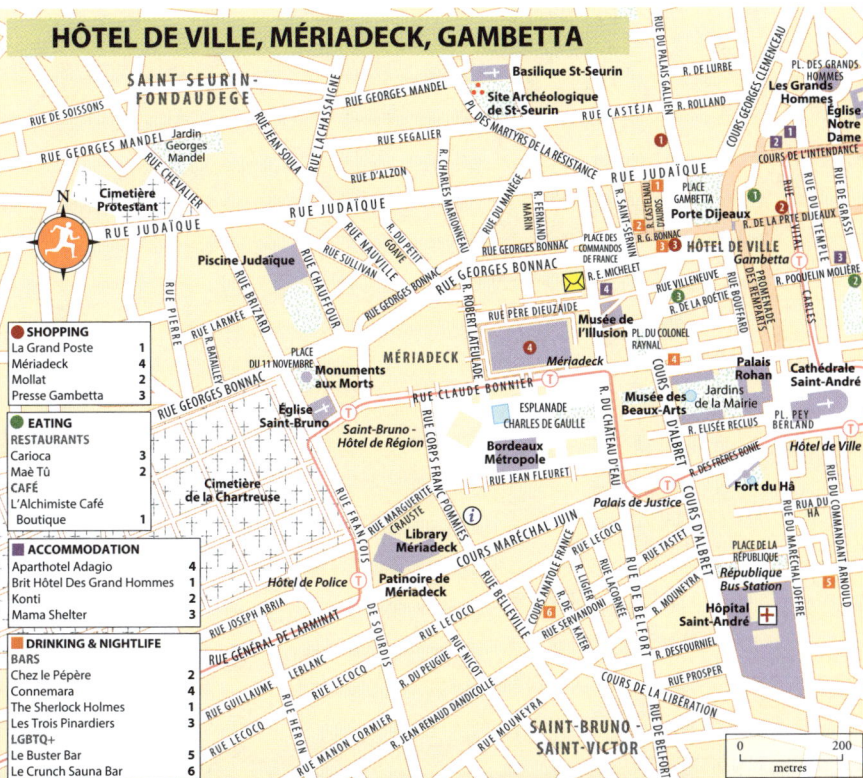

HÔTEL DE VILLE, MÉRIADECK, GAMBETTA

SHOPPING
La Grand Poste	1
Mériadeck	4
Mollat	2
Presse Gambetta	3

EATING
RESTAURANTS
| Carioca | 3 |
| Maè Tû | 2 |
CAFÉ
| L'Alchimiste Café Boutique | 1 |

ACCOMMODATION
Aparthotel Adagio	4
Brit Hôtel Des Grand Hommes	1
Konti	2
Mama Shelter	3

DRINKING & NIGHTLIFE
BARS
Chez le Pépère	2
Connemara	4
The Sherlock Holmes	1
Les Trois Pinardiers	3
LGBTQ+
Le Buster Bar	5
Le Crunch Sauna Bar	6

Église Saint-Bruno

5 place du 11 Novembre • https://fssp-bordeaux.fr • Free • ⊤ Saint-Bruno

In 1383, Carthusian monks seeking to escape the Hundred Years' War arrived in Bordeaux, settling near the river – it is from their order that the name of the Chartrons district is derived. In the early seventeenth century, a bequest from a wealthy nobleman gave the Carthusians sufficient funds to construct a new convent and church. Although the convent was largely destroyed in the Revolution, the church remains. Dedicated to Saint Bruno, the founder of the Carthusian order, it's a grand baroque building, with a magnificent altarpiece and splendid carvings running the whole length of the church's ceiling.

Cimetière de la Chartreuse

Rue François de Sourdis • Free • ⊤ Saint-Bruno

Just across the road from the Saint Bruno church is the enormous gateway to the Chartreuse Cemetery, a large burial ground containing some quite elaborate mausoleums. Among the worthies at rest here are Flora Tristan – an early feminist writer and grandmother of the painter Paul Gauguin – and the Spanish painter Francisco Goya.

SAINT SEURIN-FONDAUDEGE

EATING
RESTAURANTS
Baud et Millet — 2
Le Pavillon des Boulevards — 1
Peppone — 3

ACCOMMODATION
Le Boutique Hôtel Bordeaux — 2
Yndo Hotel — 1

BRUTALIST BORDEAUX

Somewhat at odds with much of Bordeaux's architecture, fans of twentieth century brutalism will find a couple of gems here. The area around the Mériadeck shopping centre is a great place to start a mini brutalist tour, with the rather splendid **Tour Devèze**, a government office which looks rather like a stack of cross-shaped pancakes. Across the road is the **Ancienne Caisse d'Epargne des Architectes**, which spirals upwards in three floors of increasingly generous concrete. East from here, you'll easily spot the **Cité municipale de Bordeaux**, which – although it has less to offer concrete enthusiasts – is a very fine piece of modern architecture, looking as if someone has snapped the last Lego brick into place without due care. Arguably the finest brutalist structure in Bordeaux, though, is down by the river, not far from Gare Saint-Jean: the **Jacques Thibaud Conservatory** offers a vast circular dome of concrete sat atop a square concrete plinth.

2

Institut Culturel Bernard Magrez

16 rue de Tivoli • http://institut-bernard-magrez.com • Charge • 🚇 Barrière du Médoc

Inside a grand eighteenth-century mansion, the Hôtel Labottière, is the **Institut Culturel Bernard Magrez** (Bernard Magrez Cultural Institute) a showcase for exhibitions of modern and contemporary works from both public and private collections. Check the website to see what exhibitions are taking place. Even if you don't go inside, the small formal gardens are a nice place to relax.

The cultural centre is the initiative of local man, Bernard Magrez, who is one of the biggest names in French wine and known as 'the man with 41 châteaux', in reference to the number of chateaux he owns.

Parc Rivière

Rue Mandron • Free • 🚇 Barriere du Médoc

A small but attractive park offering a leafy retreat from the city streets, **Parc Rivière** was once the grounds of a mansion built in mock-medieval castle style in the mid-nineteenth century by a wealthy wine merchant. Remains of the chateau can still be found in the park, as can the stables, which have now been converted into a popular café.

St-Michel and Capucins-Victoire

Grand old buildings and historic monuments surround elegant squares filled with pavement cafés in this charming part of the city and this is an area in which you will likely find yourself time and again during your visit to Bordeaux. It is noted for being home to two important churches, the Basilique St-Michel and the Église Sainte-Croix, as well as hosting the best food market in Bordeaux.

Porte de Bourgogne

Place Bir-Hakeim • Free • ⊙ Porte de Bourgogne

On the southern fringe of Vieux Bordeaux, and just back from the river, is the large and free-standing **Porte de Bourgogne**. Built in 1757 in honour of the Duke of Burgundy in a neoclassical style, but without any ornamentation or other decorative elements, it's grand rather than beautiful.

Pont de Pierre

Pont de Pierre • Free • ⊙ Porte de Bourgogne

Crossing the river opposite the Porte de Bourgogne is the impressive **Pont de Pierre** – "Stone Bridge". Napoleon ordered its construction during the Spanish campaigns, though it wasn't actually built until the 1820s. The bridge boasts seventeen arches – differing sources will tell you this is either in honour of Napoleon's victories or the number of letters in his name. The elegant bridge is now closed to traffic, other than public transport, and is an excellent place to take in views of the river and quays, especially at dusk.

3

Basilique St-Michel

Place Meynard/Place Canteloup • Charge • ⊙ St-Michel

The **Basilique St-Michel** is typical of medieval-era churches designed to overwhelm the people into subservience to God and the church. Work on the basilica began in the 1400s but it took two hundred years until workmen were finally able to put down their tools and call it complete.

The most notable feature is the long, tapering fifteenth-century bell tower which, at 114m tall, is the fourth tallest in France and the tallest in the south. It's also notable for standing free of the main building. Over two hundred steps wind up to the top, but at time of writing, the tower was covered in scaffolding for extensive renovations, so your legs will be spared the climb. It's expected to reopen in 2026.

As you explore the interior, you'll find no less than seventeen side chapels, which were funded by wealthy families in the fourteenth and fifteenth centuries. Each one is dedicated to a different saint and trade, with the St Fort Chapel representing fishermen, St Joseph looking out for carpenters, and so forth. Perhaps the most interesting of them is the Chapelle Ste-Catherine, which is dedicated to sailors, in which you'll find a statue to St Ursula representing the 11,000 virgins who were killed by the Huns in the fourth century.

Up until World War II the basilica was known for its 53 stained glass windows but sadly all but one set were destroyed during the war. The only surviving original windows are those in the Chapelle de Mons. All the other windows are modern replacements, but are no less impressive.

The bell tower stands close to what was a fifteenth-century mass grave. In the eighteenth century, some seventy shockingly well-preserved – if rather macabre – mummies were exhumed from the site and placed on public display in the crypt. With their tense, horror movie faces, these dried bodies attracted many visitors over the years including some famous writers such as Victor Hugo, Gustave Flaubert, Théophile Gautier and Ferdinand Céline. Some of the mummies had a specific story attached to them, including a person who had been buried alive, a whole family poisoned by mushrooms and a general killed in a dual. In 1990 the mummies were all removed from public viewing but you can continue to learn all about them through an audiovisual presentation.

ST MICHEL AND CAPUCINS-VICTOIRE

SHOPPING	
L'Entrepôt Saint Germain	2
Marché des Capucins	1

ACCOMMODATION	
Auberge de Jeunesse	4
B&B Bordeaux St Michel	3
Hôtel 56	1
Hôtel la Zoologie	2

EATING	
RESTAURANTS	
Chez Thérèse	1
Monkey Mood	3
Passage Saint-Michel	4
Samos Greek Food	6
Tuk Tik Thai Food District	5
La Tupina	2

DRINKING & NIGHTLIFE	
BARS	
Balthazar	2
Couleurs du Vin	1
Le Lucifer	4
LGBTQ+	
Ultra Klubs	3

0   300   metres

Parc des Sports Saint-Michel

Quai des Salinières • Free • 🚊 St-Michel

The **Parc des Sports Saint-Michel** is perhaps not worth a special visit in itself, but if you're walking along the river in this area, this grassy space dotted with playgrounds and sports facilities is nicer than walking along the busy road. About halfway along, the modest Porte de la Monnaie – Bordeaux's smallest city gate – can be seen on the other side of the road.

Église Sainte-Croix

Place Pierre Renaudel • Free • 🚊 Sainte-Croix

Boasting fabulous sculptures depicting desire and greed, the **Église Sainte-Croix** (Bordeaux's oldest remaining church) is also one of the prettiest. Construction took place between the eleventh and twelfth centuries, but this is the third church to have stood on this site: the first was built on the orders of the Merovingian king Clovis in the fifth century, and gradually destroyed by Arab raids in the eighth century followed by Norman attacks one hundred years later. A replacement was built in 970, followed by the present structure some centuries later. It was originally built to serve as the church of the (now long gone) neighbouring Benedictine abbey.

The bell tower – noticeably more modern than the rest of the structure – was built in the nineteenth century.

Conservatoire Jacques Thibaud

22 Quai Sainte-Croix • https://conservatoire.bordeaux.fr • Free • 🚊 Sainte-Croix

The **Jacques Thibaud Conservatory**, just east of the Église Sainte-Croix, is one of France's foremost music schools, at which there are frequent performances – check the website for details. It's a marvellously brutalist building – even if you're not here for music, you may want to take a look at the masses of concrete on display.

Château Descas

5 quai de Paludate • www.chateaudescas.fr • Charge • 🚊 Sainte-Croix

One of the most impressive buildings on Bordeaux's waterfront, the **Château Descas** was once owned by the successful wine merchant Jean Descas in the late nineteenth century. Although the building was built some centuries previously, Descas was responsible for its transformation into the ostentatious mansion it today resembles. After a stint as a cabaret club, the château was neglected in the early twenty-first century, but from 2022 renovation works began, resulting in a reopening in 2024. It today hosts musical performances, ranging from jazz to techno.

Frac Nouvelle-Aquitaine La MÉCA

5 parv. Corto Maltese • https://fracnouvelleaquitaine-meca.fr • Charge, included with City Pass • 🚊 Saint-Jean

Housed in a dramatic white building on the riverfront, **Frac** is a cultural space offering temporary exhibitions of contemporary art, and runs workshops and programmes to support local artists. Visually striking, it was designed by Danish architect, Bjarke Ingels and is a vast improvement on the former abattoirs that were once here. After a look around, head up to the terrace to enjoy a fantastic view over the river.

BORDEAUX'S BEST MARKETS

If you enjoy poking around markets, Bordeaux has a number of excellent markets to please. Here are some of our favourites:

Marché des Capucins (Place des Capucins; https://marchedescapucins.com) The city's biggest and certainly best fresh produce market is as much a social scene as a place to pick up local delicacies. An almost essential Bordeaux experience is slurping oysters and a glass of white wine here.

Marché Royal and Marché Neuf (Quai des Salinières, Sat and Mon 6am-2pm respectively) Originally two separate markets, they have now been integrated into one. Great place to pick up super fresh fruit and vegetables.

Marché Bio des Quais (Quai des Chartrons, Thu 7am-2pm; Sun 7am-1pm) A small riverside bio market in the Chartrons district. Thursday morning only.

Les Halles de Bacalan (10 esplanade de Pontac; daily 8am-11pm; Sun until 5pm; closed Mon) Mixing a produce market with restaurant and *apéro* stop, this is a good place to take a break after exploring the nearby Cité du Vin.

3

Halle Boca

208 quai de Paludate • https://halleboca.com • Free • Ⓣ Saint-Jean

First built in the 1930s as the city's abbatoir, the **Halle Boca** enjoyed a restoration in the early years of the twenty-first century and is now a food hall offering multiple different cuisines, as well as entertainment options including a bowling alley, pinball machines, and karaoke nights. A good choice for lunch if you're in this part of town.

Place des Capucins

Ⓣ Victoire

The recently renovated and enlarged **Place des Capucins** is of little interest on its own, but the marché des Capucins held here (see page 98) is the biggest and best market in the city. Established first in 1749, the marketplace graduated to a weekly and then daily market by the early 1800s. The market hall itself was built in 1878, and although the market went into decline in the late twentieth century, it has enjoyed a revitalisation since 1999.

Promenade des Remparts

Free • Ⓣ Victoire

The old city of Bordeaux was once almost completely enclosed by high, thick **defensive walls**. When the city started to expand many of these walls were knocked down. However, scattered sections of the original wall still remain, including just behind the marché des Capucins around rue des Douves. There's a gated entry to the walls on Rue Marbotin, but since it's some eight feet above street level – and doubtless locked to boot – access is somewhat challenging. In honesty, unless the *jardin*, which used to be accessible atop this section, reopens at some point in the future, the walls are not worth a special trip.

Marché des Douves

Rue des Douves • www.douves.org • Free • Ⓣ Victoire

This former **market hall**, built in 1886 and still in use until the 1980s, is today a cultural centre that's normally only open for private events. It was designed in the style of Victor Baltard, who built the Les Halles central market in Paris, but is not especially distinctive or indeed attractive.

Musée d'Ethnographie

3 place de la Victoire • https://meb.u-bordeaux.fr • Charge • 🚇 Victoire

This oft-overlooked **ethnographic museum** contains approximately six thousand objects collected in the nineteenth and early twentieth centuries from the French colonies, many of which were brought back by military doctors. It's especially strong on Asian subjects and features exhibits such as clothing, domestic items and musical instruments. Changing temporary exhibitions explore different themes throughout the year and there is a wonderful collection of over eight thousand photographs. The museum is a part of the Bordeaux university, with the building having once been the university medical faculty.

3

Place de la Victoire

Place de la Victoire • Free • 🚇 Victoire

At the heart of central Bordeaux's student area, the **Place de la Victoire** is a large cobbled square dominated by the Porte d'Aquitaine, an eighteenth-century decorative arch on which the coat of arms of Bordeaux is carved. Somewhat smaller, but a good deal more attractive, are the two bronze tortoise sculptures which sit beside a twisting 16-metre tall pillar, designed by the Czech sculptor Ivan Theimer to symbolise the city's wine industry.

Rue Sainte-Catherine

Rue Sainte-Catherine • Free • 🚇 Victoire

Leading off the Place de la Victoire is the kilometre-long **rue Sainte-Catherine**, which traverses the city north to south to Place de la Comédie. It is the main pedestrianized shopping street in the city. The flavour of the street, which is one of the longest single shopping streets in the whole of France, changes as you advance along it. At the Victoire end it's a little unappealing and lined by fast-food joints and cut-price shops. At the opposite end it's far more upmarket with big name international fashion brands such as Zara and H&M, a branch of the Galeries Lafayette department store, cosmetics haven Spehora, a Fnac store, and a selection of French chains alongside smaller, independent boutiques.

CANELÉS

Just north of place de la Victoire is Rue Magendie, on which you'll find the Convent of the Annunciades. Now in use as a government building, the convent's chief claim to fame is as the place of origin for the Bordeaux speciality, the *canelé* pastry. These small cakes, which vaguely resemble miniature Christmas puddings, are soft on the inside, caramelised on the outside, and flavoured with rum and vanilla. It's not known exactly when the *canelé* was invented, but Bordeaux was known for them by the eighteenth century, and today you'll find them in every good pastry shop. Don't miss trying this classic Bordeaux treat while you're in the city.

Grand Synagogue

6 rue du Grand Rabbin Joseph Cohen • 05 56 91 79 39 • Free • ⊤ Musée d'Aquitaine

Around halfway up Rue Sainte-Catherine, a side road leads off to Bordeaux's principal **synagogue**. Built in the 1880s, it was criticised at the time for its close resemblance to a church. Suffering damage under the German occupation in World War II – in which Jews were confined in the synagogue prior to deportation to concentration camps – the synagogue was restored in the post-war period and now serves an active community of worshippers. Call in advance to arrange a visit.

Église du Sacré-Cœur

4 rue Lefol • www.paroissebordeauxsaintjean.fr • Free • ⊤ Saint-Jean

Drawing inspiration from its Paris namesake, the **Église du Sacré-Cœur** is a nineteenth-century church built in the Roman-Byzantine style. It's a popular stop-off for pilgrims, and is attractive from the outside, though the interior is fairly austere.

THE FABULOUS CITÉ DU VIN

Chartrons, Bassins à Flot and Bacalan

Just north of the city centre is the riverside, and village-like, neighbourhood of Chartrons. One of the more desirable parts of the city, the atmosphere here is very bourgeoisie but with a strongly bohemian streak. Immediately to the north is the Bacalan and Bassins à Flot. Just a few short years ago this was a rough and seedy dockland area which, thanks to the decline in shipping, seemed to be in a spiral of permanent decline. But a radical transformation has seen former warehouses and dockyards (and even a World War II era submarine base) transformed into superb art galleries and museums, around which have sprung up lots of new restaurants, bars and hotels. All this has helped to make the Bacalan and Bassins à Flot neighbourhood the coolest in Bordeaux, and one in which you will probably spend a good deal of your time.

La Cité du Vin

1 esplanade de Pontac • http://laciteduvin.com • Charge, included with City Pass • Ⓣ Cité du Vin

One of the city's top draws, the **Cité du Vin** occupies a remarkable piece of contemporary architecture next to the Garonne. This modern building is spectacular – some might say that it outclasses the content within – having been designed to resemble both a decanter with wine swirling inside it and the eddies of the River Garonne. Whether it does so or not is open to debate, but even so, few fail to be impressed by the **spiralling glass and aluminium form** of the riverside building.

It would be hard not to compare this building with that of the Guggenheim Museum in Bilbao just a few hours' drive down the road. That museum helped transform Bilbao from a rundown industrial city to a major international art destination. Can the Cité du Vin put Bordeaux firmly on the world stage? Quite possibly. Since its opening over 3 million people have visited (and for some of that time it was closed or under visited due to Covid travel restrictions) and the museum has already transformed the city's dock area, which had previously been very rundown and unappealing, into Bordeaux's hippest neighbourhood. New restaurants, bars and hotels have sprung up around the museum as have other quality tourist attractions.

The interior reveals a vast, high-ceilinged and light-filled space with visitor attractions set over three levels. The first floor is dedicated to **temporary exhibitions**. Previous exhibitions have centred on subjects such as Georgia, the cradle of viticulture, bistros and the essential role they have played in French society and in shaping viniculture in France, wine and music, wine in the Ancient World and the use of wine in the works of artists such as Picasso.

The second floor houses the **permanent exhibitions**. These are sub-divided into six separate yet interlinking spaces, with many interactive displays. As you wander this floor you will learn about the world's different wine regions (which you visit in an interactive 'helicopter' experience), as well as how wine is made, from soil to vine, vine to grape, grape to wine. The 'Through the Ages' exhibition delves into the long (far longer than you might realise) history of the vine, and you'll learn how to appreciate wine in the 'Art of Living and Wine Around the World'. Finally, the focus shifts to wine production in and around Bordeaux.

Afterwards, head up to the top floor – Le Belvédère – where the all-glass walls offer stunning **panoramic views** of the city and the Garonne. Impressive as that is, make sure to look up: the ceiling is made up of thousands upon thousands of wine bottles to stunning effect. There's also a 30m-long bar here where you can enjoy a complimentary glass of wine (or grape juice), included with your entry ticket. One-hour tasting workshops are also on offer by advance reservation.

Although a wine museum is inherently aimed at adults, the museum has enough interactive displays that kids will get a lot out of a visit here. They also offer a good value family ticket which dramatically reduces the cost of a visit for families, a nice touch. If you time your visit well, the ground-floor restaurant is a good place for a boozy lunch.

Les Halles de Bacalan

15 quai du Maroc • Free • Ⓣ Cité du Vin

For a quick lunch after a visit to the Cité du Vin, cross the road to the **Bacalan food market**, where you'll find numerous stalls selling various street foods. As well as Bordeaux classics such as oysters and galettes, there are international options ranging from Creole to Argentine. Outdoor seating next to the water is very popular in warmer months.

Vertigina

27 quai du Maroc • https://vertigina.com • Charge • ⓣ Cité du Vin

If you're the sort of person who can't look at a massive concrete cylinder without wondering what the view from the top is like, then **Vertigina** can help – this expert outfit runs urban climbing sessions to scale the enormous industrial silos which sit on the quayside. Routes for beginners and experienced climbers are available, and once you reach the top, you'll be rewarded with a 360 panorama that's truly earned.

Musée Mer Marine

89 rue des Étrangers • http://mmmbordeaux.com • Charge, included with City Pass • ⓣ Rue Achard

A 15-minute walk from the **Cité du Vin** will bring you to the **Musée Mer Marine**, designed to look like an ocean-going liner and set by the water in the area that was

BASSINS À FLOT AND BACALAN

AVENUE DE NONTRASTE

AVENUE DE TOURVILLE

RUE DR JEAN VINCENT

BOULEVARD ALIÉNOR D'AQUITAINE

RUE DES PELOURDES
R. LÉONIE PL. MAREIHAC
BOULEVARD ALBERT BRANDENBURG

Piscine
G. Tissot

CITÉ LAFON
RUE BLANQUI
R. PASCAL LAFARGUE
RUE DUPLEIX

RUE JOSEPH BRUNET

Cleveau
Parc du
Port de
la Lune

RUE FRANÇOIS CHAMBRELENT
RUE ARAGO

BOULEVARD ALFRED DANEY

RUE CHARLES MARTIN

BACALAN

Parc de
Bacalan
Brandenburg

PL. RENÉ
MARAN

BOULEVARD ALFRED DANEY

**Moon Harbour
Distillery**

RUE LA MOTTE PICQUET
R.F. GARNIER

**Stade C. Martin
Ferdinand-Moreau**

RUE BLANQUI
RUE AUDUBERT

RUE ACHARD

COURS DUPRÉ SAINT-MAUR

RUE PROFESSEUR VILLEMIN

**Bassins des
Lumières**

*Bassins à
Flot n° 2*

RUE DE NEW YORK

CITÉ DUTREY
New York

R. CHARLEVOIX
DE VILLERS
PL. ADOLPHE
BUSCAILLET

VOIE F. AUDEGUIL

**Le Garage
Moderne**

COURS HENRI BRUNET

RUE LUCIE AUBRAC

RUE BLANQUI

**Église
Saint Rémi**

QUAI VIRGINIE HÉRIOT

**Musée
Mer Marine**

RUE POURMANN

RUE DELBOS

RUE LUCIEN FAURE

R. JEAN HAMEAU

BASSINS À FLOT

RUE DES ÉTRANGERS

Rue Achard
R. DE OUAGADOUGOU

RUE ACHARD

PL. PIERRE
ÉTOIS

N

COURS DU RACCORDEMENT

RUE BOURBON

R. ARMAND DULAMON

Parc
Chante-
Grillon

PL. LEWIS
BROWN

*Bassins à
Flot n° 1*

QUAI LAWTON

RUE DE GIRONDE

**Les Vivres
de l'Art**

PL. VICTOR
RAULIN

Garonne

CITÉ CHANTECRIT

COURS ÉDOUARD VAILLANT

**Musée de l'Histoire
Maritime
de Bordeaux** ②

**Vertigina
The Spaceship** ②

QUAI DU MAROC

**Les Halles
de Bacalan**

La Cité du Vin

COURS LOUIS FARGUE

RUE DE LEYBARDIE

R. DU COMMANDANT HAUTROUX

COURS BALGUERIE STUTTENBERG

RUE BOURBON

RUE DE LA FAÏENCERIE

RUE LUCIEN FAURE

QUAI ARMAND
LALANDE

QUAI DU
SÉNÉGAL

QUAI DE
BACALAN

QUAI DE
BACALAN

La Cité du Vin

RUE DÉLORD

RUE CHANTECRIT

R. JOSÉPHINE

R. DUPATY

CAP Sciences

CHARTRONS

Les Hangars

PONT JACQUES CHABAN DELMAS

QUAI DE BACALAN

La Cité du Vin

🟢 **EATING**
RESTAURANTS
Café Maritime	2
Les Halles de Bacalan	1

🟪 **ACCOMMODATION**
B&B Hotel Bordeaux	
Bassins à Flot	1
Renaissance	2

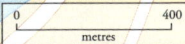

🟥 **DRINKING & NIGHTLIFE**
BARS
La Cité du Vin	3
La Dame	2
My Beers	1

0	400
	metres

– appropriately for this museum – the city's thriving port in the nineteenth century. Standing outside the front of the museum is a large sparkly sculpture of a shark hanging from fishing hooks, intended to draw attention to the tens of thousands of sharks killed each year by man and which is fast driving many shark species towards extinction. Inside, the museum has less about the aquatic denizens of the deep and more about Bordeaux's long, rich and fascinating **maritime history**. Displays combine historic maritime artefacts that run through the history of navigation, boat building and exploration, while also examining the effect climate change has on the oceans and the impact of plastic waste and overfishing. There are plenty of interactive bits and bobs for kids.

Bassins des Lumières

Impasse Brown de Colstoun • http://bassins-lumieres.com • Charge, included with City Pass • 🚇 Rue Achard

What to do with a huge, disused German-built World War II submarine base? This was the question Bordeaux faced. The bomb-proof base was one of five on the French Atlantic coast built during the height of the war by the occupying German forces. Using reinforced concrete, the base, which was constructed by prisoners of war, was used to safely protect German and Italian submarines. At the end of the war the site was largely abandoned, until the 1990s when it became a yachting conservatory. Eventually, in 2020, it became the Bassins des Lumières, a **cutting-edge art gallery** and **cultural institution** in which the exhibitions are incorporated into and around the submarine holding tanks.

What makes the gallery unusual is that it rarely has any original works of art by featured artists. Instead, it makes creative use of film, CGI and sound to create what can only be described as living, moving art projected onto the walls and water and in which the viewing public are often a part of the art themselves. Exhibitions to date have included Gaudi, Dali and Van Gogh – all showcased in a way you've never seen before. The Bassins des Lumières has proven to be a resounding success with the public, and its temporary exhibitions (there's no permanent collection) frequently sell out. As well as art installations, the space also hosts concerts. Management encourage visitors to buy tickets online in advance or via the QR codes displayed outside, but in our experience there's less queuing to be done if you just buy the tickets there and then.

Moon Harbour Distillery

492 boulevard Alfred Daney • http://moonharbour.fr • Charge, included with City Pass • 🚇 Rue Achard

If you're the sort of person who likes to confound expectations, then visiting a **whisky distillery** in the heart of France's wine region will probably appeal. Occupying a

---

SAINT LOUIS

Louis IX ascended the French throne in 1226, and over the course of his reign became widely respected across Europe as a pious and effective king – the very model of the perfect Christian monarch. As well as seeing off rebellions by fractious nobles and persistent invasions by Henry III of England, he found time to undertake widespread legal reform and go on crusade twice. Neither crusade could be described as successful: on the first, he was captured and only released after a vast ransom was paid, while on the second, he contracted dysentery and died. He was canonised in 1297, the only French king to have been made a saint.

STREET ART IN CHARTRONS AND BACALAN

Bordeaux might have a reputation for having a strong conservative streak, but the Chartrons and Bacalan neighbourhoods have always been a little more rebellious and today are a real hotspot of street art and small independent cultural spaces. Get into Bordeaux's often overlooked bohemian scene at some of the following:

LES VIVRES DE L'ART

2 bis rue Achard • http://lesvivresdelart.org • Free • ⊕ Rue Achard

Located within three renovated eighteenth-century houses, this arts and cultural space is the domain of metal sculptor and artist Jean-François Buisson and you'll see his works throughout the complex and garden courtyard. He has since been joined here by other artists which means there's always plenty of interest to see and experience. As well as the art, there are regular alternative music concerts, dance shows and fringe theatre (in French only).

LE M.U.R

Place Paul Avisseau • http://lemurdebordeaux.tumblr.com • Free • ⊕ Cours du Médoc

Le M.U.R (The Wall) is a 35m-long bit of wall that has become a canvas for Bordeaux's best **street artists**. Every month a different artist leaves his or her mark on the wall and the result is inevitably bright, bold and stunning. If visiting art galleries isn't really your thing then this is still likely to impress. There are a number of other street art walls in the vicinity including on rue André Darbon just around the corner.

LE GARAGE MODERNE

2 bis rue Achard • http://legaragemoderne.org • Free • ⊕ New York

One of our favourite spaces in Bordeaux, this is indeed a garage. But with a difference. Inside this vast hanger, a small team of **mechanics** actually help local people to do their own car or bicycle repairs whilst perusing the bizarre collection of bric-a-brac and vintage vehicles. There are also resident **artists**, a great lunchtime canteen, **cultural events** and live music, as well as summer evening parties and *apéros*. Best to come here in summer, when there's definitely a lot more going on, rather than in the cold of winter.

4

World War II bunker, Moon Harbour has been producing whisky since 2017. Tours – including tastings – of the distillery are available three times daily between Tuesday and Saturday; you'll need to book in advance on the website.

Musée de l'Histoire Maritime de Bordeaux

1 quai Armand Lalande • http://museehistoiremaritimedebordeaux.fr • Charge, included with City Pass • ⊕ Cité du Vin

If you were the kind of child who enjoyed playing with toy soldiers and wooden boats, then you'll probably look with fondness on Bordeaux's **Maritime Museum**, which tells the long story of Bordeaux's ocean-faring history through masses of toy wooden boats populated by swashbuckling soldiers and sailors. Almost all the exhibits were donated by local families. At time of writing, the museum was closed for renovation, and is expected to reopen in late 2025.

The Spaceship

Quai Lawton • Free • ⊕ Cité du Vin

Outside the Maritime Museum you'll spot a **silver UFO** seemingly hovering over the water. Once you've realised you're not in the midst of an alien invasion, you can admire

CHARTRONS

BASSINS À FLOT

Bassins à Flot n° 1

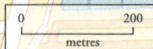

0   200
metres

QUAI VIRGINIE HÉRIOT   QUAI LAWTON

Musée de l'Histoire Maritime de Bordeaux

La Cité du Vin

RUE LUCIEN FAURE

RUE LUCIEN FAURE

CAP Sciences

R. MARCEL PAGNOL

RUE BOURBON

R. ARMAND DULAMON

RUE DE LA CHARLES DURAND

RUE DE LA FAÏENCERIE

RUE BOURBON

RUE BOURBON

COURS LOUIS FARGUE

COURS DU RACCORDEMENT

COURS ÉDOUARD VAILLANT

R. DU COMMANDANT HAUTREUX

COURS EDOUARD VAILLANT

RUE DELORD

QUAI DE BACALAN

SHOPPING
Bord'eau Village	1
Musée du Vin et du Négoce	2

DRINKING & NIGHTLIFE
BARS
BAM Karaoke Box	5
Comptoir de Saintongey	2
Gagnant Gagnant	1
Trompette	3
Wine Moment	4

CITÉ CHANTECRIT

RUE CHANTECRIT

COURS BALGUERIE STUTTENBERG

R. VIEILLARD

R. DURET

RUE DUPATY

Les Hangars

RUE JOSÉPHINE

ROND-POINT DE LA BELLE PROVINCE

ALLÉE HAUSSMANN

R. ARISTIDE SOUSA MENDÈS

RUE DE LEYBARDIE

COURS SAINT-LOUIS

RUE CHARLES PUYO

ROND-POINT DE FUKUOKA

RUE SURSON

RUE LOMBARD

RUE MAURICE

R. VICTOR SCHOELCHER

CHARTRONS

PL. SAINT-MARTIAL

RUE DENISE

Église Saint-Martial

COURS DU MÉDOC

COURS DU MÉDOC

Les Hangars (Médoc)

COURS JOURNU AUBER

COURS JOURNU AUBER

R. GUSTAVE DANDEOU

RUE POYENNE

QUAI DES CHARTRONS

Grand Parc

RUE BINAUD

R. PIERRE CHAREAU

R. ANDRÉ BAC

COURS DU JARDIN PUBLIC

RUE SAINT-LOUIS

RUE BINAUD

COURS BALGUERIE STUTTENBERG

ALLÉE STENDHAL

RUE ANDRÉ DARBON

PL. PAUL ET JEAN-PAUL AVISSEAU

Garonne

CITÉ CONRAD

RUE PRUNIER

RUE PRUNIER

Le M.U.R

R. DU FAUBOURG DES ARTS

RUE BARREYRE

RUE BARREYRE

Chartrons

Émile Counord

RUE DES FRÈRES PORTMANN

RUE ÉTIENNE HUYARD

RUE PREMETNARD

AVENUE ÉMILE COUNORD

RUE PAUL BERTHELOT

COURS DU JARDIN PUBLIC

RUE GOUFFRAND

Musée du Vin et du Négoce

RUE POMME D'OR

RUE BORIE

RUE NOTRE DAME

RUE BORIE

RUE BASTE

Marché Bio des Quais

RUE FRÉDÉRIC BENTAYOUX

RUE CONDORCET

RUE MARSAN

IMP. DE LA PRAIRIE

RUE DES RETAILLONS

COURS DE LA MARTINIQUE

RUE RAMONET

QUAI DES CHARTRONS

GRAND PARC

Camille Godard

RUE MINVIELLE

RUE MINVIELLE

RUE NOTRE DAME

RUE RAZE

COURS PORTAL

RUE SAINT-JOSEPH

Halle des Chartrons

ACCOMMODATION
Casa Blanca B&B	6
Chez Dupont	5
L'Esprit des Chartrons	4
Resid'hôtel Tatry	2
Seeko'o Hôtel Design	1
Hôtel Vatel	3

RUE DUCAU

RUE CONDORCET

COURS DE LUZE

RUE ALBERT

RUE CAMILLE GODARD

RUE DUCAU

CRÉE DE FAVOLE

RUE SICARD

Église Saint-Louis-des-Chartrons

R. DU COUVENT

R. LATOUR

Temple des Chartrons

EATING
RESTAURANTS
Alma	1
La Cabane Cent Un	3
Délices de Damas	2
Casa Gaïa	7
Chez Dupont	6
Marcellino	4
Pain Etc	5
Le P'tit Chez Moi	8

RUE PAUL VERLAINE

RUE FRÈRE

RUE MONTGOLFIER

R. SAINT-MAUR

RUE ALBERT PITRES

RUE DUCAU

RUE FRÈRE

RUE FRÈRE FONTBOUEIX

RUE CORNAC

Paul Doumer

PLACE PAUL DOUMER

RUE TOURAT

RUE CONSTANTIN

RUE NOTRE DAME

CAPC

CR XAVIER ARNOZAN

Musée d'Art Contemporain

RUE LAGRANGE

RUE GUPDET

RUE LACOUR

R. BARRENNES

R. VERGNIAUD

RUE MANDRON

SAINT SEURIN-FONDAUDEGE

RUE DE LA COURSE

PLACE MITCHELL

COURS DE VERDUN

RUE DE LA VERRERIE

RUE D'AVIAU

Jardin Public

Jardin Public

this 2018 sculpture by English artist Suzanne Treister, which was constructed from the wreckage of a German vessel from World War II.

CAP Sciences

Hanger 20, quai de Bacalan • http://cap-sciences.net • Charge • ☎ Cité du Vin

Aimed primarily at children, this **science museum** is nevertheless a fascinating visit for all ages. There's no permanent exhibition here; instead, there are normally **several temporary exhibitions** on at any one time. Previous exhibits have focused on those universal crowd pleasers: dinosaurs, robots (including R2-D2) and the galaxy, sure to appease any young visitors. Renewable energy has been a strong focus, too, and they have also hosted itchy exhibitions about lice, fleas, bacteria and bedbugs. Everything is always very well presented, with lots of hands-on exhibits, including the dreaded said lice and fleas. Be forewarned though, there is a separate admission fee for each exhibition so a visit to them all can get quite pricey. Some exhibitions also only allow in a certain number of people at any one time meaning queues can be long.

Pont Jacques Chaban-Delmas

☎ Cité du Vin

The **Pont Jacques Chaban-Delmas**, a large road bridge that spans the Garonne, is the highest vertical lift bridge in Europe. By vertical lift we mean that the entire 110m section between the towers standing on opposite sides of the river can be lifted up to 55m into the air when a large ship needs to pass under the bridge. Inaugurated in 2013, most of the time the bridge is simply just another modern bridge but if you're lucky enough to see it raise up into the skies then it's definitely pretty impressive. If you've really got a thing for elevating bridges then you can spend days on the site's live webcam waiting for the magic moment when it elevates. You'll get excellent views of it from just outside the CAP Sciences museum.

4

Musée du Vin et du Négoce

41 rue Borie • http://museedevinbordeaux.com • Charge, included with City Pass • ☎ Chartrons

The Musée du Vin et du Négoce at first glance might seem to have been rather eclipsed by the Cité du Vin. *Au contraire* – this small museum works as a perfect complement to its glitzy new sister. Specialising in the role of the wine trader over history, and occupying an atmospheric wine cellar in an old Chartrons townhouse, it's easy to spend much longer than you'd expect looking through the fascinating wine-themed memorabilia. Exhibits include boats, globes, logbooks, and some of the biggest wine bottles you're ever likely to see. There's also an interesting video about the history of the wine trade and an unexpectedly engrossing one about barrel manufacture. The visit finishes up with (an included) friendly and informative wine tasting session.

Halle des Chartrons

10 place du Marché Chartrons • Free • ☎ Chartrons

The octagonal **Halle des Chartrons** was built in 1869 as a market hall: with multiple arches and topped with an interesting cast-iron frame, it's an attractive building set in a small square surrounded by open-air cafés. It's now used primarily for concerts and exhibitions.

Église Saint-Louis-des-Chartrons

51 rue Notre Dame • www.paroissebordeauxchartrons.fr • Free • ❶ Chartrons

The **church of St Louis** – dedicated to Saint Louis, the notoriously pious thirteenth century King of France – dates from the late nineteenth century. Its twin spires on either side of the entrance give it an attractive gothic flavour, while inside there are some particularly impressive stained glass windows. In particular, check out those on the south transept, where the windows depict Saint Louis setting off on his ill-fated crusade.

Temple des Chartrons

10 rue Notre Dame • Free • ❶ Capc

Worth a quick look if you're passing, the **Temple des Chartrons** is a nineteenth-century Protestant church in neoclassical style, resembling a small Roman temple with four huge pillars surrounding the entrance. It's now used for temporary art exhibitions and the occasional concert.

4

La Bastide

Long overlooked by both visitors to the city and the Bordelais themselves, La Bastide, on the east bank of the Garonne, was once the industrial heart of Bordeaux. With the decline in fortunes of the industries here the area went into decline. Now though, thanks to an ambitious urban regeneration project, La Bastide has turned into one of the more hip neighbourhoods in the city. There may not be a lot in the way of formal tourist sights here, but the area is well worth a wander.

5

BORDEAUX AND THE SLAVE TRADE

Despite a ruling by the Parlement du Bordeaux in 1571 against a **Norman slave trader**, in which it was stated that "France, mother of freedom, does not allow slavery", by the seventeenth and eighteenth centuries, Bordeaux was fully invested in the trans-Atlantic slave trade. After Nantes, Bordeaux was France's largest slaving port, and it's estimated that over two centuries, some 1.3 million African people were transported from France to the New World destined for slave markets. The city's role in this repugnant trade is explored in a permanent exhibition in the **Musée d'Aquitaine**, see page 38.

LA BASTIDE

CHARTRONS

Chartrons

Garonne

Bastide Darwin

Fabrique Pola

Quai de Brazza

BASTIDE-BRAZZA

Rue René Char

Rue Joseph Bonnet

Rue du Commandant Cousteau

Grand Moulins de Paris

Rue Bouthier

Parc d'Activités des Queyries

Rue des Queyries

R. Dasvin de Bosmarin

R. Gustave Eiffel

Galin

Darwin Eco-Système

Rue du Maréchal Niel

Rue Hortense

BASTIDE-NIEL

Rue Édouard Mayaudon

Avenue Thiers

R. Joseph Pujol

Rue de Libourne

Rue Reignier

Rue Raymond Lavigne

Archives de Bordeaux Métropole

Rue de la Rotonde

R. du Petit Cardinal

Parc aux Angéliques

Jardin Botanique de Bordeaux

Thiers-Benauge

Rue Cazenave

LA BENAUGE

LA BASTIDE

Avenue Thiers

Rue Tranchère

Allée Jean Giono

Rue Nuyens

Rés l'Autre Quai

Avenue Abadie

Rue Laville Fatin

Rue de Tresses

R. de Cenon

Parc Pinçon

Quai des Queyries

Quinconces Jean-Jaurès

R. Jean-Paul Alaux

Rue Léonce Motelay

Rue Nuyens

Église Sainte-Marie

R. Sainte-Marie

Jardin Botanique

Rue Paul Camelle

Rue de Dijon

Cours le Rouzic

Pl. Caliste Camelie

Rue Béranger

Rue de Janeau

Allée du Paris-Orléans

Allée Serr

Rue Serr

R. Dubessan

Maison Cantonale

Rue Gabriel

Rue de Nuits

Rue de Châteauneuf

Rue Ferbugs

Rue Bonnefin

Rue Mozart

Stalingrad (Parlier)

Cinéma Megarama

R. Honoré Pijon

Rue Jardel

Stalingrad

Place de Stalingrad

Rue Montmejean

Rue de la Benauge

R. de la Tresne

R. Joseph Faure

Rue de Trégey

Rue Corot

Boulevard Ludovic Trarieux

Embarcadère des Quinconces

Quai des Queyries

Quai de Sèze

Rue de la Sauve

Rue Promis

Rue Henri Dunant

R. Joseph Faure

Rue de Cenac

Jardins des Lumières

Ponton d'honneur

Parvis Maison Écocitoyenne

Quai Richelieu

Pont de Pierre

Benauge

Sente de la Frégate

Rue René Buthaud

Quai de la Souys

Rue des Osiers

Quai Deschamps

Quai de la Garonne

Boulevard

Porte de Bourgogne

Cours Victor Hugo

Rue Auguste

Quai des Salinières

Quai de la Grave

SAINT-MICHEL

Flèche de la Basilique

Saint-Michel

Basilique Saint-Michel

Pont Saint-Jean

EATING
RESTAURANTS

Croques et Soupes	4
L'Estacade	2
Mille et une Saveurs	1
La Mona	3

DRINKING & NIGHTLIFE
BARS

Alaia	1
Caserne B	2

ACCOMMODATION

Le Clos des Queyries	1
Eklo	3
La Maison Bastide	2
Des Voyageurs	4

0 — 400

metres

Place de Stalingrad and around

Just across the Pont de Pierre is the **Place de Stalingrad**, a large square dotted with a smattering of trees. Originally named Place du Pont but renamed to honour the Russian victory over the Germans at Stalingrad, it would be quite unremarkable if it weren't for the somewhat unexpected giant, blocky lion sculpture which sits without fanfare on the plaza. Installed in 2005, the light blue big cat is the work of Parisian artist Xavier Veilhan.

Église Sainte-Marie

62 Av Thiers • www.paroisselabastidefloirac.fr • Free • ⓣ Stalingrad

A short walk along Avenue Thiers from the Place de Stalingrad is the **Église Sainte-Marie**, a sizeable church built in the late nineteenth century to serve the religious needs of the growing population of the suburb. It was designed by Paul Abadie, most famous for Paris' Basilica **Sacré-Cœur**, and it's possible to spot similarities here – Sainte-Marie's tower is topped by a dome reminiscent of that of Sacré-Cœur. It's most impressive from the outside – the interior is somewhat more sedate than some of Bordeaux's other churches, but there's some lovely stained glass to admire.

Maison Cantonale

20 rue de Châteauneuf • Free • ⓣ Jardin Botanique

Worth a quick detour, the **Maison Cantonale** comes as a bit of a surprise: it looks like a stylized fairytale house plucked from the forests of medieval Germany and deposited in the somewhat nondescript streets east of the Place de Stalingrad. Designed in the early twentieth century, it has served multiple purposes over the years, and is now used sporadically as an events venue.

Parc aux Angéliques

Quai des Queyries • Free • ⓣ Jardin Botanique

The **Parc aux Angéliques** stretches along the riverside north of the Place de Stalingrad, making a pleasant if not enormously exciting place for a wander. In the centre, there's a bust of Toussaint Louverture, a former slave and one of the leaders of the Haitian Revolution, which successfully overthrew French colonial rule in Haiti in the late eighteenth century. Louverture never visited Bordeaux, but his son Isaac lived in the city, in a house on Rue Fondaudège.

Jardin Botanique de Bordeaux

Esplanade Linné • http://jardin-botanique-bordeaux.fr • **Gardens** free; **Greenhouses** charge • ⓣ Jardin Botanique

With concrete being a key part of the architectural layout, there's perhaps not as much greenery as you might hope for in the **botanical gardens**. That said, there are some nice water features, a good range of plants and trees and – the most interesting bit of the garden – large greenhouses with impressive cacti and carnivorous plant collections.

Fabrique Pola

10 quai de Brazza • https://pola.fr • Free • ⓣ Cité du Vin

Pola is a cultural space created by local artists, which hosts a revolving programme of temporary art exhibitions and workshops – check the website to see what's on. In summer, they also run an outdoor bar with views over the river.

5

HIKING THE GR® BORDEAUX MÉTROPOLE

Hikers looking for a totally new way to experience Bordeaux will want to lace up their boots and get out on the new **Bordeaux Métropole hiking trail**. At 160km in length this GR (Grande Route) trail, the first urban GR trail in France, encircles the city taking in many of the key natural and manmade green spaces as well as river views, urban landscapes and, of course, some of the vineyards that push up against the city. It takes most people around ten days to hike the entirety of the trail but, the nice thing about it is that it's very easy to just hop on or off the route and walk as many hours or days as you wish before getting on a bus or tram to head back into the city. For more information, check out the website (https://www.bordeaux-tourism.co.uk/parcours/gr-bordeaux-metropole.html).

Grand Moulins de Paris

38 quai de Brazza • ❶ Cité du Vin

Clearly visible on the skyline, looking like the lovechild of a classic French chateau and a factory, the **Grand Moulins de Paris** is a 1920s flour mill which has acquired the nickname of the "cathedral of wheat" owing to its impressive architectural style. Still in operation, it's not open to the public, but you can't fail to spot it if you're exploring this end of the city.

Darwin Eco-Système

87 quai des Queyries • http://darwin.camp • Free • ❶ Jardin Botanique

Up until just a few years ago there wasn't a great deal of reason for a visitor to Bordeaux to cross over to the east bank of the river. But, the recent redevelopment of a nineteenth century military barracks into the **Darwin Eco-Système** (which continues to expand today), one of the city's most innovative urban regeneration projects, has changed all that. The Darwin Eco-Système is a new concept in urban living that is part experimental cultural centre, part shopping and eating zone, part social development projects. There are no tourist sights in the classic sense, but there's always plenty going on here, including art exhibitions, concerts and workshops. The complex, which incorporates modern architecture into the skeleton of the barracks has been designed in a fully eco-responsible manner with green energy used throughout. Check out the website to find out what's happening at the time of your visit. There's a really good skatepark here, too.

Archives de Bordeaux Métropole

Parvis des Archives • https://archives.bordeaux-metropole.fr • Free • ❶ Jardin Botanique

Bordeaux's archives, housed in a converted railway depot, are primarily of interest to those hoping to undertake research into **Bordeaux's historical records**, but there are regular temporary exhibitions to draw in the casual visitor. Themes of past exhibitions range from Bordeaux's role in the slave trade to the history of public transport in the city.

Bordeaux outskirts

Encircling the city centre is the main road, Boulevard du Président Wilson.
Beyond this stretch the Bordeaux suburbs. Some, such as Talence, Pessac
and Mérignac are separate towns in their own right though they've
been so consumed by Bordeaux that a short stay visitor is unlikely to
really notice where one begins and the other one ends. For the most
part sights are limited in the suburbs, but if you have time to spare
then there are a couple of places worth seeking out in the area.

Parc Bordelais

Rue de Bocage • Free • 🚇 Courbet

Covering 28 hectares and containing around three thousand trees, this well-manicured green space is both the city's largest park and its oldest. Dating from the nineteenth century, this 150-year-old park is a very popular place with Bordelais of all ages to come and relax and has water features, sculptures, spacious lawns, a petting zoo, children's playgrounds, toy trains, a puppet theatre and regular exhibitions, too.

Parc de Bourran

Avenue de Verdun • Free • Bus 1

Centred around the rather grandiose Château de Bourran, this large park was once the grounds of a vineyard estate which dates back to the seventeenth century. The park was extensively remodelled in the 1800s to create a romantic landscape, including follies such as a faux-medieval bridge and an artificial waterfall, fed by the waters of the small Devèze river, see box page 36.

Pessac

A 20-minute drive south-west of Bordeaux centre or a shot train ride will bring you to Pessac, a pleasant city suburb that has a variey of things to see and do.

Cité Frugès-Le Corbusier

Pessac • Free • 🚇 Pessac or Bus 1

Constructed in 1926 as a visionary housing estate by Henry Frugès, a wealthy Bordeaux industrialist and devotee of modern architecture, who wanted to create a housing estate where anyone, regardless of their financial situation, could afford to live. In the end, of the 127 houses envisaged, only fifty were completed. The architectural style used was completely different to anything people of the time had seen before. The strict geometric shapes, panoramic terraces, and vibrant colours had little in common with the very traditional style of the rest of Bordeaux. Not just was the architecture unprecedented but the houses were built with the needs of the occupants in mind, and all came with new-fangled inventions such as running water, heating and septic tanks. In such a conservative city as Bordeaux, these daring new designs caused instant scandal with some people claiming that Frugès was insane.

Although the estate never quite lived up to expectations, it has now been awarded UNESCO World Heritage status. The houses are all privately owned and you can't go inside any, but the neighbourhood is pleasant to walk around and you can learn more about the project in the **Corbusier Maison** (https://citefrugeslecorbusier.pessac. fr, free). Note that the Cité Frugès-Le Corbusier is in the suburb of Pessac.

Château Pape Clément

216 avenue Dr Nancel Penard, Pessac • www.chateau-pape-clement.fr • Charge • 🚇 Pessac or Bus 1

The first harvest at **Château Pape Clément** was in 1252, making this the oldest wine estate in the Bordeaux region. The estate takes its name from its first owner Bertrand de Goth, who subsequently became Pope Clement V – notorious for his ruthless crushing of the Knights Templar order. Luckily, the only crushing that goes on here today is of grapes: the estate is considered one of Bordeaux's most important vineyards. A visit involves wandering the attractive gardens, tasting the wines and even the chance

BORDEAUX OUTSKIRTS

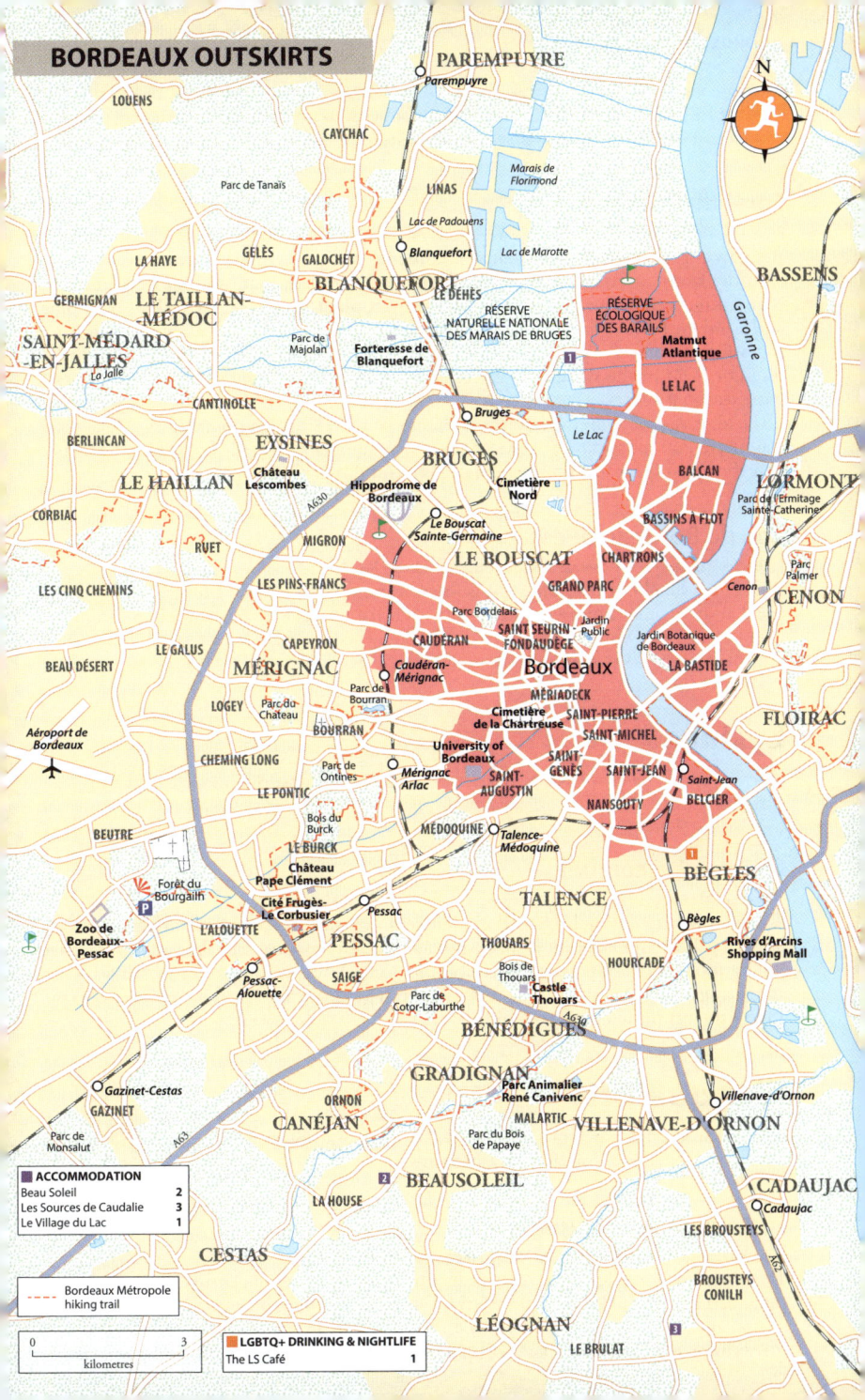

N

PAREMPUYRE
Parempuyre

LOUENS

CAYCHAC

Marais de
Florimond

LINAS

Parc de Tanaïs

Lac de Padouens

Lac de Marotte

GELÈS   GALOCHET

Blanquefort

BASSENS

LA HAYE

GERMIGNAN   LE TAILLAN-
MÉDOC

BLANQUEFORT

LE DÉHÈS

RÉSERVE
ÉCOLOGIQUE
DES BARAILS

SAINT-MÉDARD
-EN-JALLES

Parc de
Majolan

RÉSERVE
NATURELLE NATIONALE
DES MARAIS DE BRUGES

Matmut
Atlantique

La Jalle

Forteresse de
Blanquefort

Garonne

LE LAC

CANTINOLLE

Bruges

BERLINCAN   EYSINES

Le Lac

LORMONT

BALCAN

LE HAILLAN

Château
Lescombes

Hippodrome de
Bordeaux

BRUGES

Cimetière
Nord

Parc de l'Ermitage
Sainte-Catherine

CORBIAC

A630

*Le Bouscat
Sainte-Germaine*

BASSINS À FLOT

RUET

MIGRON

LES PINS-FRANCS

LE BOUSCAT

CHARTRONS

Parc
Palmer

LES CINQ CHEMINS

Parc Bordelais

GRAND PARC

Cenon

CENON

BEAU DÉSERT

LE GALUS

CAPEYRON

CAUDÉRAN

SAINT SEURIN-
FONDAUDÈGE

Jardin
Public

Jardin Botanique
de Bordeaux

MÉRIGNAC

*Caudéran-
Mérignac*

Parc de
Bourran

Bordeaux

LA BASTIDE

LOGEY

Parc du
Château

BOURRAN

MÉRIADECK

Cimetière
de la Chartreuse

SAINT-PIERRE

FLOIRAC

Aéroport de
Bordeaux

CHEMING LONG

Parc de
Ontines

University of
Bordeaux

SAINT-MICHEL

*Mérignac
Arlac*

SAINT-
AUGUSTIN

SAINT-
GENÈS

SAINT-JEAN

LE PONTIC

Saint-Jean

Bois du
Burck

NANSOUTY

BELCIER

BEUTRE

LE BURCK

MÉDOQUINE   *Talence-
Médoquine*

Château
Pape Clément

Forêt du
Bourgailh

Cité Frugès-
Le Corbusier

Pessac

BÈGLES

Zoo de
Bordeaux-
Pessac

L'ALOUETTE

PESSAC

TALENCE

Bègles

Rives d'Arcins
Shopping Mall

*Pessac-
Alouette*

SAIGE

THOUARS

HOURCADE

Parc de
Cotor-Laburthe

Bois de
Thouars

Castle
Thouars

A631

BÉNÉDIGUES

Gazinet-Cestas

GRADIGNAN

Parc Animalier
René Canivenc

Villenave-d'Ornon

GAZINET

ORNON

MALARTIC

VILLENAVE-D'ORNON

Parc de
Monsalut

A63

CANÉJAN

Parc du Bois
de Papaye

CADAUJAC

BEAUSOLEIL

Cadaujac

LA HOUSE

LES BROUSTEYS

CESTAS

BROUSTEYS
CONILH

LÉOGNAN

LE BRULAT

ACCOMMODATION

Beau Soleil	2
Les Sources de Caudalie	3
Le Village du Lac	1

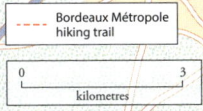

— Bordeaux Métropole
hiking trail

0   3
kilometres

LGBTQ+ DRINKING & NIGHTLIFE

The LS Café	1

to create your own bottle. A variety of (advance reservation) workshops and tasting options feature on the website. For those who wish to prolong the experience, there are rooms and suites available to book in the château, too.

Forêt du Bourgailh

Pessac • Free • Bus 77

A sprawling 65-hectare forest, this reclaimed green space offers a breath of fresh air away from city traffic. Once a dingy landfill, the area is another of Bordeaux's successful regeneration projects thanks to mass planting of species such as oak, pine and heather. Follow the multiple forest trails on foot or by bike (many of which are accessible for travellers with disabilities), enjoy the children's playground with little ones, or head to the skatepark. There is also a greenhouse containing exotic plants with seasonal access.

The biggest attraction here, however, has to be the 18m-high observatory. Make your way to the top for stunning views of the surrounding area, greatly helped by the fact that the forest is located on the highest point on the left bank.

Zoo de Bordeaux-Pessac

3 chemin du Transvaal, Pessac • www.zoo-bordeaux-pessac.com • Charge • Bus 77

Bordeaux's small but enjoyable zoo is found close to the Forêt du Bourgailh. There's the usual array of crowd-pleasers such as lions and lemurs, as well as a few less commonly seen beasties like white tigers and moose. Some enclosures are a little small, but improvement works are underway.

Eysines

North-west of the city, Eysines is a sleepy town in the midst of vineyards and dotted with châteaux.

Château Lescombes

198 avenue du Taillan, Av. du Médoc, Eysines • www.eysines-culture.fr • Charge • 🚏 Eysines Centre

A former winery dating back to the seventeenth century, **Château Lescombes** is now in use as a gallery and exhibition space displaying contemporary art. There's an impressive rolling programme of temporary exhibitions – check the website to see what's on. The attached gardens are attractive, containing both a historically listed dovecote and a (by appointment) museum of gardening.

Blanquefort

A 30-minute drive north of Bordeaux will bring you to Blanquefort, an historic town with a great medieval fort and pleasnat park.

Forteresse de Blanquefort

65 rue de la Forteresse, Blanquefort • http://gahble.org • Charge • 🚏 Frankton

This impressive medieval fortress was first built in the eleventh century, but greatly expanded by the English king Edward I. Over the subsequent centuries it fell into disuse, and is now a picturesque ruin. Opening times are extremely sporadic – check the website and contact the GAHBLE archaeological group before attempting a visit.

Finds from the site can be seen in the Maison du Patrimoine, a kilometre north in Blanquefort town centre.

Parc de Majolan

Avenue du Général de Gaulle, Blanquefort • Free • Bus 38

The large **Parc de Majolan** was created in the nineteenth century as part of a private estate for a wealthy banker, with an attractive central lake surrounded by artificial caves and canyons. Open to the public since the 1980s, the park is dotted with picturesque bridges, follies and fountains, and makes a fine place for a relaxing stroll.

Réserve écologique des Barails

Avenue de Pernon • Free • Bus 75

On the northern outskirts of the city, **Les Barails Nature Reserve** is Bordeaux's largest green space. The wetlands make it a good spot for birders: frequent winged visitors include white storks, kingfishers and egrets. The floral park, meanwhile, is a riot of colour during spring and summer.

Cenon

East of the city is Cenon, a town in the throes of regeneration. It's situated on the banks of the Garonne River and offers more green refuge in the guise of the very musically-orientated Parc palmer.

Parc Palmer

1 rue Aristide Briand • Free • 🚋 Buttinière

On the east side of the river, **Parc Palmer** sits atop a small hill, offering panoramic views over the city. The park is home to Le Rocher de Palmer (https://lerocherdepalmer.fr), a strikingly red live music venue containing three concert halls which has hosted artists ranging from the theatrical Swedish glam-metal outfit Ghost to the Tuareg desert blues band Tinariwen.

Lormont

Easily combined with a visit to nearby Cenon, the main attraction here is its park offering suberb views of Bordeaux.

Parc de l'Ermitage Sainte-Catherine

Rue Saint-Cricq • Free • 🚋 Iris

A former quarry to the city's northeast, the **Parc de l'Ermitage** centres around a small lake. Its principal attraction is a viewing platform which allows great views back towards the city centre: the Chaban-Delmas bridge and the Cité du Vin are clearly visible, with the spires of the cathedral and churches piercing the skyline beyond.

Accommodation

Finding a hotel vacancy in Bordeaux is easy at any time of year, but between Easter and October the situation is very different in more popular wine towns, and in summer accommodation in beach resorts is booked solid months in advance. Fortunately, everywhere in this book is within easy day trip reach of Bordeaux so if you can't find anything then you can always return to the city for the night. There's a wide range of overnight options in the city, from youth hostels and budget hotels to glam five-star hotels. In the wine regions you can also stay in some fabulous *châteaux*. If you're looking for the home-from-home experience then Bordeaux also has lots of self-contained apartments for rent, though many of these are only available in school holidays when the city's large university student population heads home.

At most times of the year, you can turn up in Bordeaux and the wine villages and find a room or, at least, a place in a campsite. Booking a couple of nights in advance can be reassuring, however, as it saves you the effort of trudging round and ensures that you know what you'll be paying; many hoteliers, campsite managers and hostel managers speak at least a little English.

Outside of the Easter and summer school holidays, you'll be able to get a simple double from €70, although it might not be very central. By paying at least €90 you can be assured of a reasonable level of comfort and a more central location. During the main school holidays (especially Easter and the summer holidays) room rates rise. In Bordeaux itself it's not too dramatic an increase as not many people spend their whole summer holiday in the city. Easter and, to a lesser extent, the October holidays, sees more people coming for a short break in Bordeaux and room availability can become tighter. The same goes for the wine areas around the city.

The real problems start if you're looking for beachside accommodation between mid-July and the end of August when the French take their own vacations en masse. If you're planning to stay close to any of the beautiful beaches near Bordeaux and down into Les Landes at this time of year it's vital to book accommodation as far ahead as possible (six months in advance would be sensible). With only a limited number of hotels and room rentals, many people stay on campsites but in the summer even these can be fully booked far in advance. If you turn up somewhere without a booking then the local tourist office might be able to help.

Hotels

French hotels are graded in five bands, in addition to which there is a further designation called a palace hotel – truly regal establishments (and with correspondingly regal prices). There are several of these in and around Bordeaux and the wine areas. The price more or less corresponds to the number of stars, though the system is a little haphazard, having more to do with ratios of bathrooms per guest and so forth than genuine quality; some unclassified and single-star hotels can be very good. Single rooms – if the hotel has any – are only marginally cheaper than doubles, so sharing slashes costs, especially since many hotels willingly provide rooms with extra beds for three or more people. If you're staying for more than three nights in a hotel it's sometimes possible to negotiate a lower price, particularly out of season.

7

Breakfast will often add anything between €7 and €30 per person to a bill – though there is no obligation to take it.

Note that many **family-run hotels** close for two or three weeks a year in low season. In smaller towns and villages they may also close for one or two nights a week, usually Sunday or Monday. Details are given where relevant in the text, but dates change from year to year; the best precaution is to phone ahead to be sure.

As with most of western Europe there are a growing number of reasonable value chain hotels. Often these are located out of town or near train stations and the airport in Bordeaux. They may be soulless, but you can usually count on a decent and reliable standard. Among the cheapest is the one-star *Formule 1* chain (http://hotelf1.accorhotels.com). Other budget chains include *B&B* (http://hotel-bb.com), the slightly more comfortable *Première Classe* (http://premiereclasse.com) and *Ibis* (part of the Accor group), which incorporates three brands: *Ibis Budget*, *Ibis*, and the more design-oriented *Ibis Styles* hotels (http://accorhotels.com). Slightly more upmarket is *Campanile* (http://campanile.com).

There are a number of well-respected **hotel federations** in France. The biggest and most useful of these is *Logis de France* (http://logishotels.com), an association of over 2800 hotels nationwide. They produce a free annual guide, available in French tourist offices, from *Logis de France* itself and from member hotels. Two other, more upmarket federations worth mentioning are *Châteaux & Hôtels de France* (www.relaischateaux.com) and the *Relais du Silence* (http://relaisdusilence.com), both of which offer high-class accommodation in beautiful older properties, often in rural locations.

Bed and breakfast and self-catering

In addition to standard hotels are *chambres d'hôtes* (http://chambres-hotes.fr) – bed-and-breakfast accommodation in someone's house, château or farm. By and large there are more common in the countryside around Bordeaux than in the city itself, though some options do exist in Bordeaux. Wherever the location though, the quality varies widely. On the whole standards are pretty high, and the best can offer more character and greater value for money than an equivalently priced hotel. If you're lucky, the owners may also provide traditional home cooking and a great insight into French life. Prices generally range between €80 and €130 for two people including breakfast; payment is almost always expected in cash. Some offer meals on request (*tables d'hôtes*), usually evenings only.

If you're planning to stay a week or more in any one place it's worth considering renting self-catering accommodation. In Bordeaux itself these normally take the form of apartments. It's important to check how close they are to the city centre because many will be in the southern student suburbs focused around Talence, which entails a 20–30-minute bus or tram ride into the city centre. In beach resorts apartments are also common. In general, you will pay a lot for beachside apartments in summer and the quality won't match the price paid. Inland, away from the beach and the city things are very different and you can expect to come across some gorgeous *chambres d'hôtes* **or** self-contained country cottages known as *gîtes*. Many *gîtes* are in converted barns or farm outbuildings, though some can be quite grand. "Gîtes Panda" are *gîtes* located in a national park or other protected area and are run on environmentally friendly lines. The government-funded agency Gîtes de France has a list of *gîtes* (http://gites-de-france.com), which are available by location or theme (for example, *gîtes* near fishing or riding opportunities). In addition, every year the organization publishes a number of national guides, such as *Nouveaux Gîtes* (listing new addresses); these guides are available to buy online or from departmental offices of Gîtes de France, as well as from bookstores and tourist offices. Tourist offices will also have lists of places in their area which are not affiliated to Gîtes de France. Nowadays almost all self-catering apartments and houses are advertised through Airbnb (www.airbnb.com) and other similar services. This is especially the case if looking for self-catering accommodation in Bordeaux itself.

Hostels

At around €12–26 per night for a **dormitory bed**, sometimes with breakfast thrown in, youth hostels – *auberges de jeunesse* – are invaluable for single travellers of any age on a budget. Many now offer rooms, occasionally en suite, but they don't necessarily work out cheaper than hotels – particularly if you've had to pay a taxi fare to reach them. However, many allow you to cut costs by eating in the hostels' cheap canteens, while in a few you can prepare your own meals in the communal kitchens. In the text we give the cost of a dormitory bed.

In addition to those belonging to the two French hostelling associations listed below, there are now also several independent hostels, particularly in Paris (for example, MIJE: http://mije.com). At these, dorm beds cost €30–40, with breakfast sometimes extra.

Youth hostel associations

Slightly confusingly, there are two rival **French hostelling associations** – the *Fédération Unie des Auberges de Jeunesse* (FUAJ: http://fuaj.org) and the much smaller *Ligue Française* (LFAJ: http://auberges-de-jeunesse.com). In either case, you normally have to show a current Hostelling International (HI) **membership card**. It's usually cheaper and easier to join before you leave home, provided your national youth hostel association is a full member of HI. Alternatively, you can purchase an HI card in certain French hostels.

7

Gîtes d'étape

In the countryside, another hostel-style option exists in the form of **gîtes d'étape** (http://gites-refuges.com). Aimed primarily at hikers and long-distance bikers, *gîtes d'étape* are often run by the local village or municipality and are less formal than hostels, providing bunk beds and primitive kitchen and washing facilities for around €15–25 per person. They are marked on the large-scale IGN walkers' maps and listed in the individual Topo guides. There are very few in the area covered by this guidebook.

VIEUX BORDEAUX SEE MAP PAGE 34

Hôtel Bleu de Mer Bordeaux 12 rue Saint-Rémi, www. hotel-bleudemer.com, ⓣ Place de la Bourse. A good budget option for those who want to be in the thick of it, this fairly basic hotel is just a couple of steps off place de la Bourse. Rooms vary: some are looking rather tired so ask to see a few. €

Central Hostel 2 place Saint-Projet, https://centralhostel. fr/nos-destinations/bordeaux/dortoir-bordeaux, ⓣ Sainte Catherine. Probably the city's top choice for those on a budget, the *Central Hostel* has dorms sleeping six or eight, including mixed and women-only options. There are also a couple of private rooms available. It's a sociable spot too, with events organised on a regular basis. €

L'InterContinental Bordeaux – Le Grand Hôtel place de la Comédie, http://ihg.com, ⓣ Grand Théâtre. A great city hotel, right in the centre. It's timeless luxury all the way here, with brass-buttoned porters, concierge service, two bars (including a summer-only rooftop one), two Gordon Ramsay restaurants and valet parking, as well as an excellent breakfast, an opulent spa and pool, a Jacuzzi on the roof, and rooms equipped with everything imaginable. €€€€

Hôtel Majestic 2 rue de Condé, https://hotelmajestic-bordeaux.com, ⓣ Quinconces. A very good central choice, the *Hôtel Majestic* is on an unexpectedly quiet street just a block from the place de la Comédie. Rooms are simply but stylishly decorated, and some have balconies overlooking the street. €€

Le Miroir aux Fées 3 rue du Mulet, www.le-miroir-aux-fees.fr, ⓣ Place de la Bourse. A good value and central B&B with just four rooms, all individually and eclectically decorated. The continental breakfast is excellent, and the owners are welcoming and friendly. €

Quality Hotel Bordeaux Centre 27 rue Parlement Sainte-Catherine, https://www.choicehotels.com/fr-ca/france/bordeaux/quality-inn-hotels/, ⓣ Grand Théâtre. With 86 rooms, this large hotel occupies an attractive nineteenth century building. The rooms are fairly standard international business hotel-style, but the location – right in the heart of the city – makes up for any blandness of character. €€

★ **Du Théâtre** 10 rue Maison-Daurade, http://hotel-du-theatre.com, ⓣ Grand Théâtre. A personality-packed budget choice that has been carefully thought out to maximize space and add a personal touch. Bright wall stencils, a few choice kitsch furnishings and well-designed bathrooms mean even the tiny single rooms are perfectly comfortable, plus there's a 24-hr English-speaking reception and an unbeatable location, right in the heart of town. Breakfast costs extra. €€

7

CAMPING

Camping is very popular in France. Campsites range from a field on a farm where you can pitch a tent to huge complexes with multiple swimming pools, shops, restaurants and lots of organised activities. While there are no official campsites within the Bordeaux city limits the countryside, and the coast in particular, has lots of options. Most sites open from around Easter to September or October. Most are graded – from one to four stars – by the local authority. One-star sites are basic, with toilets and showers (not necessarily with hot water) but little else, and standards of cleanliness are not always brilliant. Facilities improve with more stars: at the top end of the scale, four-star sites are far more spacious, have hot-water showers and electrical hook-ups; most will also have a swimming pool (sometimes heated), washing machines, a shop and sports facilities, and will provide refreshments or meals in high season. A further designation, **Camping Qualité** (http://campingqualite.com), indicates campsites with particularly high standards of hygiene, service and privacy, while the **Clef Verte** (http://laclefverte.org) label is awarded to sites (and also hostels and hotels) run along environmentally friendly lines. For those who really like to get away from it all, **camping à la ferme** – on somebody's farm – is a good, simple option. Lists of sites are available at local tourist offices or from Gîtes de France (see page 76).

The Fédération Française de Camping et de Caravaning (http://ffcc.fr) has some 1200 affiliated sites and publishes an annual **guide**, details of which can also be found online on the excellent Camping France website (http://campingfrance.com), which lists thousands of sites, with themed categories (campsite with beach access, with water parks, and so on). If you'd rather have everything organized for you, note that there are a number of companies that specialize in camping holidays (see page 23).

Most campsites charge per emplacement and per person, usually including a car, with extra charges for electricity. As a rough guide, two people with a tent and car might pay as little as €12 per day at an out-of-the-way rural one-star site, or as much as €70 at a four-star on the Côte d'Azur in July or August. In peak season it's wise to book ahead and note that at many of the big sites the emphasis is more on letting caravans or chalet bungalows.

Lastly, a word of caution: always ask permission before **wild camping** (*camping sauvage*) on anyone's land. If the dogs don't get you, the guns might – farmers have been known to shoot first and ask later. Camping on public land is not officially permitted and is often strongly discouraged, particularly in the south where in summer the risk of forest fires is high.

PLACE GAMBETTA AND SAINT SEURIN-FONDAUDÈGE **SEE MAPS PAGES 48 AND 47**

Aparthotel Adagio 40 rue Edmond Michelet, www.adagio-city.com/gb/hotel-6643-aparthotel-adagio-bordeaux-gambetta/index.shtml, 🚇 Mériadeck. A combination of hotel and self-catering accommodation, the Aparthotel offers rooms to accommodate up to four people, all equipped with kitchens and with access to a gym and sauna. A touch impersonal perhaps, but well-located and good value. €€

Le Boutique Hôtel Bordeaux 3 rue Lafaurie de Monbadon, www.hotelbordeauxcentre.com, 🚇 Gambetta. For a touch of luxury, try *Le Boutique*, a top-notch hotel occupying a beautiful eighteenth century mansion. Rooms are impeccably decorated, the spa facilities are excellent, and if you really want a romantic getaway, nab the room with the enormous bathtub. €€€€

Brit Hôtel Des Grand Hommes 7 rue Franklin, http://bordeaux-centre.brithotel.fr, 🚇 Gambetta. In a really handy, central location, this unfussy two-star hotel is a decent option for a short stay. Rooms are on the small side, but comfortable, bright and modern. Breakfast (not included) can be served in your room for no extra charge. €

Konti 10 rue Montesquieu, http://hotel-konti.com,

UNUSUAL ACCOMMODATION

Refuges Périurbains http://lesrefuges.bordeaux-metropole.fr. Without doubt the most unusual accommodation in Bordeaux, this is a series of refuges (basically hiking huts) situated in parks in and around the periphery of the city. Each is radically different (and unlike anywhere you will have stayed before) ranging from a giant wooden owl to what appears to be an upright seashell, treehouses and something being eaten by a snake. Book in advance through the website. None of the refuges are open year-round but each has different opening dates. €€

Gambetta. Brilliantly retro hotel (but with more than enough twenty-first century additions to make it comfortable!) in a two-hundred-year-old former brasserie. Breakfast is served in a dining room filled with curled chairs and leather sofas. €€

★ **Mama Shelter** 19 rue Poquelin-Molière, http://mama shelter.com/bordeaux, Gambetta. Fashionably eclectic, with sleek decor, stunning spacious rooms and a show-stopping rooftop terrace, *Mama Shelter* is hands-down one of the city's coolest hotels. Rooms are bang up to date, including iMac computers with internet, radio and movies

on demand, minibars, plump duvets and million-dollar views. Book online for cheapest rates. Breakfast and parking costs extra. €€

Yndo Hotel 108 rue Abbé de l'Épée, www.yndohotel bordeaux.fr, Gambetta. An absolutely gorgeous hotel, occupying an old mansion which thanks to its witch's hat turret bears more than a slight resemblance to a fairytale castle. Inside, it's furnished in a luxurious but tasteful style, melding nineteenth century grandeur with excellent modern touches. There's an exclusive restaurant for hotel guests serving locally sourced cuisine. €€€€

SAINT MICHEL AND CAPUCINS-VICTOIRE

SEE MAP PAGE 52

Auberge de Jeunesse 22 cours Barbey, http://auberge barbey.com, Bordeaux Saint-Jean. A decent private hostel with a warm, relaxed vibe and a mix of modern dorms and doubles. Located just off cours de la Marne, it's a 10min walk from gare St-Jean. Kitchen and laundry facilities are available, and breakfast is included. €

B&B Bordeaux St Michel 24 rue des Fours, www. bordeauxsaintmichel.com, Saint-Michel. There are four studio apartments available at this little B&B, just a block away from Basilique Saint Michel. A tasty continental breakfast is included, and all the studios have a kitchen if you fancy a spot of self-catering. €

Hôtel 56 56 quai de Paludate, https://56paludate.com, Bordeaux Saint-Jean. A smart and good-value business-

class hotel, this is a decent choice if you need to be close to the central train station. There are great views over the Garonne from the sixth-floor restaurant, and the hotel seems very proud of the artwork by Hervé Di Rosa found throughout the building. €

Hotel la Zoologie 151 cours de la Marne, www. hotelzoologie.com, Tauzia. This early twentieth-century building was once home to the Bordeaux Institute of Zoology, and an effort has been made to take influence from the building's past in its conversion to a hotel – some rooms have nature-themed murals on the walls, and the lobby feels somehow like a university hall. Beds are comfy, service is friendly, and there's a good restaurant and bar. €€€

CHARTRONS

SEE MAP PAGE 62

Casa Blanca B&B 39 rue de la Course, http://casablanca-bordeaux.com, Paul Doumer. Superb boutique B&B in the Chartrons district. The five-rooms here are tastefully decorated in pale tones with much use of exposed timber. Some rooms have free-standing bathtubs. A copious gourmet breakfast is included, and they'll even pack you up a picnic hamper for out-of-town explorations. The rooftop room offers wonderful views over the city. €€€

Chez Dupont 45 rue Notre-Dame, www.chez-dupont.com, Capc. Just round the corner from the Église Saint-Louis-des-Chartrons, the ten rooms at this small hotel are each decorated with an individual style. The pick of the bunch is the Kergomard suite, which enjoys its own private terrace. The restaurant on the ground floor is excellent too. €€

L'Esprit des Chartrons 17 rue Borie, http://lesprit deschartrons.fr, Chartrons. Located on a quiet road in Chartrons, a 10min walk from the centre, the three rooms in this B&B are delightfully and individually styled with up-cycled furniture and bold art. A great breakfast is served and

there's a secure garage. Breakfast included. €€

Resid'hôtel Tatry 174 cours du Médoc, http://residhotel. com, Grand Parc. Blurring the line between hotel and Airbnb, this apartment-hotel complex, which is inside an old wine storage warehouse, is well located in between the city centre and the Bacalan neighbourhood. Each of the small apartments has a basic kitchen. €

Seeko'o Hôtel Design 54 quai de Bacalan, https:// seekoo-hotel.com, Les Hangars. Occupying an impressive modern white building which provides an exciting architectural contrast with its neighbours along the waterfront, the Seeko'o offers 44 sleek and shiny rooms with attractive design. It's a good place to base yourself if you're planning to explore Chartons and the Bassins area thoroughly. €€

Hôtel Vatel 4 cours du Médoc, www.hotelvatel.fr/fr/ bordeaux, Cours du Médoc. A friendly international-standard hotel in a convenient location, with comfy if unremarkable rooms and a decent breakfast. €€

BASSINS À FLOT AND BACALAN

SEE MAP PAGE 59

B&B Hotel Bordeaux Bassins à Flot 147 rue Lucien Faure, www.hotel-bb.com/fr/hotel/bordeaux-bassins-flot, Cité du Vin. Don't be deceived: despite the name, this isn't a B&B – it's a fairly standard hotel in a tower block, which

offers slightly bland but clean rooms opposite the Bassins des Lumières. Its chief selling point is its price, which is very reasonable. €

Renaissance 16 rue de Gironde, www.marriott.com/en-

7

us/hotels/bodbr-renaissance-bordeaux-hotel/overview, ⊕ Cité du Vin. Set alongside a collection of monolithic industrial silos, through which you reach the lobby, the Marriott-owned Renaissance certainly makes an impression on the skyline. From the upper floors there are fantastic views of the Cité du Vin, and the hotel also boasts Bordeaux's highest swimming pool. €€€€

LA BASTIDE AND AROUND   SEE MAP PAGE 66

Le Clos des Queyries 38 rue André Degain, www.leclos desqueyries.com, ⊕ Jean Jaurès. Looking to spend the night in a castle? Check into *Le Clos des Queyries*, which occupies an eighteenth century mansion – there are five beautifully decorated rooms to choose from, and extensive gardens to relax in. It's an atmospheric and relaxing stay. €€€€

Eklo 10 rue de la Gare-d'Orléans, http://eklohotels.com, ⊕ Jardin Botanique. In the Bastide neighbourhood on the right bank of the river, and close to the botanical gardens, this hotel has been cleverly designed with eco-responsibility in mind. There are solar panels on the roof, steps have been put in to reduce water consumption, short supply chains are used and emphasis is placed on recycling. As well as having comfortable rooms they also offer dorms for more budget conscious travellers. The breakfast is extra. €

La Maison Bastide 8 cours Le Rouzic, http://lamaison bastide.fr, ⊕ Jardin Botanique. Five-bedroom guesthouse in a nineteenth-century building that's been carefully renovated in an environmentally friendly manner. Although it's only a ten-minute tram ride from the city centre, the owners grow vegetables and make their own jam, which you will get to enjoy at breakfast time. €€

Des Voyageurs 3bis av Thiers, http://hotel-voyageurs-bordeaux.com, ⊕ Stalingrad. This small, two-star hotel is a short, picturesque walk from the centre across the Pont de Pierre, and represents the best value for money in Bordeaux. It has helpful staff and clean, well-furnished rooms. Breakfast is extra. €

BORDEAUX OUTSKIRTS   SEE MAP PAGE 71

Beau Soleil 371 cours du Général de Gaulle, www.camping-beausoleil-gradignan.fr. 12km south of Bordeaux's centre, *Beau Soleil* offers 31 pitches for caravan and motorhome drivers. The facilities are all clean and well-maintained, and there's a nearby bus stop offering access to the centre. €

Les Sources de Caudalie Château Smith Haut Lafitte, Martillac, http://sources-caudalie.com. 15min drive from Bordeaux, *Les Sources* is a five-star spa hotel, part of the Château Smith Haut Lafitte empire, that specializes in grape-based spa treatments. The setting is luxuriously faux-rustic, there's a Michelin-starred restaurant, tranquil grounds, and vineyards on every side, giving the air a vinous sweetness. €€€€

Le Village du Lac bd Jacques Chaban-Delmas, http://camping-bordeauxlac.com. A lovely lakeside campsite located 8km north of the centre near the tramline, with rental cottages (kitchenette, TV, a/c, bathroom, terrace), camping, camper vans, swimming pool, shops, laundrette and secure parking. €

Eating

The French seldom separate the major pleasures of eating and drinking, and there are hundreds of establishments in Bordeaux where you can do both or either, as you wish. Eating out is generally excellent value for money, and it is still difficult to get a bad meal, except occasionally in popular beach resorts in summer. Southwestern specialties include duck, hearty cassoulet and bean stews, and the more controversial *foie gras*. Meat in general is a heavy focus on menus everywhere. A restaurant may call itself a brasserie, bistrot, café or indeed restaurant; equally, a café can be a place to eat, drink or listen to music. Most cafés and wine bars remain open until late and are perfect for a beer, glass of wine or digestif; if you're looking for cocktails or nightlife, you'll need to head for the city's bars and clubs (see page 88).

The cuisine of this part of southwest France is predominantly simple, country cooking (*cuisine de terroir*), revolving around duck and goose, seafood, garlic, a host of mushrooms, and whatever else the land has to offer. Although Bordeaux and some of the wine villages have some superb, multi-Michelin starred gourmet restaurants, overall, this is the sort of cuisine best sampled in little family-run places, where it's still possible to eat well for €17 or less.

Bordeaux itself is famed for its classic brasseries while in the countryside there's an endless choice of atmospheric village or farm restaurants and cafés. Along the beaches it can be harder to find decent value places to eat – many are simply overpriced tourist cafés, but there are exceptions and you only have to move a couple of kilometres away from the sea to find local people tucking into delicious seafood meals with barely another tourist in sight.

Breakfast and light meals

For most French people, **breakfast** is a quick no frills affair consisting of a bit of baguette with jam or a croissant and a coffee. In hotels though it's often a different story and the standard hotel breakfast comprises cereals, yoghurt, bread and/or pastries, jam, orange juice and a jug of coffee or tea. More expensive hotels typically offer fresh fruit, cheeses and hot and cold meats in addition to the above. If you're not staying in a hotel (or don't want to fork out that much), head to a café-bar and grab a croissant or *pain au chocolat* (chocolate croissant) with coffee or a hot chocolate.

Restaurant meals

There's no difference between restaurants (or *auberges* or *relais* as they sometimes call themselves) and brasseries in terms of quality or price range. The distinction is that **brasseries**, which resemble cafés, serve quicker meals at most hours of the day, while **restaurants** tend to stick to the traditional mealtimes of noon to 2pm, and 7pm to 9pm or 9.30pm. Bordeaux has some truly outstanding **brasseries that fill with locals at lunch time**. In touristy areas in high season, and for all the more upmarket places, it's wise to make reservations – easily done on the same day in most cases.

When hunting for places to eat, don't forget that **hotel restaurants** are open to non-residents, and can be very good value. In country areas keep an eye out for **fermes auberges**, farm restaurants where the majority of ingredients are produced on the farm itself. These are often the best places to sample really traditional local cuisine at very reasonable prices; a four-course meal for between €18 and €35 is the norm, including an apéritif and wine, but reservations are a must.

Traditionally the big meal of the day for the French is **lunch**, and while this is changing in cities, in rural areas a long, a leisurely lunch is still the cornerstone of the day. Wherever you eat, remember, always call the waiter or waitress *Monsieur* or *Madame* (*Mademoiselle* if a young woman), never *Garçon*.

EATING OUT PRICE CODES

Throughout the guide, eating out listings are categorized according to a price code, which roughly corresponds to the following price ranges. Where available, this price code is based on the cost of a standard weekday lunchtime 3-course menu. These price codes are:

€ = below €17
€€ = €17–€25
€€€ = €25–€45
€€€€ = above €46

LE PIQUE-NIQUE

For **picnics**, the local outdoor market or supermarket will provide you with almost everything you need. Cooked meat, prepared snacks, ready-made dishes and assorted salads are also available at *charcuteries* (delicatessens), which you'll find in some villages, and in most supermarkets. You'll find *boulangeries* (bakeries) just about everywhere – often several in one village – and it's here you can pick up some delicious breads and, usually, a mouthwatering array of cakes and pastries too, though a *pâtisserie* is more of a specialist cake shop. If a boulangerie or *pâtisserie* has the word *artisanal* after it then it means their bread or cakes are homemade so go for one of these instead.

Costs

Prices, and what you get for them, must be posted outside by law. Normally there's a choice between one or more **menus fixes** – with a set number of courses and a limited choice – and choosing individually from the *carte* (menu). *Menus fixes*, often referred to simply as *menus*, are normally the cheapest option – at between €15 and €20 for a three-course lunch with wine, the *menu du jour* (menu of the day) is great value. Eating in restaurants at lunchtime is almost always much cheaper than eating the same meal in the evening and most restaurants offer a weekday, **lunchtime**, *plat du jour* (daily special). At the upper end of the price scale, going **à la carte** offers greater choice and, in the better restaurants, unlimited access to the chef's inventiveness.

In the vast majority of restaurants, a **service charge** of fifteen percent is included in prices listed on the menu – in which case it should say *service compris* (*s.c.*) or *prix nets*. Very occasionally you'll see *service non compris* (*s.n.c.*) or *servis en sus*, which means that it's up to you whether you leave a tip or not. Most French leave just a couple of euros in loose change as a tip unless it's a more upmarket establishment in which a more substantial tip is expected. In either case tipping is not deemed as important as in the US.

There are good restaurants pretty much everywhere you turn in Bordeaux: in the centre, there are options to suit all budgets, ranging from brasseries and little galette shops to Michelin-star cuisine. When on the hunt for something to eat, the streets around rue du Parlement St-Pierre and rue St-Rémi are a good place to start, and you'll find the more upmarket options around place du Parlement and northward towards Chartrons.

VIEUX BORDEAUX   SEE MAP PAGE 34

CAFÉS

Books & Coffee 26 rue Saint-James, www.booksandcoffee.fr, ☎ Rue Sainte-Catherine. No prizes for guessing what's on offer here, but the advertised perfect combination of books and coffee is further enhanced by the location: a stone's throw from the Grosse Cloche, with outdoor seating providing a perfect view while you enjoy your drink.

Cafecito 7 Rue Parlement Saint-Pierre, https://cafecito-bordeaux.com, ☎ Place de la Bourse. On the corner of Place Saint-Pierre, this friendly café is a perfect stop for a glass or two of wine, accompanied by an excellent cheese and charcuterie board.

RESTAURANTS

Le Bouchon Bordelais 2 rue Courbin, http://bouchon-bordelais.com, ☎ Grand Théâtre. Bordeaux is full of excellent little brasseries, but this one stands out from the pack due to its imaginative take on old southwest classics. The menu gets a revamp with each new season. The royal cheesecake is a classic that never changes. Great value weekday menu du jour. €€€

Le Bouquet Saint-Pierre 6 rue des Bahutiers, https://le-bouquet-saint-pierre.fr, ☎ Place de la Bourse. Friendly no frills little place serving up a small menu of tasty galettes,

EATING OUT WITH CHILDREN

With the exception of some gourmet restaurants (where you probably wouldn't want to take children anyway) most restaurants have kid's menus and baby chairs and the French are, in general, laid back about taking children to restaurants.

Perfect for a lighter lunch. €

Chez Bibi 62 rue du Há, http://instagram.com/bibi_resto_ cave, 🚇 Hôtel de Ville. From clams to octopus, the seafood heavy menu at this place never fails to disappoint. It's actually two places in one here, with half the building being a café and wine bar and the other the restaurant. €€€

Echo 18 rue de la Cour-des-Aides, http://facebook.com/ echo.cavemanger, 🚇 Place de la Bourse. Run by a former oenologist (someone who studies wine and wine making) for one of the grand châteaux of the Médoc and his father, the little place specialises in 'sharing dishes'. The deco is delightfully rustic, with the tables and chairs looking like they were rescued from a school room in 1950, but the food entirely modern and full of unexpected twists. As to be expected the wine is first rate. €€€

Frida 27–29 rue Buhan, http://frida.fr, 🚇 Sainte Catherine. Named after Mexican artist Frida Kahlo (whose face adorns the walls), this bo-ho chic place run by a group of friends draws on their wide ranging travel experiences to create a menu filled with wonderful worldwide tastes (and yes, that includes proper Mexican mole sauces). €€

Fufu 37 rue St-Rémi, http://restaurantfufu.com, 🚇 Place de la Bourse. A well-loved Japanese noodle bar in the heart of town; eat at the long bar, watching the chefs fry your noodles, or take away a hot box of ramen and perch on a bench next to the Garonne, a few minutes' walk away. €

Madame Pang 16 rue de la Devise, https://madamepang. com, 🚇 Place de la Bourse. Taking Chinese as its starting point, *Madame Pang*'s menu offers some interesting fusion dishes amongst the dim sum tapas, with influences as diverse as Thai and Peruvian. It's also a great spot for cocktails. €€

Le Marrakech 15 rue Saint-Rémi, https://lemarrakech- bordeaux.fr, 🚇 Place de la Bourse. Hearty North African fare is on the menu here, in an atmospheric restaurant named after the famous Moroccan city. Expect tagines, cous- cous, merguez sausages and slow-cooked lamb shoulder. Reservations advised. €€€

Le Michel's 15 rue du Pas-Saint-Georges, www. michelsbistro.fr, 🚇 Place de la Bourse. Popular restaurant serving up regional specialities such as duck confit and steak

FAST FOOD

More popular for lunch with foreign tourists than most French are snacks such as *croques-monsieur* and *croques- madame* (variations on the toasted-cheese sandwich), along with *frites*, *gaufres* (waffles) and fresh-filled baguettes. However, one of these with a drink and some kind of dessert is likely only going to cost a little less than a *menu du jour* in a restaurant. You could also try a **crêpe** (pancake with a filling) – the savoury buckwheat variety (*galettes*) are the main course; sweet, white-flour crêpes are dessert. **Pizzerias**, usually *au feu de bois* (wood-fired), are also very common though more popular with the French in the evening.

and frites, as well as a few slightly more out-there choices such as shakshuka. Street entertainers will often stop at the outdoor seating and you may well be serenaded. €€€

Orta 3 bis rue du Há, http://instagram.com/ortabordeaux, 🚇 Musée d'Aquitaine. Low-key and welcoming, the frequently changing menu here is heavy on bio, veggie, fair-trade and locally sourced ingredients and dishes. Everything is served with artistic flair. Leave room for one of the super desserts. €€

Le Petit Commerce 22 rue du Parlement-Saint-Pierre, http://lepetit-commerce-restaurant.com, 🚇 Place de la Bourse. Seafood fans will enjoy this one. The menu changes daily and is largely dependent on what the boats hauled into the ports of nearby Arcachon and other coastal towns. It's particularly strong on shellfish and likewise the crab is excellent. €€€

★ **Le Pressoir d'Argent Gordon Ramsay** 2-5 place de la Comédie, http://gordonramsayrestaurants.com, 🚇 Grand Théâtre. Talk about putting the cat among the pigeons. British super chef Gordon Ramsay has come to Bordeaux, taken classic local produce such as duck, oysters and other

VEGETARIAN FOOD

On the whole, **vegetarians** can expect a fairly lean time in this part of southwest France, although Bordeaux itself – and some of the beach resorts – do have veggie-only restaurants. That said, in many of the better restaurants you'll often find one or two fantastically creative vegetarian dishes on the menu. Otherwise, your best bet is to head for a crêperie or pizzeria, while Chinese or North African restaurants can be good standbys. Occasionally they'll be willing to replace a meat dish on the fixed-price menu (*menu fixe*); at other times you'll have to pick your way through the *carte*. Remember to ask "*Je suis végétarien(ne); est-ce qu'il y a quelques plats sans viande?*" (I'm a vegetarian; are there any non-meat dishes?). **Vegans**, however, should probably forget about eating in restaurants and stick to self-catering. Food trends in general are not as embraced here as in the Anglo-Saxon world.

CHEESE

Charles de Gaulle famously commented "How can you govern a country that has 246 kinds of cheese?" For serious **cheese**-lovers, France is the ultimate paradise. Other countries may produce individual cheeses which are as good as, or even better than, the best of the French, but no country offers a range that comes anywhere near them in terms of sheer inventiveness. In fact, there are officially over 350 types of French cheese, and the methods used to make them are jealously guarded secrets. Many cheese-makers have successfully protected their products by gaining the right to label their produce **AOP** (*appellation d'origine protégée*), covered by laws similar to those for wines, which – among other things – controls the amount of cheese that a particular area can produce. As a result, the subtle differences between French local cheeses have not been overwhelmed by the industrialized uniformity that has plagued other countries.

The best, or most traditional, restaurants offer a well-stocked *plateau de fromages* (cheeseboard), served at room temperature with bread, but not butter. Apart from the ubiquitous Brie, Camembert and numerous varieties of goat's cheese (*chèvre*), there will usually be one or two local cheeses on offer – these are the ones to go for. While the Bordeaux area itself doesn't produce any regarded local cheeses, the southwest of France does have some excellent local varieties including the ewe's milk cheese known as *brebis* from the western Pyrenees. If you want to buy cheese, local markets are always the best bet, while in larger towns you'll generally find a *fromagerie*, a shop with dozens of varieties to choose from.

---

shellfish and shown the locals how to cook it! This superb, and very formal, two-star Michelin restaurant is located within the Intercontinental hotel. Reservations essential. €€€€

★ **Le Quatrième Mur** 2 place de la Comédie, http://quatrieme-mur.com, ☻ Grand Théâtre. Within the Grand-Théâtre is this truly magnificent brasserie full of turn of nineteenth-entury columns, gold frills and painted ceilings. The cuisine of chef Philippe Etchebest is equally ornate with a menu that changes weekly. If you really want to go to town reserve a table at the Michelin starred table d'hôtes. €€€€

Santosha 2 place Fernand Lafargue, 0970182085, ☻ Sainte Catherine. The food of southwest France is good. No, the food of southwest France is superb. But sometimes you just need something a little spicier and this is where Santosha, which specialises in Thai, Indonesian, Malaysian and Vietnamese dishes, comes to the rescue. The *pad thai* is recommended. €€

Soif 35 rue du Cancera, http://soif-bordeaux.com, ☻ Place de la Bourse. A brilliantly vintage style flows throughout this friendly place using largely bio and market fresh produce. The menu changes with the seasons. Artichokes are a favourite with the chef. €€€

★ **Tante Charlotte** 7 rue des Bahutiers, www.kalendes.com/site/tante-charlotte/welcome, ☻ Place de la Bourse. This popular restaurant has a hip bourgeois feel to it, with silver chairs and cushions, black and white photos on the walls and candlelit tables. Stick with the theme and order the *menu à boudoir*, which includes succulent meat dishes, delicious home-made desserts and a huge range of aperitifs to choose from. €€

Totto 10 place du Parlement, www.totto-restaurant-bordeaux.fr, ☻ Place de la Bourse. You might expect an Italian restaurant on one of Bordeaux's prettiest squares to be a bit of a mediocre tourist trap, but Totto defies expectations with top-notch pizzas and pastas, and unbeatable people-watching opportunities from the outdoor seating. €€

La Toque Cuivrée 5 rue Sainte-Catherine, www.la-toque-cuivree.fr, ☻ Grand Théâtre. Excellent little pastry shop specialising in Bordeaux's iconic canelés – if you've not tried one yet, this is a perfect place to sample. It's a small chain, with plenty of outlets in Bordeaux and the surrounding areas, including Arcachon and Cap Ferret. €

8

PLACE GAMBETTA AND SAINT SUERIN-FONDAUDÈGE   SEE MAPS PAGES 47 AND 48

CAFÉ

L'Alchimiste Café Boutique 12 rue de la Vieille Tour, www.alchimiste-cafes.com, ☻ Gambetta. Minimalist coffee shop with great coffee, pavement seating, and some very tasty pastries. A good place for a quick caffeine hit.

RESTAURANTS

★ **Baud et Millet** 19 rue Huguerie, http://baudetmillet.

com, ☻ Fondaudège - Muséum. Running since 1986, this local institution takes guests on a journey through the cheeses of France, with a mind-boggling array of cheese-inspired dishes. Select a bottle of wine from the shelf and order *langres* profiteroles or splash out on unlimited access to the cheese cave. Portions are generous and staff are keen to guide you. €€

Carioca 30 rue du Dr Charles Nancel Penard, www.carioca-bordeaux.com, ☻ Gambetta. Popular Brazilian restaurant, serving excellent steaks and mixed grills, as well as some delicious fish dishes. There's also a fine selection of cocktails, of which the caipirinha is the best choice. €€€

Maè Tû 12 rue Poquelin Molière, http://facebook.com/maetubordeaux, 🚇 Gambetta. Specialising in delightfully light Vietnamese spring rolls, this cheerful restaurant makes for a welcome sight thanks to the flowers covering the doorway and the walls and tables within. The prawn spring rolls are particularly worthwhile, and prices are low. Plenty of options for veggies as well. €€

Le Pavillon des Boulevards 120 rue Croix-de-Seguey, http://lepavillondesboulevards.fr, 🚇 Barrière du Médoc. The elegant setting and exemplary service are to be expected at this Michelin-starred restaurant, but there's nothing traditional about the menu. Dishes are inventive, sometimes surprising and always delicious, with plenty of fish and seafood. €€€

Peppone 31 cours Georges-Clemenceau, http://groupe-peppone.fr, 🚇 Gambetta. This cosy Italian restaurant has been in business for more than fifty years. The pasta dishes are creative and the pizzas excellent. Prices are reasonable and the welcome is warm. €

SAINT MICHEL AND CAPUCINS-VICTOIRE

SEE MAP PAGE 52

RESTAURANTS

Chez Thérèse 28 place Meynard, http://cheztherese.fr, 🚇 Saint Michel. This place, which is inside an old wine cellar, manages to have a relaxed, casual atmosphere yet serve fancy remixes of traditional southwestern cuisine. The menu, which uses local products as much as possible, changes with the seasons. €€

Monkey Mood 11 rue Camille Sauvageau, http://monkey-mood.fr, 🚇 Saint Michel. Although the main focus of this restaurant is Indonesian, it's a bit of a world tour with *nasi goreng*, *sambal manis* and *gado gado* being joined by veggie burgers and peanut brownies. Everything on the menu is vegan. €

Passage Saint-Michel 14–15 place Canteloup, http://lepassagesaintmichel.fr, 🚇 Saint Michel. This is one of those wonderfully classic French brasserie's serving reliable dishes such as steaks with pepper sauce and thick cut home-made chips and burgers containing so much burger the bun can't contain it all! Eat out on the sunny pavement terrace or inside in the 1920's styled dining room. €€

Samos Greek Food 2 place du Séminaire, http://instagram.com/samos.greekfood, 🚇 Saint Michel. Sit out on the terrace on a warm sunny day hemmed in by flowerpots full of herbs and olive saplings, and you could almost imagine yourself in a Greek town (admittedly without a view over the Mediterranean). The food at this friendly place is more Greek fast-food than proper meals. Think pita breads stuffed with chicken and home-made chips. Finish off with the Greek yogurt with fruit. €

Tuk Tik Thai Food District 1 rue Clare, http://tuktik-thaifood.fr, 🚇 Saint Michel. While calling this tiny place, which has just a couple of chairs lined up against the counter (most people come for takeaway), an entire district might be misleading, it certainly dishes up delicious, cheap and fairly authentic Thai dishes. Dishes can be modified for those with dietary requirements. €

La Tupina 6 rue Porte-de-la-Monnaie, http://latupina.com, 🚇 Saint Croix. *La Tupina* has been a legend in the Bordeaux dining scene since it opened in 1968. The chef has been at the helm since 2019, but the formula hasn't changed. A *tupina* is a big kettle-like saucepan used to slowly cook a soup-like casserole over an open fire. Afterwards tuck into delights such as milk-fed lamb, tripe and other very traditional southwestern fare. Come on a weekday lunchtime for an affordable *menu du jour*. Reservations advised. €€€

CHARTRONS

SEE MAP PAGE 62

RESTAURANTS

Alma 59 quai de Bacalan, www.alma-bordeaux.com, 🚇 Les Hangars. Excellent Portuguese café where you can enjoy a tasty breakfast or lunch. Don't miss the classic Portuguese pastel de nata custard tarts. €

La Cabane Cent Un 7 rue Rode, https://cabanecentun.fr, 🚇 Paul Doumer. Well-regarded place for fresh seafood on the Chartrons market square. The oysters are the star of the show, but crab and octopus feature too. €€€

Délices de Damas 85 cours Balguerie Stuttenberg, https://www.delicesdedamas.com, 🚇 Cours du Médoc. Get a taste of the Middle East at this popular Syrian restaurant, with a menu taking in mezze, falafel and perfectly charcoal-cooked kebabs, among much else. If you fancy a break from Bordeaux wine, try some of the Lebanese vintages on offer. €€€

Casa Gaïa 16 bis rue Latour, www.casagaia.fr, 🚇 Capc. Modern restaurant focussed on dishes made from local organic produce, resulting in a regularly-changing menu of seasonal dishes, much of it cooked in the wood-fired oven. Order a selection of tapas and a bottle of wine, and settle in for the afternoon. €€€

Chez Dupont 45 rue Notre-Dame, www.chez-dupont.com, 🚇 Capc. A romantic, old-fashioned restaurant in Chartrons, with wooden floors, vintage posters and waistcoated waiters. Ingredients are fresh from the market, with huge portions. €

Marcellino 11 rue Sicard, https://pastificio-marcellino-bordeaux.fr, 🚇 Capc. Marvellous Italian restaurant serving

a daily-changing menu of delicious freshly-cooked pasta. Don't miss the focaccia, and if you've got room, the tiramisu is perfect for afters. It has limited opening hours – check the website, but at time of writing it's open at lunchtime Monday to Friday, as well as in the evenings on Thursday and Friday. €€
Pain Etc 49 rue Notre Dame, 05 56 52 73 92, ⊕ Capc. Top-notch little bakery with great croissants and pastries for

breakfast, or good paninis and sandwiches for lunch. Good coffee too. €
Le P'tit Chez Moi 46 rue Notre Dame, 05 56 06 47 56, ⊕ Capc. Vegans can get a bit of a raw deal in the meat-heavy restaurants of Bordeaux, so this little spot is rather welcome. With a freshly-cooked buffet, you can try a little of everything from the varied vegan dishes on offer. €€

BASSINS À FLOT AND BACALAN   SEE MAP PAGE 59

RESTAURANTS
Café Maritime 1 quai Armand Lalande, www.cafe maritime.fr/cafe-maritime-bordeaux.html, ⊕ Cité du Vin. An upmarket restaurant on the quayside of the Bassins, with outdoor seating offering a front-row view of the spaceship sculpture hovering in the harbour. Menus revolve around local specialities, such as oysters and duck. There's a very

popular brunch buffet on Sundays. €€€
Les Halles de Bacalan 15 quai du Maroc, ⊕ Cité du Vin. In a convenient spot across the road from the Cité du Vin, the Bacalan market is a large food hall with multiple small kitchens offering a variety of street foods. A great place for picking up an easy lunch. €

LA BASTIDE AND AROUND   SEE MAP PAGE 66

RESTAURANTS
Croques et Soupes 5 rue Calvimont, https://croques etsoupes.fr, ⊕ Stalingrad. Friendly little café, perfect for a light lunch of sandwiches or soup. It's all handmade on the premises, and delicious. €
L'Estacade quai des Queyries, www.estacade-restaurant. com, ⊕ Stalingrad. Well-regarded waterfront restaurant, with a panoramic terrace offering views across the Garonne onto the place de la Bourse. It's particularly known for its fish and seafood, especially the scallops, but there are some hearty meat options too. (Note the vegetarian menu is very

limited.) There's a splendid selection of wines. €€€
Mille et une Saveurs 96 avenue Thiers, 05 57 61 38 58, ⊕ Stalingrad. No-frills excellent Lebanese spot, with an extensive menu ranging from mezze snacks such as falafel and sambousek to larger meals like barbecued skewers of meat. €€
La Mona 1 rue Sainte-Marie, www.pizzerialamona.fr, ⊕ Stalingrad. Deservedly popular Italian spot, which is particularly good on the pizza side of proceedings: think lovely authentic thin crusts and generous toppings. Pastas, risottos, meat dishes and salads are all good shouts too. €€

8

Drinking and nightlife

Bordeaux may be known as the "sleeping Beauty" and for good reason. While the city has a huge student population and lots of student bars, especially around place de la Victoire, the nightlife scene beyond that demographic is rather ordinary. Indeed, for a city of its size, there are few standout options and a glass of wine or a beer on a terrace in a pretty, cobbled street may well be your best bet.

In France **drinking** is done at a leisurely pace whether it's a prelude to food (**apéritif**), or a sequel (**digestif**), and cafés are the standard places to do it. Every bar or café has to display its full price list, including service charges. You normally pay when you leave, and it's usually perfectly acceptable to sit for hours over just one cup of coffee. Note that the minimum age for buying alcohol is 18, though younger teenagers may drink wine in a restaurant if accompanied by their parents. Public displays of drunkenness are very much frowned upon.

> ### SALUT !
> Wine (*vin*) or a drink (*boisson*) is sometimes included in the cost of a *menu fixe*. Otherwise, the cheapest option will be the house wine, usually served in a jug (*pichet*) or carafe; you'll be asked if you want *un quart* (0.25 litre), *un demi* (0.5 litre) or *un litre* (1 litre).

WINE

French wine (*vin*), drunk at just about every meal or social occasion, is unrivalled in the world for its range, sophistication, diversity and status and nowhere is this more the case than in the Bordeaux region. The house wine served in restaurants can be very good value in this wine-producing region or opt for a bottle of AOP (*appellation d'origine protégée*) wine if you want a more sophisticated taste. You can buy a very decent bottle of wine for €6 in a shop or from the producer, while €10 and over will get you something worth savouring. A glass of wine in a bar will typically cost around €3 to €5.

BEER

Light Belgian and German **beers**, plus various French brands, including a growing range of small, local breweries making craft beer, account for most of the beer you'll find. Draught beer (*à la pression*) – very often Kronenbourg – is the cheapest drink you can have next to coffee and wine. For a wider choice of draught and bottled beer you need to go to special beer-drinking establishments. Bordeaux now has a number of craft beer bars. A small bottle at one of these places can cost up to twice as much as a *demi* in an ordinary café-bar.

SPIRITS AND LIQUEURS

Strong alcohol, including **spirits** (*eaux-de-vie*), such as cognac and armagnac, and **liqueurs** such as locally made walnut liqueurs (*vins de noix*), are always available. Refreshing *pastis* – the generic name for aniseed drinks

KNOW YOUR WINE
The most obvious guide to the quality of a wine is its **classification**, and in 2012 the system used to classify French wines changed. At the lowest level is now **vin de France**, suitable for everyday drinking, replacing the old **vin de table** but now allowing growers to provide information on vintage and grape variety. Then there's **Indication Géographique Protégée** (IGP), a new intermediate category indicating quaffable fare. IGP replaces the old Vin de Pays category. AOP – **appellation d'origine protégée** – is the highest category, taking the place of the old AOC classification. Within this category a number of exceptional wines qualify for the superior labels of **Premier Cru** or **Grand Cru**.

Within each wine region there's enormous diversity, with differences generated by the type of grape grown (there are over sixty varieties), the individual skill of the *vigneron* (producer) and something the French refer to as *terroir*, an almost untranslatable term meaning the combination of soil, lie of the land and climate.

The Bordeaux wine-producing region produces a huge quantity of very fine, medium-bodied reds, delicious, sweet whites, notably **Sauternes**, and dry whites of varying quality. The best-known area is the Médoc, known for its long-lived, rich reds, including such legendary names as **Margaux** and Lafitte, which are made from a blend of wines, chiefly the blackcurranty **Cabernet Sauvignon**. Graves produces the best of the area's dry white wines, while St-Émilion, where the **Merlot** grape thrives, yields warmer, fruitier wines.

9

such as Pernod or Ricard – is served diluted with water and ice (*glace* or *glaçons*). Among less familiar names, try Poire William (pear brandy), or Marc (a spirit distilled from grape pulp). Measures are generous, but they don't come cheap: the same applies for imported spirits such as whisky (known as *"Scotch"* in France). Two drinks designed to stimulate the appetite – *un apéritif* – are Pineau (cognac and grape juice) and Kir (white wine with a dash of cassis – blackcurrant liqueur – or with champagne instead of wine for a Kir Royal). For a post-meal *digestif*, don't miss out on armagnac, oak-aged brandy from the south of the Garonne but available in bars and restaurants throughout the region. **Cocktails** are served at most late-night bars, discos and clubs, as well as at upmarket hotel bars.

SOFT DRINKS

On the **soft drink** front, you can buy cartons of unsweetened fruit juice in supermarkets, although in cafés, the bottled (sweetened) nectars such as apricot (*jus d'abricot*) and blackcurrant (*cassis*) still hold sway. Fresh orange or lemon juice (*orange/citron pressé*) is a much more refreshing choice on a hot day. Other soft drinks to try are syrups (*sirops*) of mint, grenadine and other flavours mixed with water. The standard fizzy drinks of lemonade (*limonade*), Coke (*coca*) and so forth are all available. Bottles of **mineral water** (*eau minérale*) and spring water (*eau de source*) – either sparkling (*gazeuse*) or still (*plate*) – abound. But there's not much wrong with the tap water (*l'eau de robinet*) which will always be brought free to your table if you ask for it.

COFFEE, TEA AND HOT CHOCOLATE

After a meal, **coffee** is always espresso – small, black and very strong. You can also get it with a dash of milk (noisette). *Un café or un express* is the regular. The only time of the day that French drink milky coffee is in the morning with breakfast when you could ask for *un café au lait* – espresso in a large cup or bowl filled up with hot milk. *Un déca* is decaffeinated and is available everywhere. Ordinary **tea** (*thé*) – Lipton's nine times out of ten – is normally served black (*nature*) or with a slice of lemon (*au citron*); the French never add milk to their tea but if you prefer it like that then ask for *un peu de lait frais* (some fresh milk), but expect the result to be a dishwater weak brew. *Chocolat chaud* – **hot chocolate** – lives up to the high standards of French food and drink and is available at any café and some specialist chocolate shops where it's invariably superb. After meals, **herbal teas** (*infusions* or *tisanes*), are offered by most restaurants – most commonly *verveine* (verbena), *tilleul* (lime blossom), *menthe* (mint) and *camomille* (camomile).

VIEUX BORDEAUX   SEE MAP PAGE 34

★ **Aux 4 Coins du Vin** 8 rue de la Devise, http://aux4 coinsduvin.com, ⊕ Place de la Bourse. Where good grapes go when they die. There are forty wines available, mostly red and mostly French, but a few whites and foreign wines, and you can taste by the glass, half-glass or quarter-glass. Pleasing tasting plates accompany the wine, big enough for two or three to share.

Bar à Vin du CIVB 1 cours du 30-juillet, http://baravin. bordeaux.com, ⊕ Quinconces Fleuve. On the ground floor of the Maison du Vin de Bordeaux, the wine bar of the CIVB (Bordeaux Wine Council) offers two parts edification to one part intoxication. Not surprisingly, a full range of Bordeaux wines (ranging from reds to sparkling whites, via dry and sweet whites, rosés and clarets) are available.

Calle Ocho 24 rue des Piliers-de-Tutelle, ⊕ Place de la Bourse. Bordeaux's best-known salsa bar has an unrivalled party vibe and is packed out most nights till 2am. There's bonafide Cuban rum and mojitos, too.

Sonate 18 rue Parlement Saint-Pierre, www.sonate-bordeaux.com, ⊕ Place de la Bourse. A classy cavernous wine bar, offering local vintages by the glass and bottle. The bar staff know their wines very well and can help you choose.

Le Sur Mesure 17 place du Palais, www.facebook.com/ lesurmesurebordeaux, ⊕ Place du Palais. Bordeaux may be a wine-focused destination, but it doesn't neglect beer: this friendly no-frills bar has an extensive menu of more than thirty craft beers, both local and imported. Porte Cailhau is visible from the pavement seating.

Wash Bar 39 rue Ausone, https://washbar.fr, ⊕ Porte de Bourgogne. Picture the scene: you need to do your laundry, but you really want to go out on the town. Luckily, *Wash Bar* has you covered: this café-bar also contains a long line of washing machines, allowing you to combine two previously unrelated activities. Not only that, but most evenings see stand-up comedy, improvised theatre or even a burlesque show.

PLACE GAMBETTA AND SAINT SEURIN-FONDAUDÈGE   SEE MAP PAGE 48

Chez le Pépère 19 rue Georges Bonnac, www. chezlepepere.com, ⊕ Gambetta. A top-notch wine bar, with friendly staff who can help you choose from the almost bewildering array of options. There's also a very good tapas menu to accompany your wine.

Connemara 18 cours d'Albret, http://connemara-pub. com, ⊕ Palais de Justice. As Irish a pub as ever you'll find outside of Ireland. The Guinness is cold and the football always pulls a good crowd. Happy hour 6–8pm daily, and weekly live music and open-mic nights.

The Sherlock Holmes 16 rue Judaïque, www.sherlockholmespub.fr, ⊙ Gambetta. One of Bordeaux's many British-style pubs, the *Sherlock Holmes* is a welcoming spot with good beers on tap, decent food, and regular live music.

Les Trois Pinardiers 2 rue Georges Bonnac, https://les3pinardiers.com, ⊙ Gambetta. Cosy little wine bar just off place Gambetta, with an excellent range of Bordeaux wines. Get a bottle and a charcuterie plate and settle in for the evening.

SAINT MICHEL AND CAPUCINS-VICTOIRE   SEE MAP PAGE 52

Balthazar 8 rue des Augustins https://vintagegroup.fr/balthazar-bar-sport-bordeaux, ⊙ Victoire. Popular with students from the nearby university, this pub-style place offers a good range of draft beers and decent cocktails. Sometimes hosts live music and DJ sets.

Couleurs du Vin 1 place Duburg, https://baravinbordeaux.fr, ⊙ Saint Michel. Small wine bar with pavement seating offering lovely views of the Basilique St Michel. All wines on

sale are local and organic, and there are tasting experiences available.

Le Lucifer 35 rue Pessac, ⊙ Victoire. A lively pub-style joint with a good mix of students and locals, *Le Lucifer* is a hit with beer-lovers thanks to its huge range of bottled and draught brews (mostly Belgian) and hosts regular live music nights. They don't accept cards, so be sure to bring cash.

CHARTRONS   SEE MAP PAGE 62

BAM Karaoke Box 36 rue Cornac, https://fr.bam-karaokebox.com/en/bordeaux, ⊙ Paul Doumer. "It's thrilling, it's joyful – it's BAM!" says the website, and while that may depend somewhat on your mileage for karaoke, there's no denying that the punters have a great time here. Private rooms are available if you want to get up there and sing but don't want anyone to see you do it.

Comptoir de Saintongey 34 cours du Médoc, https://comptoir-de-saintongey.fr, ⊙ Les Hangars. Friendly wine bar with a great selection of bottles from both nearby and further afield. Small plates available, and sometimes hosts live music.

Gagnant Gagnant 39 quai de Bacalan, https://gg33.fr/le-bar-a-jeux, ⊙ Les Hangars. Choose a board game from the well-stocked shelves, order some drinks, and settle in

for a competitive evening. The staff will happily teach rules for games you don't already know.

Trompette 107 quai des Chartrons, ⊙ Cours du Médoc. With a vibe that somehow hits the sweet spot between pavement café, billiards bar and 1920s speakeasy, Trompette is an enjoyable place to while away an hour or two over wine, cocktails or – slightly unexpectedly – hot dogs.

Wine Moment 86 quai des Chartrons, www.winemomentbyba.fr, ⊙ Chartrons. A friendly wine bar which operates a blind tasting policy – you tell the staff a little about what kind of wines you enjoy, and they will pick one out for you, without telling you what it is or where it comes from. The idea is to try the wine without any preconceptions – an approach which really works, resulting in an extremely enjoyable experience.

BASSINS À FLOT AND BACALAN   SEE MAP PAGE 59

La Cité du Vin 1 esplanade de Pontac, http://laciteduvin.com, ⊙ Cité du Vin. Your visit to *La Cité du Vin* includes a glass of wine, but there are plenty more on offer, and the views from the terrace are good, so it may be tempting to stay for another. The staff know wine very well and can help you choose the best option for you.

La Dame 1 quai Armand-Lalande1, ⊙ Cité du Vin. An old petrol barge moored in the north of the city provides one

of Bordeaux's liveliest nightlife spots. Come for above-board or port-side cocktails, or head below deck to the popular nightclub.

My Beers 63 quai Virginie Hériot, www.mybeers.fr/etablissements/bordeaux-bassins-a-flot, ⊙ Cité du Vin. Right opposite the Bassins des Lumières, the enjoyably industrial-themed My Beers has a great selection of bottled beers from all over Europe. It operates as a shop, too.

LA BASTIDE AND AROUND   SEE MAP PAGE 66

Alaia 12 quai des Queyries, https://alaia-bordeaux.fr, ⊙ Stalingrad. A restaurant-bar with views over the river, *Alaia* has a vaguely surfy Hawaiian vibe. Perhaps better for drinks than food, it's got a great selection of cocktails and beers.

Caserne B 1 quai Deschamps, www.instagram.com/casernebbordeaux, ⊙ Stalingrad. In a former barracks near Place de Stalingrad is the quirky *Caserne B*, where you can enjoy a drink or a light meal while surrounded by vintage fire engines. There's also table football and old-fashioned pinball machines here, offering plenty of distraction.

THE INTERIOR OF THE GRAND THÉÂTRE

Film and the performing arts

When it comes to the performing arts and film, Bordeaux is not exactly a cultural powerhouse. There are only a small number of theatres, although some of them do put on some rather avant-garde performances. The Grand Théâtre is classic Bordeaux: stately and usually fairly conservative, but what a place to take in a performance! All performances will be in French and while this means that many of the theatre productions might be lost on non-French speakers, the opera and ballet performances at the Grand Théâtre and elsewhere can be understood by anyone.

PROGRAMMES AND TICKETS

Séances (programmes) run throughout the day, sometimes as early as 10am, and can continue until 10.30pm or so. Tickets (*billets*) rarely need to be bought in advance, and they're not expensive by European standards – many cinemas also offer discounts for seniors and students.

CINEMA

There are lots of cinemas throughout the city and its suburbs. Many have an eclectic mix of Hollywood blockbusters and interesting art-house films. While many films are subtitled or dubbed, you can also often see original-language (*version originale* or *v.o.*) films. Check the free weekly *Bordeaux Plus* for listings.

Cinema Utopia 5 place Camille-Jullian, http://cinemas-utopia.org, ⊕ Place de la Bourse. Watch original-language films at this wonderful art-house cinema housed in a converted church.

Megarama 7 quai des Queyries, http://megarama.fr ⊕ Stalingrad. Arguably Bordeaux's best spot for Hollywood blockbusters is the seventeen-screen Megarama, which occupies the old gare d'Orléans train station.

UGC 13-15 rue Georges Bonnac (city centre) or 6 Quai Virginie Hériot (Bassins), www.ugc.fr, ⊕ Gambetta or

⊕ Cité du Vin. There are two branches of the UGC cinema chain in Bordeaux, at which you can see both French films and Hollywood flicks.

BORDEAUX'S FILM FESTIVALS

The **Festival International du Film Independent** (FIFIB) (https://www.fifib.com) is the city's annual film festival. It has taken place every October since 2012: expect lots of atmospheric, well-shot arty films. Check out the programme online to see what's on and where online.

The **European Short Film Festival of Bordeaux** (https://filmmakers.festhome.com/en/festival/festival-europeen-du-court-metrage-de-bordeaux), meanwhile, has been running since 1997, and presents non-documentary films which range from 5 to 25 minutes long. As such, it offers quite a varied programme. It's usually hosted by one of the city's multiplexes.

10

OPERA, THEATRE AND DANCE

Auditorium 8-13 cours Georges Clemenceau, https://opera-bordeaux.com, ⊕ Gambetta. The Auditorium has perfect acoustics, and as such, is the best place in town for classical music and opera performances.

Théâtre des Chartrons Galeries Tatry, 170 cours du Médoc, www.theatredeschartrons.fr, ⊕ Grand Parc. A small and relaxed theatre found in a converted wine warehouse, the Théâtre des Chartrons focuses largely on comedy plays.

Théâtre Fémina 10 rue de Grassi, www.theatrefemina.com, ⊕ Grand Théâtre. The gorgeous Théâtre Fémina is an atmospheric place to catch a performance, with its red velvet seats and sumptuous ceiling evoking a bygone age. It plays host to a range of shows, from concerts to stand-up comedy.

Grand Théâtre place de la Comédie, http://opera-bordeaux.com, ⊕ Grand Théâtre. If you're going to go to the theatre or see an opera while in Bordeaux then for sheer magnificence there's nowhere better than here. Dominating the place de la Comédie, the splendid neoclassical Grand Théâtre was built in 1780 and in its time has hosted concerts

by Liszt and Plácido Domingo.

La Grand Poste 7 rue du Palais Gallien, https://lagrandeposte.com, ⊕ Gambetta. Just off Place Gambetta, the former post office – a lovely Art Deco building in its own right – is now a venue for all manner of performances, from stand-up comedy to flamenco. There's a restaurant and bar too, and even pop-up shops selling art and fashion.

La Manufacture 226 boulevard Albert 1er, http://lamaufacture-cdcn.org, ⊕ Terres Neuves. Housed inside an old shoe factory and showing highly artistic and alternative theatre and dance.

TnBA place Renaudel, http://tnba.org, ⊕ Sainte-Croix. The Bordeaux national theatre has an eclectic mix of contemporary and classic theatre as well as dance and even circus. The building is quite a sight too.

Théâtre Trianon 6 rue Franklin, www.bordeauxtheatres.com, ⊕ Grand Théâtre. Théâtre Trianon has been going strong since its opening in 1913: behind its grandiose façade you'll find performances which range from jazz to flamenco.

MUSIC

Arkea Arena 48-50 avenue Jean Alfonséa, www.arkeaarena.com/fr/arkea-arena, Bus 25. If a big name in the music biz comes to Bordeaux, they'll probably play at this large arena to the city's southeast. Past performers include Shakira and Massive Attack.

Le Rocher de Palmer Parc Palmer, 1 rue Aristide Briand, https://lerocherdepalmer.fr, ⊕ Buttinière. There are three

concert halls at this venue on the east side of the river, which has played host to everyone from English indie darlings The Libertines to German headbangers Powerwolf.

Rock School Barbey 18 cours Barbey, www.rockschool-barbey.com, ⊕ Bordeaux Saint-Jean. A 700-person capacity venue, Rock School Barbey is where you'll catch up-and-coming bands and artists.

Festivals and events

There's a year-round busy festival calendar in Bordeaux and surrounding areas and, throughout the summer months there will always be a festival or event worth building into your itinerary. Classical and contemporary music, as well as wine themed events get the most attention. Major international rock and pop artists are yet to really discover Bordeaux but every now and then you might catch a big name act. There are also a few festivals and events focused more on local culture held throughout the year.

It's hard to beat the experience of arriving in a small French village to discover the streets decked out with flags and streamers, a band playing in the square and the entire population out celebrating the feast of their patron saint. As well as the country-wide Fête de la Musique (June 21) and Bastille Day (July 14), Bordeaux city hosts dozens of festivals (mainly in the summer), from giant music festivals to ones celebrating literature, dance, classical music and cinema. Many of the classical music, jazz and theatre festivals often take place in churches and châteaux.

The following are only the biggest or otherwise most important. Towns throughout the area often host low-key local events, which can be great fun if you happen to stumble into one. Local tourist offices can help point you in the right direction.

> ### CELEBRATING WINE
>
> In such dedicated **wine** country, there are inevitably festivals coinciding with the grape harvest, when each village stages its own celebrations. While we have mentioned some of the more important festivals within the text it's worth asking in tourist offices for a full list.

11

JANUARY

Bordeaux Rock Bordeaux, http://bordeauxrock.com. Two-day mini festival featuring local Bordeaux rock groups.

MARCH

Carnaval des 2 Rives Bordeaux, http://carnavaldesdeuxrives.fr. Popular city-wide carnival celebration.
Portes Ouvertes des Châteaux en Médoc Pauillac, http://medocvignobles.com. Some of the biggest châteaux in the Médoc swing open their doors to the public.

APRIL

Printemps des Vins de Blaye Blaye, http://vin-blaye.com. A dozen local wine producers present their tipples in the citadelle of Blaye.

MAY

Saint-Émilion Portes Ouvertes Saint-Émilion. Producers in the world's most famous wine town open to the public.

JUNE

Fête le Vin Bordeaux, http://bordeaux-fete-le-vin.com. Huge four-day wine festival with producers from across the region. Various evening events are also put on to celebrate the grapes that helped make Bordeaux rich.

JULY

Estivales de musique en Médoc Médoc, http://estivales-musique-medoc.com. Big name classical music performers put on a show in some of the best known Médoc châteaux.
Festival Musicalarue Luxey Luxey, http://musicalarue.com. The biggest street festival in the southwest takes over the small town of Luxey in the north of Les Landes. Expect street theatre, dance, world music and all manner of other performers.

AUGUST

Fest'arts Libourne, http://festarts.com. Hundreds of artists, musicians and performers descend on the town of Libourne, for a feast of theatre, concerts, dance and circus.
Reggae Sun Ska Vertheuil, http://reggaesunska.com. By far the biggest and most prestigious reggae and ska festival in France. A three-day event with thousands of attendees.

OCTOBER

Festival International du Film independent de Bordeaux Bordeaux, http://fifib.com. Small film festival.

DECEMBER

Marché de Noël Bordeaux, http://marche-de-noel-bordeaux.com. Impressive Christmas market that fills les allées de Tourny throughout the month.

> ### UPCOMING EVENTS
>
> Check out http://bordeaux-tourism.co.uk/agenda for a complete list of upcoming events.

Shopping

The obvious souvenir to bring back from a visit to Bordeaux is wine, and you'll find any number of places to buy it: wine shops are everywhere in the city centre. Other souvenir options also tend toward the edible – cheese in particular is always popular – but you'll also find a good range of places selling locally-made jewellery and art.

The most upmarket place to shop in Bordeaux is the so-called "Golden Triangle": the area bordered by the cours de l'Intendance, allées de Tourny and cours Clemenceau, which is lined with designer stores, jewellery boutiques and wine shops. Alternatively, head to the pedestrianized rue Sainte-Catherine, which has all the usual high street brands and outlets, as well as a Galeries Lafayette department store. A popular Sunday market is held along quai des Chartrons.

For food, the quickest and most convenient places to shop are the hypermarkets and supermarkets you'll find all over the place. The biggest ones in Bordeaux are all in out-of-town locations, but the city centre is dotted with smaller minimarkets. But more interesting by far are the specialist food shops of which Bordeaux excels and, of course, the markets. There are daily food markets in Bordeaux and weekly ones in surrounding towns and villages. Tourist offices can give you a full list of produce markets. Coastal towns such as Arcachon have seafood markets.

In winter, you'll find that some of the inland towns and villages around Bordeaux hold *marchés aux gras* when whole fattened livers of duck and goose are put up for sale alongside the other edible bits of the fowl. Often these events double up as truffle or *cèpe* markets.

ANTIQUES

L'Entrepôt Saint Germain 96 rue Amédée Saint-Germain, ⊕ Bordeaux Saint-Jean; see map page 52. If you love rifling through antiques and second-hand goods, head down to this warehouse southwest of the station. Specialising in furniture, decoration and clothing, a visit will keep vintage hunters happy for hours.

BOOKS

La Machine à Lire 8 place du Parlement, www.lamachinealire.com, ⊕ Place de la Bourse; see map page 34. Atmospheric bookshop with an impressive vaulted ceiling. Some books in English available, and also sells lovely greetings cards.

Mollat 15 rue Vital-Carles; see map page 34. It's easy to get absorbed browsing in Bordeaux's largest bookshop. Most titles are in French, but there's still a decent selection of books in other languages.

Presse Gambetta place Gambetta; see map page 34. Sells all the main English-language papers in addition to some regional guides and maps.

Pulp's Bordeaux 56 rue du Loup, www.pulps.fr, ⊕ Hôtel de Ville; see map page 34. Comic book fans rejoice – here's your temple in Bordeaux. With a wide selection in both French and English, Pulp's offers both current and back issues, as well as a decent range of other collectibles.

CLOTHES AND ACCESSORIES

Bord'eau Village quai de Bacalan www.bord-eau-village.com, ⊕ Les Hangars; see map page 62. On the riverfront north of the centre, the Bord'eau Village is home to numerous interesting boutiquey shops to browse – mostly clothing, but also cooking and furniture. There are plenty of waterside cafés to relax in when you need a refreshment stop.

De Grimm 4 rue Michel Montaigne, www.degrimm.com, ⊕ Grand Théâtre; see map page 34. Local business producing high-quality leather goods, particularly handbags but also belts, wallets and smartphone cases. Fittingly for Bordeaux, they also have a range of wine-related products – coasters and bottle carriers, among much else.

Parenthese 6 rue Jean Jacques Rousseau, https://www.parenthesebordeaux.com, ⊕ Grand Théâtre; see map page 34. A boutique store selling luxury fashion items – pop in to check out the designer handbags, shoes and accessories.

12

ANTIQUES AND FLEA MARKETS

Place des Quinconces is where to head for the city's best flea market in Bordeaux held bi-annually in spring (end Apr-early May) and winter (end Nov-early Dec). Meanwhile, the The Saint-Michel flea market operates weekly (Tue-Fri and Sun, 4-6pm; http://lespucesdestmichel.com). The nouveau wine and flea market festival in **Les Chartrons** is brocante heaven with stalls spilled out along rue Notre Dame and takes place at the end of October annually.

DEPARTMENT STORES AND MALLS

Galeries Lafayette 11–19 rue Sainte-Catherine, http://galerieslafayette.com, ⊕ Sainte-Catherine; see map page 34. France's most famous department store has a huge range of women's clothing, including a number of top-name designers, plus a gigantic cosmetic and perfume floor, luxury foods and souvenirs. There's a men's store on rue de la Porte-Dijeaux, and the tourist office offers 10 percent discount coupons.

Les Grands Hommes 12 place des Grands-Hommes, http://lesgrandshommes.com, ⊕ Grand Théâtre; see map page 34. An elegant domed shopping mall at the epicentre of the "Golden Triangle", *Les Grands Hommes* has a small selection of upmarket jewellery, accessories and homeware boutiques, plus a *Carrefour* supermarket. Head to the ground floor, where the artisan food stalls are excellent quality, if slightly overpriced.

> ### FOOD AND WINE CLASSIFICATIONS
>
> AOP, Appellation d'Origine Protegée, is a legal regulation for cheeses, poultry and other food items such as lentils and walnuts as well as wines, and it ensures the products conform to a particular standard.

Mériadeck 57 rue du Château d'Eau, http://meriadeck.com, ⊕ Mériadeck; see map page 52. Bordeaux's biggest shopping centre, with three floors of shops and restaurants, including clothing stores like H&M, Zara and Mango, and a gigantic two-floor Auchan supermarket. Parking is free for the first 90 minutes.

FOOD AND WINE

Fromagerie Deruelle 66 rue du Pas-St-Georges, http://fromagerie-deruelle.com, ⊕ Sainte-Catherine; see map page 34. There are seemingly endless *fromageries* (cheese shops) in Bordeaux, but this small shop is one of the best. Here you'll find an extensive range of 150 different cheeses, with knowledgeable, friendly staff who can help you find the perfect choice. As well as *fromage*, Deruelle also sells other dairy products such as yoghurts and eggs, plus charcuterie, wine and oils – and don't forget to check out the fabulous home-made (and cheese-based) desserts.

L'Intendant 2 allées de Tourny, http://intendant.com, ⊕ Grand Théâtre; see map page 34. One of the city's best wine shops, with over 1200 Bordeaux wines straight from the châteaux. It's worth a peek just to marvel at the grand spiral stair-well, which towers with neatly stacked wines.

Marché des Capucins Place des Capucins ⊕ Victoire; see map page 52. Bordeaux's main covered market hall is an epicurean journey through France, with fresh fruits, vegetables, meats, fish and seafood, breads and pastries from around the country. Stock up on edible souvenirs like Bordeaux speciality *canelés* or enjoy lunch at one of the many food stalls.

MiAM 33 rue des Argentiers, 05 57 14 98 61, ⊕ Place de la Bourse; see map page 34. Well-stocked deli packed with goodies, ranging from cheese and charcuterie to cakes and wine. An excellent place to stock up for a very French picnic – or you can simply eat your purchases there and then at the small café in-store.

Musée du Vin et du Négoce 41 rue Borie, http://musee devinbordeaux.com, ⊕ Chartrons; see map page 62. The gift shop of this wine museum sells, predictably enough, an excellent selection of wines, as well as other tasty treats: the chocolate-coated raisins are delicious and make a perfect pairing with a Bordeaux red wine.

> ### SHOPPING FOR WINE
>
> The best way of **buying wine** is directly from the producers (*vignerons*) at their vineyards or at Maisons or Syndicats du Vin (representing a group of wine-producers), or Coopératifs Vinicoles (producers' co-ops). At all of these you can usually sample the wines first. The most interesting option is to visit the vineyard itself, where the owner will often include a tour of the *chais* in which the wine is produced and aged. The most economical method is to buy *en vrac*, which you can do at some wine shops (*caves*), filling a plastic five- or ten-litre container (generally sold on the premises) straight from the barrel. Supermarkets often have good bargains, too.
>
> There are strict limitations on the extent to which winegrowers can interfere in the natural process – it's illegal even to water vines. The result is that, far more than in other countries, French wines are the product of a very specific bit of land or *terroir*, and there will often be significant differences in taste between the wines of two neighbouring producers. This makes tasting wines a real joy, and even if you're not an expert, it's well worth trying to establish which grape types you particularly like or dislike, and whether you like your wine fruity or dry, light or heavy. For basic wine distinctions, see page 89.

Saunion Chocolats 56 cours Clemenceau, http://saunion.fr, ⊕ Grand Théâtre; see map page 34. Decadent chocolates and confectionary hand-crafted by one of Bordeaux's most renowned chocolatiers, with products starting at just a few euros, plus delicious artisan ice creams in summer.

MUSIC

Diabolo Menthe 30 rue de Cheverus, https://diabolo-menthe-bordeaux-33.fr, ⊕ Hôtel de Ville; see map page 34. A treasure trove for crate diggers, *Diabolo Menthe* is one of Bordeaux's best record stores, with an eclectic selection of new and second-hand vinyl ranging from jazz to punk.

MISCELLANEOUS AND GIFTS

La Grand Poste 7 rue du Palais Gallien, https://lagrandeposte.com, ⊕ Gambetta; see map page 34. The attractive former post office is now a cultural centre which plays host to a regularly changing line-up of pop-up shops. It's a good place to browse works by local artists and fashion designers.

Petit Pouces 3 rue du Pas-Saint-Georges, https://petitspouces.com, ⊕ Place de la Bourse; see map page 34. A lovely traditional toy shop, selling wooden toys and stuffed animals. If you're looking for a child's gift, this is the place to head.

w.a.n. 1 rue des Lauriers, www.wanweb.fr, ⊕ Place de la Bourse; see map page 34. Standing for "we are nothing", *w.a.n.*_sells locally-made, sustainable and zero-waste products, with a particular emphasis on cosmetics. The owner is passionate and always up for a chat.

12

Activities and sports

Bordeaux is like many other cities when it comes to sporting opportunities: there are numerous gyms, running tracks and sports centres but in many cases they're aimed at residents. The running tracks and sports facilities in the parks are free to use though for everyone and many gyms offer single session entry, as do the swimming pools. The real sporting interest of the region, however, lies beyond the city. Southwest France is something of a giant adventure playground and just a short way outside of Bordeaux or within a couple of hours' driving out of the city you can enjoy world class surfing, superb cycle paths, kayaking, sailing, horse-riding and hiking – make a side trip to the Pyrenees to enjoy some of the world's finest, least spoilt and most varied hiking trails or a spot of skiing or snow shoeing.

13

BOULES

The classic French game, revered throughout the whole country, boules (or pétanque), is a common sight on balmy summer evenings in many of the city's parks and gardens. You could search for 'Terrain de boules' online to find a court near you, but you'll certainly see it played at the Quinconces (see page 42), Place de la République (enclosed by l'hôpital Saint-André) and Place du Cardinal-Donnet, near Gare St-Jean. The principle is the same as British bowls but the terrain is always rough – usually gravel or sand, and never grass – and the area much smaller. The metal ball is also smaller than a bowling ball, usually thrown upwards from a distance of about 10m, with a strong backspin in order to stop it skidding away from the wooden marker (cochonnet). Though traditionally the social equivalent of darts or perhaps pool, the game is becoming far less male-dominated; there are café or neighbourhood teams and many local championships.

COOKERY AND WINE COURSES

Many of the vineyards outside the city will offer wine tasting experiences and offer some form of educational experience. For a more concentrated, hands-on experience though you can book a French cookery or wine course that runs for over a few hours.

Cooking School Château Kirwan https://www. chateau-kirwan.com. In the village of Margaux 30km north of Bordeaux, *Château Kirwan* offers culinary courses involving cooking dishes, pairing wines, and even making macaroons. There's also an interesting course on creating perfume.

Cooking School Le Saint James www.saintjames-bouliac.com. *Le Saint James* is an excellent hotel and restaurant in the commune of Bouliac, about 7km southeast of Bordeaux's city centre. Cookery classes offer a look into the chefs' kitchens to learn their techniques.

The Gastronome http://thegastronome.fr. Wine and French cooking classes run by an American chef and his wife. All classes are in English and cover everything from duck to deserts and of course wine pairings to go with every menu. The Capucins food market tour includes a five-course lunch.

CYCLING

A web of superbly maintained cycle paths (which are often like shrunk down versions of proper roads) spider web across Bordeaux and out into the countryside. Bike hire is available in every tourist town in summer. Cycling between wine villages and up and down the coast is especially rewarding.

Gravel Explore www.gravelexplore.com/gravel-bike-tours-bordeaux-france. *Gravel Explore* run cycling tours both in Bordeaux centre and in the surrounding countryside, also involving stops at restaurants and vineyards.

Véloce http://veloce-location.fr. Bike hire for adults and children available in branches in Bordeaux, Saint-Emilion and Cap Ferret. One-way hire is an option.

FOOD TOURS

If you're interested in local cuisine but don't want to take a cookery class, try one of the walking tours of Bordeaux with a focus on food. These will often take you to markets and delis, as well as reveal some excellent local foodie hangouts.

Do Eat Better https://doeatbetterexperience.com/france-food-tour/what-to-do-in-bordeaux/bordeaux-food-tour. *Do Eat Better* run food-themed walking tours of multiple French cities, and certainly know what they're doing in Bordeaux. Among much else, they can help you perfectly pair chocolate and wine for a truly decadent experience.

Miam https://miamevent.fr/en/bordeaux-2. With experiences such as "The Epicurious", *Miam* runs walking tours of Bordeaux visiting local markets to purchase produce which you'll then cook – or simply eat there and then. Wine tastings are often involved too.

HAMMAMS

Turkish baths, or hammams, are one thing that is done very well in France in general, and Bordeaux is no exception. More luxurious than the standard Swedish sauna, but less soothingly upmarket than a spa, these are places to linger, meet up and chat, and exit glowing and sparklingly clean. You can usually pay extra for a massage and/or a *gommage* (scrub) followed by a refreshing mint tea or a cool drink to complete the experience. You're often given a strip of linen and modest towel on entry, and usually some slippers, but bring your own swimsuit for mixed men-and women sessions.

Les Cents Ciels 16, cours du Médoc, Charge, http://bordeaux.hammam-lescentciels.com. Mixed hamman that is less luxe than le Grand Hammam but it's open daily for anyone over 13 years. All sessions are mixed and a range of care packages are available.

Le Grand Hamman de Bordeaux 45 rue des Menuts, Charge, http://legrandhammamdebordeaux.fr. Gorgeous opulent hammam in the city with luxurious treatment packages. Women and girls over 12 years only. Open Mon–Sat. Closed every second Wednesday.

13

HIKING

Although generally flat, there are some fine hiking trails in the countryside around Bordeaux and the city has its very own long-distance trail – the GR Bordeaux Metropole, a multi-day hike encircling the city. See the box on page 68. The coastal forests have good hiking trails as do the villages in the wine regions. Tourist offices can give full details.

HORSE RIDING

Many of the inland villages have horse riding stables catering to all abilities. Try the below, or ask at tourist offices for details. **Ecuries du Lac Hostens** https://equitation-aquitaine. com. This riding school to the south of Bordeaux can arrange pony trekking or horse riding for an afternoon, a day or lengthier courses.

Les Sabots du Temple www.centre-equestre-le-temple. com. Offering horse-riding trips either through forest or along the beach, these stables can accommodate riders of all ages and abilities.

KAYAKING

The giant, shallow coastal lakes are the most obvious place to take to a kayak and they can be hired in many places. Another very rewarding place is the Bassin d'Arcachon. In Bordeaux itself kayaks can be hired from the Bordeaux-Lac in the city's western fringes. This lake also has a busy beach in summer and is ringed by cycle paths.

Les Marins de la Lune https://lesmarinsdelalune.fr. Based on the Garonne's east bank, this is the place to come for plenty of water-based action –besides kayaking and stand-up paddleboarding, surfing and sailing get a look in too. Their canoeing excursions can be booked at https://bordeauxcanoe.com.

RIVER CRUISING

If you want to get out on the water but would prefer to let someone else do the hard work, consider a river cruise on the Garonne. It's a relaxing way to see Bordeaux's sights, and there are plenty of operators offering guided tours with commentary – a selection of them is listed below. A cheaper alternative is to use the river ferry (www.infotbm.com/fr/ le_bato_par_tbm.html) which trundles up and down the Garonne – picking it up from place de la Bourse and heading north is a great way to reach Cité du Vin.

Les Bateau Bordelais https://en.lesbateauxbordelais. com. Boat trips with guided commentary, which can include wine tasting while aboard ship.
Bordeaux Be Boat https://bordeauxbeboat.fr. Cruises for small groups, including culinary trips or rides at sunset.
Burdigala Cruises www.croisieresburdigala.fr. Offers 90-minute tours along the Garonne, departing from place de la Bourse and taking in all Bordeaux's riverside highlights.

SAILING

The Atlantic is often rough and wild but the Bassin d'Arcachon offers wonderful sailing opportunities. Smaller one- and two-man sail boats bob about the larger lakes and lessons are normally available. Try the Arcachon Sailing Circle (www.voile-arcachon.fr) or the Bombannes Aventures sailing school (www.ucpa.com/centres-sportifs/ bombannes) if you want to get out on the water.

SURFING

For surfing the best-known spot close to Bordeaux is Lacanau but almost any beach town will have multiple surf schools and camps. The best season for learning to surf is June to early September. The best season for those with experience is mid-September through to early November.
Arcagliss www.ecoledesurf-arcachon.com. Based in Arcachon, this excellent surf school can rent boards and run classes. Stand-up paddleboarding and kayaking are also available.

Big Mama Surf School www.ecole-surf-lacanau.com. Relaxed and child-friendly surf school offering courses and excursions suitable for all ages from 5 years up.
Bordeaux Surf School https://bordeaux-surf-school. com. Half-day or full-day surfing courses, including travel to and from the beach and the hire of boards and wet suits. The small group sizes are a plus.

SWIMMING

Piscine Galin 80 rue Galin, 05 56 86 25 01, ☻ Galin; daily; Charge. Nice, recently revamped pool with curved glass ceiling. Disabled accessible.
Piscine Judaïque 164 rue Judaïque, 05 56 51 48 31, ☻ Judaïque; daily; Charge. Probably the best bathing place in the city, this pool has an open-air terrace as well as a covered pool.

Piscine Stéhelin 200-288 avenue Maréchal De Lattre de Tassigny, 05 56 08 38 03, Charge. Take the bus line G to St Aubin Villepreux to this open-air pool that operates from the beginning of June to the end of August.

SPECTATOR SPORTS

Oddly for a city of its size, Bordeaux doesn't have a great sporting presence, apart from its excellent rugby team. Although it has two football teams, neither of them is currently a heavyweight – though Girondins has an impressive pedigree and both teams boast some loyal supporters. Rugby is a somewhat different story, with its local team among the best in France. The city also has a basketball team and hosts an annual tennis tournament.

BNP Paribas Primrose Tennis Tournament http://tournoi-primrosebordeaux.com. is held over five days every May at Villa Primrose featuring top players and hosting over thirty thousand spectators at the oldest, most prestigious tennis club in the city.

FC Girondins de Bordeaux www.girondins.com/fr. Based at the Matmut Atlantique stadium (☻ Parc des Expositions), Girondins are Bordeaux's top football team. They were formed in 1881 and enjoyed considerable success over the twentieth century, but due to financial difficulties in the early 2020s they currently play in the Championnat National 2, France's fourth tier.

JSA Bordeaux Métropole Basket www.jsa-bmb.fr. Bordeaux's basketball team doesn't tend to trouble the big leagues. They play at the Arkea Arena (bus 25).

Stade Bordelais https://stade-bordelais.com. Bordeaux's smaller team, Stade Bordelais compete in France's fifth tier and are based at the Sainte Germain (☻ Sainte Germaine) stadium.

Union Bordeaux Bègles (https://www.ubbrugby.com. Bordeaux's rugby union team formed in 2006 when two previous clubs merged, and have gone from strength to strength since – in 2024, for example, they took second place in the national championship, losing to Toulouse's Stade Toulousain. They play at Stade Chaban-Delmas (☻ Chaban-Delmas).

Bordeaux for children

For most adults a Bordeaux city break is all about food, drink, architecture and touring the vineyards – hardly riveting stuff for the little people in your life. But Bordeaux also has many child-friendly activities and sights. Some of the vineyards offer special activities for kids, while many others have plenty of space for them to run around and burn off some energy. Cycling between vineyards (the roads are generally quiet and there are lots of cycle tracks) is also a good way to keep younger visitors engaged. All but the most highbrow of restaurants in the city welcome children, and there are normally kids' menus and highchairs for smaller ones. Restaurants with play areas, such as you might find in the UK, are very rare, as French children are normally expected to be engaged in a family meal.

Bordeaux and surrounding areas have a lot to offer travelling families. For a compact city, there is plenty to entertain little ones in Bordeaux well into their teen years. There are lots of child-friendly activities and sights for the little members of your team including some great museums in Bordeaux, as well as boat rides, cycle paths and chateaux, gardens and castles throughout the countryside to explore. There are even child-friendly vineyards. And then there are the beaches. These vast stretches of endless golden sand, heaped up dunes and pleasantly warm waters are one of the worlds most famed surf destinations. Older kids especially will love the chance to learn to surf here. Just back from the beaches are a series of sprawling lakes and meandering rivers and streams with kayaking, sailing and wind surfing all on offer. All this makes the coastal regions of Bordeaux one giant adventure playground for children of all ages, though great care should be taken of the currents and shore breaks along the whole coastline.

In season, almost every tourist town, and major sight puts on special children's activities which can range from dedicated children's guided tours to art classes, face painting, and more. Ask at tourist offices for suggestions. For Sports and Activities, see page 100.

14

OUTDOOR ACTIVITES, PARKS AND TRAILS

Aquapark Biscarrosse Lake Biscarrosse, https://aquapark.fr. It's about 90 minutes' drive from Bordeaux, but the lure of the world's largest aquapark may tempt you and the kids out of the city. Expect a veritable maze of inflatable obstacles floating on the surface of the lake. It's for adults as much as kids, but there are dedicated sessions for younger children. June to September only.

City parks Bordeaux offers numerous parks which are ideal for letting off steam, some of them with interesting structures to explore – try Parc de Majolan for its artificial caves or the puppet show at Jardin Public.

Cycle along the riverfront An excellent cycle path runs along the riverfront and bikes (including ones for kids) can be hired from Véloce (33 rue Notre Dame; http://veloce-location.fr). The traffic-free riverfront is also extremely popular for e-scooter riders and roller-skaters.

Darwin Eco-Système 87 quai de Queyries, http://darwin.camp. For teens this is a great hang out with skate parks (and boards to rent), street art and a trainer recycling plant. Other activities include stand-up paddleboarding, roller-skating and the intriguing bike polo.

Dotto train Departing from the tourist office, 12 cours du 30 Juillet. See the sights of Bordeaux from the road train, which follows a 45 minute circuit past the city's highlights, starting from the tourist office.

Miroir d'Eau place de la Bourse. On a hot summer day, kids of all ages will relish the cooling jets of fine mist sprayed up from the vast shallow pool on the riverfront.

Parc de la Coccinelle Archachon, www.la-coccinelle.fr. Close to Archachon to the west of Bordeaux is this amusement park, which boasts rollercoasters and log flumes, carousels and a petting farm-zoo at which you'll meet rabbits, llamas and Shetland ponies, among much else.

Piscine Judaïque 164 rue Judaïque, 05 56 51 48 31. Head to this gorgeous art-deco swimming pool for a splash about. The exterior terrace is lovely in fine weather.

Pop Corn Labyrinthe Parempuyre, www.popcornlabyrinthe.fr/bordeaux. Just north of Bordeaux, this giant corn maze (July to September only) will provide a couple of hours' entertainment as you attempt to navigate its paths to solve cryptic riddles.

Robin's city trail Available from the tourist office, 12 Cr du 30 Juillet. A free treasure trail for kids between the age of 7 and 12, designed to lead families on a route through the city centre's top sights.

Surfing There are numerous surf schools on the Atlantic coast for kids who want to get out among the waves. The most child-friendly is Big Mama Surf School (www.ecole-surf-lacanau.com), which runs family-oriented classes.

Tépacap 5 rue Hipparque Entrée à Décathlon, Mérignac https://tepacap-bordeaux.com. Explore zipwires, swings and rope bridges at this vast treetops adventure park.

Tèrra Aventura www.terra-aventura.fr. A free app-based treasure hunt for everyone aged 7 and up, Tèrra Aventura offers seven trails to follow in and around Bordeaux.

ATTRACTIONS AND MUSEUMS

Bassins des Lumières impasse Brown de Colstou, http://bassins-lumieres.com. Incredible digital art projected onto the giant walls of a former WWII submarine base make for such a memorable way to experience art that even the most bored teen might grudgingly remark that "It's okay".

CAP Sciences Hanger 20, quai de Bacalan, http://cap-sciences.net. Depending on the exhibitions on at the time, children (and adults) visiting the city's science museum might learn all about bed bugs, dinosaurs, Star Wars, Egyptian mummies and more. Everything is extremely

14

engaging and presented in a very hands-on way.

La Cité du Vin 134 quai de Bacalan, http://laciteduvin. com. A state-of-the-art museum dedicated to wine might seem an unusual choice of day out for children, but a genuine effort has been made here to get kids on side. The child-focused tablet helps younger visitors enjoy the wonders of wine, and there are numerous interactive displays which may also prove diverting. The virtual grape-crushing exhibit – at which visitors must stamp all over the floor – is likely to be a hit. Younger visitors can even join in the wine tasting session, albeit with a glass of grape juice.

Musée Mer Marine 89 rue des Étrangers, http://mmm bordeaux.com. For the would-be pirate in your family, the hundreds of model boats in this museum will provide hours of wonder.

Musée de l'Illusion 4 rue Bonneaffé, http:// museedelillusion.fr. One of Bordeaux's most kid-friendly museums, children – and adults – will be enthralled by the visual illusions on display here.

Museum Bordeaux Sciences et Nature Jardin Public, http://museum-bordeaux.fr. The natural history museum enjoyed a renovation in 2022 and is now far from a stuffy display of, well, stuffed animals – it's full of engaging displays on various themes, many of which have been specifically designed with younger visitors in mind.

Zoo de Bordeaux-Pessac 3 chemin du Transvaal, Pessac, www.zoo-bordeaux-pessac.com. At Bordeaux's zoo, kids can come face-to-face with lions and jaguars, as well as enter the lemur enclosure.

LGBTQ+ Bordeaux

With a large and young student population Bordeaux has a fairly open attitude to LGBTQ+ travellers, but there aren't all that many bars and clubs aimed specifically at an LGBTQ+ audience. Likewise, restaurants and accommodation city-wide are generally all-inclusive rather than targeted to any one sexual orientation. Outside of the city, don't expect to find any special welcome or facilities. The Bordeaux Pride festival, organized by Le Girofard Centre, takes place annually in June and sees several thousand dance and sing their way through the city centre.

In general, France is more liberal on homosexuality than many other European countries. The legal age of consent is 15 and civil unions between same-sex couples were made legal in 1999 and marriage in 2013, as well as the right for stepchild adoption by same sex couples.

On a day-to-day level, the French mostly consider sexuality to be a private matter, and homophobic assaults are extremely rare. Nevertheless, **gay men** tend to be discreet outside specific gay venues, **gay women** even more so. You can expect to be received with tolerance, but not necessarily a warm welcome.

ESSENTIALS

INFORMATION CENTRES

Le Girofard 21 rue du Loup, http://le-girofard.org, ⊕ Place de La Bourse. This centre covers everything from health information and free counselling to sports and social activities, as well as offering support and advice to its members. Lots of social events are posted on their social media pages. Open every Wednesday and Friday evening for meet-and-greet sessions; by appointment at all other times. In French only.

PRINT AND ONLINE MEDIA

Spartacus International Gay Guide https://spartacus. gayguide.travel. Has an extensive section on France and contains some info for lesbians.

Têtu http://tetu.com. France's best-selling gay/lesbian magazine, with events listings and contact addresses; you can buy it in bookshops, newsagents or through their website, which is also an excellent source of information.

Wake Up! http://assowakeup.org. This is a local online association for LGBTQ+ students, but the website contains plenty of information for those just passing through the city.

DRINKING AND NIGHTLIFE

In terms of nightlife, Bordeaux does not have a gay centre or area as such and exclusively gay bars and clubs are thin on the ground. Here are a few recommendations.

Le Buster Bar 34 rue de Cursol, http://facebook.com/ CocoLokoBar, ⓜ Hôtel de Ville; see map page 47. Spread across two floors and with big party nights, this is another popular gay bar.

Le Coco Loko 203 rue Duffour Dubergier, http://www. facebook.com/BusterBarOfficial, ⓜ Hôtel de Ville; see map page 34. Bordeaux's best-known gay bar has happy hours, single nights, quizzes and drag queen evenings.

Le Crunch Sauna Bar 62 cours Anatole France, https:// sauna-crunch.com, ⊕ Bourse du Travail; see map page 47. A fairly risqué offering in Bordeaux's gay scene at this men-only, fully licensed bar centred around a sauna, Jacuzzi

and hammam. Background tunes and movies play to suit the time of the day. Enter dressed as you wish, shower, towel up (you'll be given one on entry, plus a locker for your things) and stay until late.

The LS Café 297 boulevard Albert 1er 2, 05 56 49 69 52, ⊕ Bègles; see map page 71. All-female bar in Bègles with a cosy interior and nice terrace. Early evenings are suited to long chats and discussions while as the night goes on, the music goes up a few notches, the cocktails are flowing and the party starts.

Ultra Klubs 22 place André Meunier dit Mureine; www. facebook.com/ultraklubs, ⓜ Tauzia; see map page 52. The most gay-friendly nightclub in the city has a giant dancefloor and puts on drag shows. Frequent theme nights.

15

Day-trips from Bordeaux

The region's most prestigious vineyards lie just beyond the city's periphery, close to picturesque riverside towns with citadels and cobbled streets. Further afield, upmarket beach resorts like Arcachon and Cap Ferret, attractions such as the famous Dune du Pyla and the excellent surfing along the coast of the Côte d'Argent are a major draw, especially in the balmy summer months. Cycle your way around vineyards and pine forested trails at leisure, boat along rivers and hit the beach – this is the ideal way to enjoy the slow pace of life that southwest France has to offer.

The Bordeaux wine region

It's pretty much unthinkable to visit Bordeaux without spending some time in the surrounding wine region, which occupies much of the countryside on the eastern side of the city. The most frequently-visited areas include the **Médoc** in the north, **St-Émilion** due east, and the **Sauternes** to the south. Other less well-known but equally worthwhile areas include **Blaye**, to the north of Bordeaux, and **Entre-Deux-Mers**, to the east.

Although one of the greatest pleasures of visiting the region is, of course, touring the local **vineyards** and sampling a few home-grown wines, that's not all there is to this part of the country. The Médoc is home to a fine collection of beautiful eighteenth-century châteaux, while for earlier architecture it's worth checking out Blaye's vast fortress, the ruined castle at Villandraut near Sauternes, or the remains of the **La Sauve-Majeur** abbey at Entre-Deux-Mers. For sheer out-and-out prettiness, you're best turning to St-Émilion, an impossibly picturesque little wine town, which also offers the unexpected bonus of a cavernous underground church.

ARRIVAL AND GETTING AROUND   THE BORDEAUX WINE REGION

By train There are train lines from Bordeaux running north through the Médoc to Margaux and Pauillac, and south through the Garonne valley to St-Macaire and La Réole. St-Émilion lies on the Bordeaux–Sarlat line, but the station is a couple of kilometres from the town.

By bus There's a comprehensive regional bus network – pick up timetables at the tourist office. Several different companies operate buses; the largest is Citram Aquitaine (http://citram.fr).

By car Clear the Bordeaux suburbs and you'll find yourself in a very rural area which invariably means that getting around by public transport can be hard work. For this reason, most people touring the wine regions do so by private car. Most of the roads are gentle N roads and driving is normally a pleasure.

By bike Cycling is an appealing mode of transport, and many of the towns are connected by well-marked tarmac cycle paths. Cycling to the wine regions direct from Bordeaux would be a bit much for most people but many of the more popular wine towns and villages have bicycle rental shops.

The Médoc

Taking its name from the Medulli, the Celtic tribe who occupied the region until the Roman period, **THE MÉDOC** is not the prettiest of the wine regions, consisting largely of flat plains and gravelly soil, interspersed by the brown water of the estuary. The landscape is, however, enlivened by the presence of beautiful wine-producing châteaux, most of which make for excellent views. From Bordeaux, driving the D2 road to Margaux, St-Julien, Pauillac and St-Estèphe will allow you to reach many of the more famous châteaux.

Margaux

The small village of **Margaux**, 30km north of Bordeaux, is no great shakes. The **Maison du Vin** (7 place de la Trémoille; http://maisonduvindemargaux.com), can help find accommodation, and advise on visits to the *appellation*'s châteaux, plus it has a few small wine themed exhibitions. A little further down the road is **La Cave d'Ulysse** (http://caveulysse.com), which gives free tastings from a variety of Margaux châteaux. The village has created **La Boucle des Châteaux de Margaux**, a short (8.5km) long walking or cycling trail that loops past eighteen of the better-known châteaux in the vicinity of the village. More information on the route can be obtained from the tourist office website (margaux-tourisme.com). Not an official sight – but perhaps the chocolate fountains and other chocolate creations should be – **Mademoiselle de Margaux** (37 rue de la Tremoille; mademoiselledemargaux.com) is a wonderful chocolate shop at the northern end of the village.

Tonnellerie Nadalié
Ludon-Médoc · www.nadalie.fr · Charge

16

DAY-TRIPS

N

BAY OF
BISCAY

**CHARENTE-
MARITIME**

Saintes
Cognac
Angoulême

Saujon
Royan
Gémozac
Pons
Archiac
Charente

PARC NATUREL
MARIN DE L'ESTUAIRE
DE LA GIRONDE
Pointe de Grave
Cozes
Jonzac
Barbezieux-
St-Hilaire

Plage St Nicolas
Soulac-
sur-Mer
Pointe de la Négade
St-Vivien-
de-Médoc
Mirambeau

CHARENTE

Plage Vensac
Montendre
Chalais

Gironde

Lesparre-
Médoc
St-Estèphe
St-Ciers-
sur-Gironde
Montlieu-
la-Garde

Plage du Pin Sec
Château Lafite
Rothschild
Île de Patiras
St-Savin

NOUVELLE-AQUITAINE

La Roche-
Chalais

Hourtin
Pauillac
Île de Nouvelle
Château Latour
Fort Médoc
St-Laurent-
Médoc
Île Margaux
Blaye
St-Savin

Lac
d'Hourtin
Château Margaux
Île Margaux
Bourg-sur-Gironde
Guîtres
Coutras
Montpon-
Ménestérol

Médoc
Castelnau-
de-Médoc
Margaux

Lacanau
Océan
Lacanau
Libourne
Château
Cheval Blanc

Sainte-Hélène
Blanquefort
St-Émilion
Château
Angélus
Montcaret

Lac de
Lacanau
St-Médard-
en-Jalles
Castillon-
la-Bataille

Le Porge Océan
Bordeaux Airport
Bordeaux
Créon
Château
Altagaia
Sauveterre-
de-Guyenne

Lège-Cap-Ferret
Cestas
GIRONDE

Bassin
d'Arcachon
Audenge
La Brède
Podensac
Garonne
La Réole

Cap-Ferret
Arcachon
Château de
Malle
St-Macaire

Dune du Pyla
Gujan-
Mestras
Graves
Guillos
Sauternes
Langon

Biscarrosse-
Plage
Lac de
Cazaux
Belin-
Béliet
Château Filhot
Château de
Roquetaille
Marmande

Parentis-
en-Born
St-Symphorien
Villandraut
Bazas
Grignols

Landes
Pissos
Sore
Captieux
Casteljaloux

Plage Remember
Labouheyre
**PARC
DES LANDES
DE GASCOGNE**
Houeillès

Mimizan
Sabres
Labrit

St-Girons
en Marensin
Morcenx
Roquefort
Saint-Justin
Labastide d'Armagnac

Castels
LES LANDES
Cazaubon
Eauze

La Midouze
Villeneuve-
de-Marsan
Douze

Tartas
Mont-de-
Marsan
Nogaro

Adour
Grenade-
sur-l'Adour
OCCITANIE

Dax
St-Sever
Aire-
sur-l'Adour

0   20
kilometres

While the art of turning grape to wine is the focus of almost every tourist's interest in these parts there are many other aspects of wine making that tend to get overlooked by most visitors. One of those is the creation of the giant wine wooden wine barrels. At the **Tonnellerie Nadalié**, 9km southeast of Margaux in the village of Ludon-Médoc, the same passionate family have been bending oak into wine barrels since 1902. On a fascinating one-hour tour (By appointment only. Tours in French only) you can learn some of what's involved. Tours start outside in the woodland park where a guide explains how the tree is used, before moving indoors to watch the magic happening and then finishes with a short tasting. Stay for lunch in the decent attached restaurant, the Brasserie Le 1902 (brasserie-1902.com; €€€).

Château Margaux

1km east of Margaux • By appointment only Mon–Fri; closed Aug and during harvest • http://chateau-margaux.com • Free

The Margaux estate has been in viticulture since at least the fifteenth century, though the current **châteaux** - one of the loveliest in the Médoc, set in extensive, sculpture-dotted gardens close to the west bank of the Gironde – was built in the early nineteenth century following the inevitable ownership shake-up in the wake of the French Revolution. Its wine, a classified Premier Grand Cru, was world-famous by the 1940s and 1950s, but went through a rough patch in the two succeeding decades. A return to grace came in the 1980s, after the estate was bought by a Greek family. Tours are by appointment only and tastings are only given to wine professionals.

Parc du Château Kirwan

16

3km southeast of Margaux • http://chateau-kirwan.com • Charge

More receptive to casual visitors than the Châteaux Margaux, this eighteenth-century château is set within a large woodland **park** with more formal gardens. Self-guided tours (they give you a tablet) allow you to explore the grounds before a tasting inside the château. There are a variety of different tasting packages on offer. Check out the website for details.

ACCOMMODATION   **MARGAUX AND AROUND**

Domaine Quittignan Brillette 148 av de la Gironde, Moulis-en-Médoc, http://quittignanbrillette.com. This eighteenth century stone house has been turned into a charming *chambre d'hôte* set within a pretty garden surrounded by vineyards. €€
Relais de Margaux 5 route de L'île-Vincent, Margaux, http://relais-margaux.fr. A beautiful old château transformed into a 'wellness resort' set beside the Gironde on a small golf course and surrounded by vines. The large rooms, with floral wallpaper, have an old-fashioned feel and panoramic views that all makes for a good weekend break from Bordeaux. Excellent in-house restaurant. €€€

Marais d'Arcins

7km north of Margaux, the marais d'Arcins is a fascinating area of woodland, marsh and flood prairie. A couple of short walking trails allow you to discover this wildlife rich habitat, in which you might be fortunate enough to spot otters or European pond turtles. Dedicated birdwatchers can set themselves up in the observation tower for a day's twitching.

Lamarque

The pretty village of Lamarque, which is full of flowers and has a distinctive, minaret-like church tower, is worth a stop to explore the nearby châteaux – Château Malescasse (www.chateau-malescasse.com), for example, offers tastings as well as top-notch accommodation, while Château Chasse Spleen (www.chasse-spleen.com) also runs vineyard tours and enjoys some quirky decoration in the gardens.

From Lamarque's port, a couple of kilometres from the village centre, you can take a ferry (4–9 daily; charge) across the muddy Gironde to Blaye. The ferries carry passengers and motor vehicles, and are ideal for avoiding a long detour round the estuary.

Fort Médoc

32 Avenue du Fort-Médoc, Cussac Fort-Médoc • www.cussac-fort-medoc.fr/tourisme/visiter-le-fort-medoc-2 • Charge

The ruins of **Fort Médoc** sit just east of the village of Cussac Fort-Médoc. It was designed by prolific military architect Vauban in the seventeenth century, and is now inscribed on the UNESCO World Heritage list alongside other Vauban works as part of the Fortifications of Vauban ensemble. Perhaps the most impressive part of the star-shaped fortress is the ostentatious coat of arms carved above the entranceway.

Pauillac

PAUILLAC, the largest and most attractive town in the Médoc, is perched on the banks of the Gironde estuary. With its pleasant waterfront cafés and restaurants, it makes an excellent base for exploring the wine-growing region, thanks to its proximity to some of Bordeaux's most important vineyards; no fewer than three of the top five Grands Crus hail from here. As with Margaux, Pauillac has its own cycling and walking trail that loops past a number of the areas best known chateaux. There are three different versions of the **Boucle des Châteaux de Pauillac** (8, 13 or 16km) all of which begin from behind the Maison du Tourisme et du Vin. The trails are waymarked in blue and white but do be careful not to veer onto the private land of the chateaux. Bikes can be hired from L'Atelier Vélo (6 Passage du Desquet; http://funbike.fr)

Musée du Vin dans l'Art

Château Mouton Rothschild • www.chateau-mouton-rothschild.com • Charge

16

Inside a former wine barreling hall (chai), this **museum** at the Chateau Mouton Rothschild contains a small but utterly exquisite collection of antique wine related art that includes silverware and goblets from the kings of Naples, medieval tapestries, glassware and porcelain from China, Japan and the Persian Empire and eighteenth-century carved ivory. There are also contributions from more modern-day masters including Dalí and Andy Warhol.

INFORMATION   PAUILLAC

Maison du Tourisme et du Vin On the waterfront (http://pauillac-medoc.com); they can provide a list of *gîtes* and arrange bike hire and châteaux visits.

ACCOMMODATION

Camping les Gabarreys route de la Rivière, http://campinglesgabarreys.com. Small municipal campsite with ample shade and riverside views. Facilities include a minigolf, play area and sauna. €

★**Château Cordeillan-Bages** route des Châteaux, Bages, http://cordeillanbages.com. Live like the other half in this stunning chateau just south of Pauillac centre. As you would expect of such a place, everything is very refined and prim. The 28 bedrooms have signature art works and Frank Gehry designed deco. The beautiful gardens meld gently into lines of vines which can be appreciated from the fabulous swimming pool. €€€€

★**Le Coeur des Vignes** 19 chemin du Marronnier, St-Lambert, http://coeurdesvignes.com. Just under 4km south of Pauillac is this utterly delightful B&B. The four individually decorated rooms are modern and light-filled, while retaining a sense of the nineteenth-century house itself. There's a lovely garden, a terrace with a pool, and a lounge with a fireplace – plenty of places to relax after choosing a bottle of wine from their well-curated list. €€

Les Phoenix 21 rue Jean-Mermoz, http://lesphoenix pauillac.jimdofree.com. This is a budget B&B with simple

---

VISITING THE MÉDOC CHÂTEAUX FROM PAUILLAC

Organize a visit to the most famous of the **Médoc châteaux** – Château Lafite-Rothschild (4km northwest of Pauillac; http://lafite.com), and Château Latour (3km south of Pauillac; http://chateau-latour.com) – either directly or through the Maison du Vin.

A ROUGH GUIDE TO THE WINES OF BORDEAUX

The Bordeaux **wine region** circles the city, enjoying near-perfect climatic conditions and soils ranging from limestone to sand and pebbles. It's the largest quality wine district in the world, producing around five hundred million bottles a year – over half of France's quality wine output and ten percent, by value, of the world's wine trade.

CLASSIFYING WINES

Wines in France are ordered in a strict hierarchical structure based upon quality. The lowliest category is *vin de table*, or plonk in plain English. These wines are anonymous as their labels cannot include where they were made, the grape varieties used or the vintage. There are, however, no restrictions on yield. In France this wine is normally used for cooking.

The next step up is vin de pays, which is an increasingly important category although it was only created in 1973. These are wines that come from a specific region. Many are often sold as varietal wines, for example Chardonnay *vin de pays d'Oc*. Growers have greater freedom of choice over what varieties of grapes they can use.

The top category is the *appellation d'origine contrôlée* (AOC). Such wines are governed by strict rules covering such aspects as the grape varieties that can be planted, the way the vines are trained and the amount of grapes that can be produced.

There is also an intermediate category, the *vin delimité de qualité supérieure* (VDQS). This was introduced as a stepping stone to full appellation status. Many such wines have now been promoted to AOC status, although a number remain in the Southwest.

The massive and complex Bordeaux wine region has its own further hierarchy within the *appellation contrôlée*. At the base is plain Bordeaux AOC, which covers the whole region. A step up are sub-regional appellations like the Médoc or the Entre-Deux-Mers. At the top are the communal appellations such as Pomerol, Pauillac and Sauternes. It has to be said that this official hierarchy of quality is often notional in practice. There are plenty of *vins de pays* that are better than supposedly *superior appellation contrôlée* wines. The most crucial information on any wine label is the name of the producer.

BORDEAUX

Despite the emergence of new quality wine-producing countries and regions, Bordeaux remains the largest and most important quality wine-producing region in the world. A number of the world's most famous wines, such as Château Lafite, Château Latour, Château Pétrus and Château d'Yquem are made here. These wines, however, represent only a small fraction of the some 6–7 million hectolitres (15 million gallons) of wine that are produced in Bordeaux annually from the 115,000 hectares (285,000 acres) planted.

Around 90 percent of the wines are red. The chief red grape varieties are Cabernet Sauvignon, Cabernet Franc and Merlot. These grapes are invariably blended together, the proportions varying from district to district and between individual estates.

On the right bank (St-Émilion and Pomerol) Merlot is the dominant variety with quite a high proportion of Cabernet Franc used. On the left bank, especially in the Médoc, Cabernet Sauvignon is dominant, with Merlot playing a secondary role. Some producers also use a small amount of Malbec and Petit Verdot. The classic Bordeaux blend of Cabernet and Merlot has been copied around the world for many top reds, especially those in California, Chile and South Africa. Cabernet, especially Sauvignon, gives structure to the wine, while Merlot softens the tannins and often angular fruit of Cabernet.

For the white wines, Sémillon is the most widely planted grape followed by Sauvignon Blanc, which has been gaining in popularity over the past twenty years, especially in the Entre-Deux-Mers region. It is rare to find a pure Sémillon, while a pure Sauvignon Blanc is increasingly common. Muscadelle is also planted and is mainly used as one of the components in the sweet wines from the regions of Sauternes and Barsac.

REGIONAL BORDEAUX WINES

The regional *appellations* account for half of the wine made in Bordeaux. As well as plain Bordeaux, these are Bordeaux Sec (white), Bordeaux Rosé, Bordeaux Clairet (a slightly deeper-coloured style of rosé), Bordeaux Supérieur (a red with slightly more alcohol than plain Bordeaux) and the small production of sparkling wine, Crémant de Bordeaux. There are some good regional wines made, but they need searching out, for much of regional Bordeaux is made to a price that encourages over-production and the tendency to pick before the grapes are properly ripe, especially in difficult years.

GRAVES AND SAUTERNES

Bordeaux can be divided into four sub-regions: Graves and Sauternes; the Entre-Deux-Mers; St-Émilion and Pomerol with its various satellite appellations; and the Médoc.

The vineyards of the Graves begin in the suburbs of Bordeaux – the original Haut Brion winery is now totally enclosed by housing developments. Vines continue intermittently for 40km (25 miles) southwards along the western bank of the Garonne. They are mainly planted on gravel, hence the name Graves. Bordeaux's best dry white is made here, especially in the superior appellation of Pessac-Leognan. Even so, red wines are in the majority in the Graves. At the southern end are Sauternes and Barsac, their sweet wines made with the assistance of noble rot which concentrates the grape's juice. The Château d'Yquem here makes one of the most expensive wines in the world. On the other side of the Garonne at the southern end of the Premières Côtes de Bordeaux are the three small, sweet wine appellations of Cérons, Cadillac and Ste-Croix-du-Mont.

ENTRE-DEUX-MERS AND ST-ÉMILION

The Entre-Deux-Mers, the land between the Garonne and the Dordogne, provides an interlude between the Graves and the St-Émilion area. This is rolling country and its rich soils are devoted to mixed farming. Red, white and rosé wines are made here but the appellation Entre-Deux-Mers is reserved for white.

Much of Bordeaux is not very picturesque. However, the pretty little town of St-Émilion is an exception. The wines here and from neighbouring Pomerol are softer and rounder than those of the Médoc because of the higher proportion of Merlot used. These wines have become increasingly fashionable recently because of their soft appealing fruit and the fact that they are ready to drink earlier than the more tannic wines of the Médoc.

The various satellite appellation groups around St-Émilion, such as St-Georges-St-Émilion, offer similar wines at lower prices and are good value, as are those from nearby Lalande de Pomerol, Fronsac and Côtes de Fronsac. The vineyards of the right bank continue northwards up the Gironde with the Côtes de Bourg and Premières Côtes de Blaye.

THE MÉDOC

Although, with Château Lafite, Château Latour, Château Margaux and Château Mouton-Rothschild, the Médoc (the land stretching north from the city of Bordeaux, along the Gironde estuary) has four of the most important estates, it is the youngest vineyard of Bordeaux. Until it was drained by the Dutch in the seventeenth century much of this region was marshy. The best properties here are on gravel beds close to the Gironde. The communes of Margaux, St-Julien, Pauillac and St-Estèphe form the quality heart of the Médoc. Because of the high proportion of Cabernet Sauvignon used, the top wines can age for fifty years and more.

BUYING WINE AND VISITING CHÂTEAUX

If you're interested in **buying wine**, head for the châteaux, where you'll get the best price and the opportunity to sample and receive expert advice before purchasing. To visit the **châteaux**, ask at the Maison du Vin or tourist office in each wine-producing village.

16

ISLANDS OF THE ESTUARY

The stretch of the **Garonne** that runs north of Bordeaux to the mouth of the river is dotted with a number of **islands**. Mostly uninhabited yet often still used for growing vines, a couple of these islands can be visited. While it's true that none contain anything that can't be seen on the mainland there's something inherently romantic about the islands that make them well worth visiting.

Six kilometres long but just 750m wide, the **Île Nouvelle**, just offshore of Blaye, is one of the larger islands. It's actually born out of two islands that joined together in the nineteenth century, it was inhabited and used for wine production for a time before being abandoned. Local authorities turned it into a nature reserve and today thousands of waterbirds nest here. Visits are led by naturalists and as well as seeing the birdlife you will be taken to the old village. Arrange visits through the tourist office in Blaye.

The **Île Margaux** off the village of Margaux is a private island used for vine production. Visits aren't permitted but river cruises will take you close to shore.

Further north is little **Île de Patiras** off Pauillac, which rose up out of the river waters in 1625 and is again used for vine production. Visits can be arranged from Pauillac and once on the island you can climb to the top of a lighthouse for epic views.

but spacious rooms and shared bathrooms, as well as friendly hosts, free parking and an excellent breakfast (included). €
La Villa Nady 43 rue de la République, https://villanady.

fr. A welcoming B&B with just two rooms in an impeccably decorated house close to the centre of Pauillac. A continental breakfast with homemade produce is included, and lunch and dinner are available on request. €€

EATING

Les Blés Du Mascaret 5 quai Albert Pichon, 05 56 59 37 43. Perfect for a light lunch, *Les Blés Du Mascaret* offers a range of baguette sandwiches, but make sure to leave room for a pastry for afters. €
La Cambuse 2 quai Léon Perrier, 05 56 59 28 90. *La Cambuse* offers a short menu of excellent French dishes – duck confit being a particular highlight – accompanied by well-chosen wines. If it's warm, sit out on the pavement seating, and if not, enjoy the atmospheric vaulted interior. €€€
Café Lavinal passage Desquet, Bages, https://www.jmcazes.com/en/cafe-lavinal. With its sunny terrace and

English-speaking waiters, this bright, pleasant bistro is understandably popular with tourists, which is no reflection on the quality of the food – expect interesting, well-presented, tasty takes on the usual bistro staples, such as confit lamb with bulgur wheat. It's a five-minute drive from Pauillac in the village of Bages. €€
Château Cordeillan-Bages route des Châteaux, Bages, http://cordeillanbages.com. A first-rate two-Michelin-starred gourmet restaurant in opulent surroundings. Prices are as high as you'd expect for such an experience but it's an undeniably lovely setting, and the restaurant is refreshingly modern and unstuffy. Dress smartly. €€€€

St-Estèphe

On the D2 towards Pauillac, http://marquis-saint-estephe.fr

Next stop on the road north is the wine commune of **St-Estèphe**, Médoc's largest *appellation*. Here you'll find vineyards belonging to the local *cave coopérative*, **Marquis de St-Estèphe**, consisting predominantly of *Crus Bourgeois* – a level below *Cru Classé* (see page 114). Perhaps the most interesting of the *appellation*'s five Crus Classés is **Château Cos d'Estournel**, a fairytale-like castle built in a curious blend of neoclassical and gothic styles, with turrets, towers, and a flamboyant nineteenth-century pagoda. The château's *chais* (warehouses) can be visited by appointment (http://estournel.com; English spoken, reserve a week ahead).

St-Estèphe itself is a relaxed, slow-moving village dominated by the **Église de Saint-Étienne** (charge). The interior of this eighteenth century Baroque church, which sits on ninth century foundations, is a rainbow of vivid colours and extravagant chandeliers. Hidden in the church square is the small, homespun **Maison du Vin** (http://vins-saint-estephe.com), which is the best place in the village to buy local vintages.

16

ACCOMMODATION **ST ESTÈPHE AND AROUND**

Château Les Ormes de Pez 29 route des Ormes de Pez, http://lesormesdepez.com. A comfortable family hotel in a handsome château, with a pool (unheated) and large walled garden, surrounded by vineyards, just outside the village. Breakfast included. €€€

La Maison d'Estournel route de Poumeys, http://lamaison-estournel.com. If you're looking for a treat then this wonderful eighteenth-century chateau set within extensive grounds is the place to do it. The atmospheric rooms have period character and the restaurant is as superb as the accommodation. Oh, and we can't not mention the boiled eggs served at breakfast, which are topped with caviar no less. €€€€

La Nuit & Le Jour 1 rue de Lesquirot, 7km west of St Estèphe, https://lanuitetlejour.fr. In a converted nineteenth century stone house, this excellent B&B has three cosy rooms. The delicious breakfast is enjoyed on the outdoor terrace. €€

Abbaye de Vertheuil
www.vertheuil-medoc.com • **Church** Free; **Abbey** Charge

Around 6km west of Saint-Estèphe is this stout and austere eleventh century Romanesque **abbey** founded by Guillaume VIII d'Aquitaine. It was destroyed several times over the centuries including during the Hundred Years War and much of what you see today is an eighteenth century restoration. While the church is open year-round the abbey itself is only open to the public in summer. Next door is a small museum of dolls (many of which illustrate fairytales) – much more intriguing than it might sound – and another little museum exploring the life of craftspeople in the Middle Ages. Both are included in a visit to the abbey. The village itself is an attractive place for an aimless amble.

Phare de Richard
www.phare-richard.com • **Church** Free; **Abbey** Charge

Some 30km north of Saint-Estèphe and overlooking the Garonne close to the point at which it embraces the Atlantic, is the **Phare de Richard**. While this small lighthouse is only moderately diverting, the drive up to it from Saint-Estèphe is interesting for the sheer flatness and repetitiveness of the landscape. With ribbons of vines stretching to the distance, you get a distinct sense of the end of the road. For a small fee you can climb to the top of the lighthouse for a view over the estuary, and there are also some easy hiking paths starting from here.

16

Blaye

By far the most interesting town to the north of Bordeaux, **BLAYE** makes for a great day trip from the city, but if time permits it's worth spending a night or two here using it as a base for exploring areas north and east of Bordeaux. The town's long history dates back to the pre-Roman era, when it was used as a port by the local Celtic people, the Santones. It gained mythic status in the Middle Ages as the burial place of the great Frankish hero Roland, and later on the town played a crucial role in the Hundred Years' War as well as during the French Wars of Religion. Its superb citadel was built by the great military engineer Vauban, but has never seen action. Blaye has a long history of viniculture, as the area was originally planted by the Romans, and is also known for the messy-looking sweet confectionery, pralines, made here since the seventeenth century. Another speciality is caviar; legend has it that it was introduced to residents by noble Russians who fled to France during the Russian Revolution.

Bikes can be hired from **ABCD Cycles** (15 cours du Port, Gauriac; abcd-cycles.fr), with which you can enjoy the kilometres of cycle paths that stretch away from Blaye. The countryside here is absolutely flat and for the most part the cycle paths run through vine stripped countryside, making it an enjoyable and easy place to cycle. The tourist office has cycle route maps. A *bac* (a type of traditional boat) offers a regular ferry service across the Garonne which makes for a convenient way of visiting Fort Médoc.

Citadelle de Blaye

http://bbte.fr · **Citadel** Free; **Museums and underground citadelle** Charge, included with Bordeaux City Pass

Awarded UNESCO World Heritage status, the small town of Blaye is utterly dominated by the imposing walls of its riverside **citadel**. Constructed in the seventeenth century by mastermind military architect Vauban, to protect Bordeaux from attack by sea, it is the largest of a string of fortifications that also include Fort Médoc and Fort Pâté. This wasn't the first military structure to stand here though, with some form of castle being here since the seventh century. When Vauban constructed the citadel, he designed it in a way that gives it both landward and seaward defences, with dry ditches dug out of the rock also surrounding the walls. Today parkland surrounds much of the citadel and you are free to wander at will. People still live inside the walls of the citadel and there are also a couple of cafes and restaurants. To get a better understanding of the structure, sign up to one of the guided tours run by the tourist office, which take you into the otherwise closed underground passages that fan out under the citadel. The lively guides will explain how the defence system of the citadel worked and give you an insight into the lives of the soldiers based here. A guided tour also includes entry into the museum, which reveals wall engravings carved by soldiers and prisoners. Tours last 75 minutes but are only in French unless you pre-organise an English language tour. Even if you can't understand all that is said it's still worth joining a tour as much of it is fairly self-explanatory.

Villas gallo-romaines de Plassac

http://villagalloromaine-plassac.fr · **Ruins** free; **Museum** Charge

16

Roman **ruins** are not something that many people associate with southwest France, but just a few kilometres east of Blaye next to the church in the village of Plassac are the well-preserved remains of three Roman villas dating from between the first and fifth centuries. A guide (French language only) will show you around the site, which has some lovely floor mosaics. The site museum contains some interesting finds from the site.

INFORMATION   **BLAYE**

Tourist office The office on rue des Minimes (http:// tourisme-blaye.com) has details on wine tasting/tours and can book rooms.

VISITING THE CHÂTEAUX AROUND BLAYE

There are around a hundred **châteaux** scattered about the countryside surrounding Blaye and many of the bigger ones are open to visits (normally by advance reservation). Bookings can be made through the tourist office.

Château Monconseil Gazin (http://monconseilgazin.com; Charge) Six kilometres south of Blaye, this welcoming, family-run estate offers visits and tastings through advance reservation. It's a good one to visit with children as there's a play area and several walking trails around the château and neighbouring village.

Château Marquis de Vauban (http://vignobles-le-cone-de-vauban.fr; Charge) A few minutes' walk north of Blaye, this château offers guided visits and tastings as well as a dinner and visit package. Plus they offer visits by miniature train.

Château Peybonhomme-les-Tours (http://hubert-vigneron.com; Charge) Reinviting the wine game with its impressive bio wines, this family-run château offers visits that focus on their environmental credentials. You also get to climb to the top of a tower for panoramic views over the vines and estuary. It's walking distance east of Blaye.

Château les Chaumes (http://chateauleschaumes.com; Charge) A visit to this château, 6km northeast of Blaye, also includes a visit to the barrel making workshop as well as a guided tour around the vines and a tasting. If you want to simply enjoy the wooded grounds then picnics are also allowed here. The château also organises summer concerts and theatre.

WINES OF BLAYE

The green slopes north of the Garonne were planted long before the Médoc. Wine here is powerful, richly coloured, fruity, and cheaper than on the opposite riverbank. The **Côtes de Bourg** and **Côtes de Blaye** are quintessential pleasant, inexpensive reds. Visit the **Maison du Vin de Blaye** on cours Vauban (Mon–Sat 9am–12.30pm & 2–7pm) to stock up.

ACCOMMODATION

Camping Municipal La Citadelle Citadelle de Vauban, http://blaye.fr. Situated in green, tree-lined grounds, inside the old citadelle, and 5min from the *centre ville*, this is an old-school campsite, with room for just 36 tents, electricity and bathrooms. €

Clos Réaud de la Citadelle 8 rue des Maçons, www.closreaud-citadelle.com. A little taste of luxury close to the town centre, the converted eighteenth century *Clos Réaud* offers five beautifully decorated rooms set amongst pleasant gardens with a heated outdoor pool. Breakfast is delicious and generous. Jacuzzi and sauna also available. €€€

Domaine des Deux-Cèdres 26 route des Astéries, http://domainedesdeuxcedres.com. Striking, colourful rooms, enhanced with homely knick-knacks, and delicious home-cooked cuisine available on request. There are four rooms available, along with a *gîte*, set amid the vineyards, and a swimming pool. Breakfast included. €€

La Maison Blanche 3 rue Saint-Aulaire, www.lmblanche.com. Centrally located in the heart of Blaye, *La Maison Blanche* is a small hotel with attractive gardens and an indoor swimming pool. As well as the human staff, a team of seven cats helps to keep the place running smoothly. €€

★ **Villa Saint-Simon** 8 cours du Général-de-Gaulle, http://villastsimon.com. A skilfully renovated nineteenth-century townhouse opposite Blaye port with five tastefully decorated rooms named after local châteaux. English-speaking hosts Les and Clarissa – oenophile and artist, respectively – extend a warm welcome that goes far beyond the average B&B. Excellent value wine tours and tastings are offered exclusively to guests and tailored to both the seasoned connoisseur and the wine-loving amateur, plus there's a well-stocked wine shop. If you're on a tight budget, ask about the ground-floor room. €€

Villa Saint-Simon Apartments 9 rue St-Simon. These one- to three-bedroom fully furnished apartments, run by the same team as *Villa Saint-Simon*, have impeccable style, with chic furnishings and beautiful wooden floors, offset by striking artwork. Ask about weekly discounts. €€

EATING

Le Gavroche 14 rue Neuve, http://facebook.com/restaurantlegavroche. At the base of the citadelle, this cosy restaurant with bare stone walls and beamed ceilings is a great spot for enjoying traditional, meat-heavy dishes like duck parmentier and rabbit terrine. €€

Panda 15 cours de la République, www.facebook.com/people/Restaurant-Panda-Blaye/61566033565115. Top-notch Chinese cuisine, with plenty of options to choose from – perhaps the best choice is the satay beef skewers, but most of the usual favourites feature on the menu. €€

Bourg-sur-Gironde

Surprisingly undiscovered by most international visitors to Bordeaux, the small honey-stoned town of **Bourg-sur-Gironde** (otherwise simply known as Bourg) is one of the prettiest towns in the Bordeaux region. Partially fortified, it lies just before the point where the River Dordogne melds gently into the larger Garonne and it was a locally important port from the Middle Ages up until the nineteenth century. Today it's more of a pleasure port than anything else with small sailing boats moored up in-front of the town. The highlight of a visit is just strolling the streets and soaking up the sun by the river. On Sunday mornings there's an animated market.

Musée de la Citadelle

Parc de la Citadelle • http://bourg-gironde.fr • Charge

This fascinating **museum** within the citadel takes you deep underground through secret sixteenth century tunnels, lets you admire a fine collection of horse drawn carriages and shows you impressive WWII vestiges. All visits are led by interesting guides.

Grotte de Pair-non-Pair

http://pair-non-pair.fr • Charge

Inhabited an astonishing sixty thousand years ago, the **cave** system of **Pair-non-Pair**, which is 5km east of Bourg in the village of Prignac-et-Marcamps, contains cave paintings that pre-date those of the world-famous Lascaux caves in the nearby Dordogne. Guides will point out some of the more impressive paintings which include depictions of mammoths, horses and prehistoric cattle, all of which were painted between 33,000 and 26,000 years ago. A small museum showcases some of the findings from the site including hominoid skulls and mammoth teeth.

INFORMATION   BOURG-SUR-GIRONDE

Tourist office The tourist office (http://www.bbte.fr) is at 4 Place de la Libération.

ACCOMMODATION

Château de la Grave 1 lieu-dit La Grave, http://chateaudelagrave.com. With turrets and walled gardens, this fifteenth-century, fairytale château is a wonderful place to stay. The elegant rooms have exposed stone walls and big comfy beds, there's a lovely garden with swimming pool and the owners will show you around the vineyard. €€€€

La Grange 1 la Dupuise, Civrac-de-Blaye, http://chambres-dhotes-la-grange.com. Lovingly restored *chambre d'hôte* inside an old stone wine estate building some 12km inland of Bourg that's surrounded by utter peace. As well as tastefully decorated rooms, there's a superb restaurant. €€€

EATING

Cuisine & Dépendance 4 place Marchal, http://cuisineetdependance.fr. An urban-looking country restaurant with long, curved windows overlooking the estuary, and well-cooked dishes like monkfish with fresh pesto, or red snapper with peppers and olives. €€

16

Saint-André-de-Cubzac

Saint-André-de-Cubzac is a small and pleasant, though largely unremarkable, town 12km east of Bourg. Its claim to fame is as the birthplace of Jacques Cousteau, who – along with fellow Frenchman Émile Gagnan – invented scuba equipment, which in turn led to a long and successful career filming underwater documentaries. There's a plaque marking the house in which he was born in 1910 – look for it at the point where rue du Commandant Cousteau meets rue Nationale. On the south side of town, you'll find a further tribute to Cousteau in the form of a wooden dolphin in the centre of a roundabout.

Libourne

LIBOURNE, the largest town in the region, and within the Bordeaux commuter belt, doesn't get a huge number of visitors, but it has some interesting buildings and is a thriving commercial centre with an imposing market square, Place Abel-Surchamp, which is lined with exquisite Renaissance and baroque houses. On its eastern side is the Hôtel de Ville, which dates back to the fifteenth century: its second floor contains the town's museum and art gallery. Chiefly of interest here is an unusual collection of sporting and hunting scenes painted by René Princeteau, an artist friend of Toulouse-Lautrec. The quayside of this little riverside port is an ideal setting for a drink in the sunshine, and from which to admire the Grand Pont, an arched stone bridge almost 220 metres from end to end.

   A short drive west of Libourne (9 km), and on the opposite side of the Dordogne River, stands the splendid Château de Vayres (www.chateaudevayres.com, charge), which was once the property of King Henri IV and was rebuilt in the sixteenth century by Louis de Foix, mastermind of the great lighthouse at Cordouan. Its elegant classical gardens that reach down to the river offer a refreshing, shady walk, while the interior apartments are stocked with beautiful furniture and fine tapestries.

St-Émilion

ST-ÉMILION, 35km east of Bordeaux, and a short train trip, is easily the world's most famous wine town and an essential visit for anyone interested in the gift from the grape. But St-Émilion is about more than just wine. It's also very easy on the eye. The old grey houses of this fortified medieval town straggle down the steep south-hanging slope of a low hill, with the green froth of the summer's vines crawling over its walls and the cobbled streets lined with (expensive) wine shops, restaurants and small boutiques. To add a little extra colour to the scene, many of the growers still keep up the old tradition of planting roses at the ends of the rows of vines, which in pre-pesticide days served as an early-warning system against infection, the idea being that the most common bug, oidium, went for the roses first, giving three days' notice of its intentions.

Be warned that St Émilion's fame means that in summer, at Easter and during the September and October harvests, this small town can be overrun with visitors.

The old town
Much of St Émilion's old town can be admired on a simple wander, with the central place du Marché making a good place to start. From here, you can admire the exterior of the vast bulk of the rock-carved church: gazing upwards to take in the impossibly high spire, it's easy to appreciate the effort that went into constructing this impressive structure even if you don't visit the inside.

16

Head up the steep Rue du Tertre de la Tente to reach place du Clocher, where you can take a closer look at the church's spire, as well as gaze down from a convenient terrace on the now far-below place du Marché. From here, you can take a door o the right of the tourist office to enter the twelfth-century **collegiate church**, with a handsome but mutilated doorway, and a fourteenth-century **cloister**. The cloister is purposefully closed on all four sides so that the only real view is up, toward Heaven. The central gardens here were said to represent Eden. Today the cloisters often host small art exhibitions.

Just south of this main grouping of buildings is the **Tour du Roy** (Kings Tower; charge), which soars 32m into the sky. There's much debate over its year of

GUIDED TOURS OF ST ÉMILION

Although you can easily explore the town on your own, many of the more interesting corners are closed to the general public unless as a part of an organised tour. For this reason, the best way to see St Émilion is on a **guided tour**, most of which are organised by the tourist office (charge, included with Bordeaux City Pass). Tours generally begin at the **grotte de l'Ermitage**, where it's said that the town's namesake, St Émilion, lived as a hermit in the eighth century, sleeping on a stone ledge and performing various miracles. The tour continues in the half-ruined **Trinity Chapel**, which was converted into a cooperage (barrel-makers') during the Revolution. Striking frescoes are still visible. Across the yard is a passage beneath the **belfry** leading to the **catacombs**, where three chambers dug out of the soft limestone were used as an ossuary between the eighth and eleventh centuries. Finally, you'll reach the church itself. Simple and huge, the entire structure – barrel vaulting, great square piers and all – was hacked out of the rock. The interior was once painted, but only faint traces survived the Revolution, when it was used as a gunpowder factory. Every June the wine council – *La Jurade* – assembles here in red robes to judge last year's wine and decide whether each *viticulteur*'s produce deserves the *appellation contrôlée* rating.

construction, with some saying it was built on the instructions of Louis VIII after he conquered this part of Aquitaine. Others maintain it was actually built in 1237 by Henry III Plantagenet, King of England and Duke of Aquitaine, when England reasserted control over St Émilion. Whatever the truth of the matter, from the summit, which you can climb up to for a small fee, the views over the town and surrounding vineyards are worth a king's royal fortune.

On the opposite side of the old town is the **Cloître des Cordeliers**. These clositers, which were established by Franciscan monks, date from the fourteenth century. At the time the complex consisted of a church, the cloisters, a garden, a wine storehouse and a cellar. Much of it is today in ruins. However, the single nave church still stands and gives access to deep underground cellars (which can only be visited on a guided tour). For most visitors though, it seems the main reason to visit is the chance to relax over a glass of wine in the in-house wine bar.

ARRIVAL AND INFORMATION ST-ÉMILION

By train The small, unmanned gare de Saint-Émilion is on the Sarlat–Bergerac–Libourne–Bordeaux rail route, and about 1.6km from the village (just turn right at the station and follow the road). The nearest mainline station is at Libourne (served by the TGV), a 40-minute walk from Saint-Émilion.

Tourist office Place des Créneaux by the belfry (http://saint-emilion-tourisme.com), organizes town tours (one or two a day in English; charge) and vineyard tours by bus, tourist train or bike (June–Sept; some in English; charge). They also have bikes for rent.

ACCOMMODATION

Badon Boutique Hotel 8 rue de la Prte Bouqueyre, www.badonboutiquehotel.com. In a great location near the centre of St-Émilion, *Badon Boutique* offers classic and superior rooms, both of which are decked out with clean white decor. Discounts on wine tours are available. **€€€**

Camping Yelloh! http://camping-saint-emilion.com.

2km northwest of St-Émilion, on the road to Montagne, this four-star campsite is well-maintained and has cottages and houseboats for rent, as well as a restaurant and takeaway, corner shop, swimming pools, boating lake, bike rental and a free shuttle bus to town. **€**

Château Franc-Pourret 1 La Gomerie. This family château,

LOCAL VINEYARDS

You're in St Émilion. Of course you're going to visit a vineyard or three. Many local vineyards hold wine tastings. Most require advance reservations which can either be made directly through the château website, the tourist office or the **Maison du Vin**, next door to the tourist office (http://vins-saint-emilion.com), which can advise you on which vineyards to visit, and sells local wines at a fair price.

American-owned **Château Fonplegade** (http://fonplegade.eu; visits by appointment only and only to those who subscribe to the mailing list) is close to the train station and was an early pioneer of bio wines.

Château Canon (http://chateaucanon.com; appointment only), west of town, has splendid architecture and offers bicycle tours of the estate. Also has an excellent restaurant.

Château Caprice de Milon (http://chateaucanon.com; appointment only), 3km east of town, this small château offers guided group tours between Monday and Thursday.

Château Guillemot (http://chateauguillemot.com; appointment only), owned by the same family for six generations, this château offers entertaining visits and you can climb the castle like tower for commanding views.

Château Pavie (http://vignoblesperse.com; appointment only), just south of the town centre, this famous Premier cru producer offers a range of well organised tours that includes a look at the history of the property, a visit to the cellars and a tasting.

Château Villemaurine (http://villemaurine.com; appointment only), one-hour tours that include explanations of wine production, a visit to the vineyard and the underground cellars and tasting of two different wines. It's north of town.

a fifteen-minute walk from St-Émilion, and set amid a sea of vines and rose bushes, has two homely guestrooms. The hostess is welcoming and English-speaking, the organic, home-made breakfast (included) is delicious, and wine tours can be organized (book in advance). €€

Clos 1906 14 La Gaffelière-Ouest, https://clos1906.com. This 1700s manor house on the outskirts of town has enjoyed an extensive renovation and is now a lovely boutique hotel, with simple yet classy decoration and luxurious comfy beds. There's an antiques and vintage shop here too, selling pieces dating back to the nineteenth century. €€€

Hôtel Au Logis des Remparts 18 rue Guadet, https://logisdesremparts.com. An attractive hotel in the centre of St-Émilion, with comfortable rooms boasting stylish modern decoration. Outside, there's a lovely garden to relax in, with a swimming pool should you need to cool off in the heat of summer. Unusually for central St-Émilion, parking is available. €€

★**La Gomerie** 5 La Gomerie, http://chambreshotes saintemilion.com. A rustic cottage hidden away in the vineyards, *La Gomerie* is a quiet retreat from the bustle of St-Émilion. Bare stone walls and dark wood furnishings give the rooms a distinctive character and it is excellent value for the price. Don't arrive after dark as the turn-off is easy to miss even in daylight; free parking. Breakfast included. €

Hostellerie de Plaisance 5 place du Clocher, http://hostelleriedeplaisance.com. Those with trust funds to blow can do so with flair and extravagance here; in the heart of town, with five stars, first-class dining, spectacular views and sumptuous rooms. Breakfast costs a lot extra. €€€€

EATING

Although there are a couple of excellent places to eat in St-Émilion, there's also a lot of rather average places. If there's somewhere in particular you want to eat, making a reservation in advance is wise. Eating spots here tend to be a little more expensive than elsewhere in the region. The bakery by the carpark at the bottom of town sells hot snacks as well as the normal bakery fare and is the place to grab something for a picnic.

Chai Pascal 37 rue Guadet, http://chai-pascal.com. A welcoming family-run bistro and wine bar with a concise, quality menu of traditional dishes. €€

Cloître des Cordeliers 2 rue de la Prte Brunet, www.lescordeliers.com/fr. The large garden of this former cloister is one of the most atmospheric places in St-Émilion to relax with a glass of wine. If it's hot, there's ice cream available too, with a good range of flavours. €€

Les Girondines 5 rue des Girondins, 05 57 24 77 72. Extremely friendly and easy-to-miss spot, just around the corner from place du Clocher, boasting a relaxing terrace on which you can enjoy dishes including baked camembert and steak and chips. It's also a great place to simply unwind with a glass of wine and charcuterie plate. €€

Lard & Bouchon 22 rue Guadet, http://lardetbouchon.

fr. Hidden away in an arched brick wine cellar, this is a cool spot to escape the blazing summer sun and enjoy bistro-style meals. There's an excellent choice of local wines by the glass or bottle. €€

★**Macarons de St-Émilion** 9 rue Guadet, http://macarons-saint-emilion.fr. Beneath its unassuming red-and-white-striped awning, this tiny store is heaped with home-made *macarons*, *canelés* and artisan treats. Owner Nadia Fermingier uses an original *canelé* recipe, invented by nuns in the 1620s, and locals rave that they're the best in France. €

Café Saigon 21 rue Guadet, www.facebook.com/cafe saigon33330. If you fancy a break from French cuisine, stop by this excellent Vietnamese restaurant, which offers a daily changing menu of delicious eastern dishes. The great wine list perfectly complements the food. €€€

Restaurant Le Tertre 5 rue du Tertre-de-la-Tente, http://restaurant-le-tertre.com. Stashed halfway up a dizzyingly steep cobblestone street, you won't want to drink too much if you're eating here. It's worth the climb, though – snag a prime view on one of the cosy outdoor platforms or head into the wood-beamed, stone-walled restaurant and gorge on the hearty three-course regional menu. Book ahead. €€€

16

Entre-Deux-Mers

Entre-Deux-Mers ("between two seas") is named for its position in between the tidal waters of the Dordogne and Garonne. As far as scenery goes, it's the most attractive part of the wine region, dotted with medieval villages amongst the small hills. Local wines, including the Premières Côtes de Bordeaux, are mainly dry whites, produced by over forty *caves coopératives*. They're considered good, albeit not up to the level of Médocs or dry Graves produced to the south.

Abbaye de la Sauve-Majeure

http://abbaye-la-sauve-majeure.fr • Charge

Medieval pilgrims on their way to Santiago de Compostela in Spain tended to travel through Bordeaux, with the result that numerous important pilgrimage spots sprung up along the way. One such was **La Sauve-Majeure**, which was founded in 1079 as a Benedictine abbey by Gérard de Corbie, with the support of the local dukes of Aquitaine. Enjoying the patronage of popes, dukes and kings throughout the Middle Ages, it prospered but was already in decline by the time of the Revolution, after which the abbey fell into disrepair. Today, the abbey is a set of picturesque ruins, with the Romanesque apse and apsidal chapels remaining, as well as some marvellous capitals in the chancel. The best of these depict biblical stories, with that of Daniel in the lions' den being a particular highlight. A small **museum** at the entrance helps visitors to make sense of the site.

St-Macaire and around

30 km or so south of La Sauve-Majeure is the pretty village of **ST-MACAIRE**, which boasts attractive medieval town walls, complete with gates and battlements. The village's central feature is the church, the **Église Saint Sauveur**, which boasts outstanding medieval carvings around its doorway and some splendid frescoes inside.

It's also worth taking a side trip 18 km east to **La Réole**, another fine medieval town which is known as the home of France's oldest **town hall**, constructed in the twelfth century by Richard the Lionheart. On the edge of town is the **Château des Quat'Sos**, an impressive medieval castle which was built by England's Henry III in the mid-thirteenth century, while nearby stands the well-preserved **Abbaye des Bénédictins**, from which you can enjoy fantastic views over the River Garonne and the surrounding countryside.

16

INFORMATION	ST MACAIRE AND AROUND

Tourist office 52 rue André-Bénac, La Réole (http:// entredeuxmers.com).

EATING

Le Pampaillet 2 rue François-Bergoeing, http:// restaurant-labricotier.com. In an attractive stone building, this genial local restaurant has tasty daily menus and everything is presented in unexpectedly creative ways. €€

Sauternes

Across the Garonne from St-Macaire is the pretty village of **SAUTERNES**, worth stopping by for a visit to the excellent Maison du Sauternes (http://maisondusauternes.com). This non-profit association of local winegrowers is home to a fantastic collection of Sauterines wines (see box, page 125), all of which are sold at very competitive process. Tastings are available and highly recommended.

Around Sauternes

Head south from Sauternes to reach the little town of Villandraut, which is dominated by the ruins of the enormous **Château de Villandraut** (www.chateaudevillandraut.fr, charge). Built in the early fourteenth century by Pope Clement V, who was born in the town in the 1260s, it suffered substantial damage in the French Wars of Religion in 1592. Clement's papacy was very eventful: in cahoots with Philip IV of France, he ruthlessly suppressed the Knights Templar, and indirectly caused the Great Papal Schism by moving the seat of the papacy to Avignon. His tomb can be visited in nearby **Uzeste**, which is a convenient short stop if you're heading to **Bazas** to check out the gorgeous **St-Jean-Baptiste cathedral**, a Gothic-style beastie built in the thirteenth and fourteenth centuries.

ACCOMMODATION	SAUTERNES

Château d'Arche http://chateau-arche.fr. A luxurious château-hotel and vineyard on the D125 just outside Sauternes (heading north) with nine rooms. Breakfast costs extra. €€€

Hotel Le 23 23 rue Principale, www.hotelsauternesle23. fr. A good budget option, *Hotel Le 23* offers eight simple but

SAUTERNES WINE

The **Sauternes** region, which extends southeast from Bordeaux for 40km along the left bank of the Garonne, is an ancient winemaking area, first planted during the Roman occupation. The distinctive golden wine of the area is sweet, round, full-bodied and spicy, with a long aftertaste. It's not necessarily a dessert wine, either; try it with Roquefort cheese. Gravelly terraces with a limestone subsoil help create the delicious taste, but mostly it's due to a peculiar microclimate of morning autumn mists and afternoons of sun and heat which causes *Botrytis cinerea* fungus, or "noble rot", to flourish on the grapes, letting the sugar concentrate and introducing some intense flavours. When the grapes are picked they're not a pretty sight: carefully selected by hand, only the most shrivelled, rotting bunches are taken. The wines of Sauternes are some of the most sought-after in the world, with bottles of **Château d'Yquem**, in particular, fetching thousands of euros. Visits are by private guided tour only that must be arranged in advance. Be warned that a visit is not cheap, but you can wander around the buildings and grounds without joining a tour. It's two minutes' drive north of Sauternes.

clean and comfortable rooms in a renovated nineteenth century house. Breakfast is extra. €

★**La Sauternaise** 22 rue Principale, https://en.lasauternaise.com. Offering four individually designed, luxurious rooms with wellness facilities, this B&B is a step above the usual offerings and boasts a hard-to-beat location in the centre of the village. The main entrance is on the Place de l'Eglise side. A gourmet breakfast is included, and they offer a great selection of wines for purchase. €€

EATING

Auberge Les Vignes 23 rue Principale, Sauternes, http://aubergelesvignes.fr. Understated elegance with a sunny terrace right on the main street, this is a good place for fish and oysters, as well as local specialities like *cassolette d'escargots* (snail casserole). There's also a sizeable wine list. €

Le Cercle Guiraud 14 rue Principale, Sauternes, www.lecercleguiraud.com. With its shady garden terrace right at the foot of the vineyards, this is a romantic place to escape the sun or dine beneath the stars. The cuisine is classic French, with a good mix of meat and fish dishes. €€

Restaurant Le Médiéval 8 place Gambetta, Villandraut, https://restaurant-lemedieval.fr. Not especially medieval in decor, this place just round the corner from the Pope's castle offers a short and fairly meat-heavy menu, with honey-roasted pork belly being an excellent choice. €€€

16

The Côte d'Argent

For a taste of the seaside, head west of Bordeaux to reach the **CÔTE D'ARGENT**, which claims to be Europe's longest, straightest, sandiest stretch of coast. Extending 200km from north to south, from the mouth of the Gironde down to the Adour river at Biarritz close to the Spanish border, it's a beautiful stretch of coastline, with the Atlantic Ocean crashing against sandy beaches backed by huge dunes – making it ideal for surfing. Behind the dunes you'll find a huge expanse of pine forest, which forms one of western Europe's largest woodland areas, crisscrossed with hiking and cycle trails. The coast offers little in the way of tourist sights other than plenty of beaches, with the result that away from the main resort towns, it can be fairly quiet, even during July and August. A secluded stretch of beach can seem tempting for swimmers, but bear in mind that undertows can be extremely strong here: it's best to limit your swimming to the designated and tightly patrolled swimming areas.

Arcachon

The oldest, and still most popular, beach resort on the Côte d'Argent is **ARCACHON**, which sits 65km west of Bordeaux at the head of the large Arcachon Bay. On summer weekends, the town is full of Bordelais escaping the city heat to enjoy the beaches, the

---

OYSTERS IN GUJAN-MESTRAS

The Bassin d'Arcachon is known for its oysters. The centre of the oyster industry is the small town of Gujan-Mestras, immediately west of the **Parc Ornithologique du Teich**. On the pretty, boat lined waterfront is the Maison de l'Huître (Oyster House; free), a small museum that reveals everything you never thought you needed to know about oysters. Nearby are many summer stands selling fresh oysters that fishermen will prepare for you while you wait.

---

seafood, and the oddly fussy architecture: many of the buildings resemble strangely fairytale-like dolls' houses.

Arcachon is short on specific sights: the pleasure of a visit comes from strolling through the pretty streets and along the seafront promenade before relaxing on the beach. If you want to explore the town, you'll find it's divided into four separate little districts, named after the seasons. Chances are you'll spend most of your time in **ville d'été** (summer town), which encompasses the seafront and the attractive shopping streets just behind it, but **ville d'hiver** (winter town), with its plethora of Second Empire-era mansions, is also worth a visit. If walking on the seafront becomes tiresome, try **Parc Mauresque**, a lovely little park packed with flowers and winding pathways. If you have a head for heights, you can climb the metal tower of the **Observatoire Sainte-Cécile**, which offers sweeping views over town and out to sea.

Parc Ornithologique du Teich

16

Charge • http://reserve-ornithologique-du-teich.com

At **Le Teich**, about 14km east of Arcachon, one of the most important expanses of wetlands remaining in France has been given official protection and turned into a bird sanctuary, the **Parc Ornithologique du Teich**. Walking trails lead to bird hides and ornithological guides are on hand to point out the difference between a sparrow and an egret! Away from the birds, keep an eye out in the pools of water for the rare European pond tortoise. This is a real hot spot for them, but, unfortunately, as in many parts of southwest France, invasive North American terrapin species are also present and wiping out the local boys. There are no hotels in Le Teich, but there are campsites, and it's an easy daytrip from Arcachon by train.

INFORMATION

ARCACHON

Tourist office Théâtre Olympia, 21 av du Général-de-Gaulle (http://arcachon.com).

Boat trips The huge Bassin d'Arcachon, a virtual inland sea, is a fantastic place for nautical adventures of all kinds. The shallow – and in summer, warm – waters of the bay have a number of sand-spit islands populated by great numbers of birds. In summer boats leave the jetties of Thiers

and Eyrac in Arcachon on various cruises, including to the Île aux Oiseaux (1hr 45min), and the Dune du Pyla (4hr). There's also a regular boat service from here to Cap Ferret on the opposite peninsula (30min; charge). Discounted tickets for all excursions are available from the tourist office. Check http://bassin-arcachon-info.com for timetables.

ACCOMMODATION

Accommodation in Arcachon in summer is both very limited and very expensive. Reservations – even for campsites – should be made a good six months in advance.

Arc Hôtel sur Mer 89 bd de la Plage, www.arc-hotel-sur-mer.com. With a great spot on the seafront, the Arc's chief calling card is its location: some rooms have views looking right out onto the beach. Some parts of the hotel are beginning to look a little tired, so it's worth asking to see a few rooms before settling in. €€

Le Camping Club 5 allée de la Galaxie, http://camping-

arcachon.com. An excellent four-star campsite in town with a bar, restaurant, and shop (July & Aug only), playground, BBQs, volleyball and bike rental. €

Le Dauphin 7 av Gounod, http://dauphin-arcachon. com. This unpretentious hotel in an attractive nineteenth-century building has simple but pleasant rooms, some of which have a balcony. There's an outdoor swimming pool, and the beach is just a few streets away. €€

Hôtel Ha(a)ïtza 1 av Louis Gaume, https://haaitza.com. It's not cheap, but if you want to stay somewhere truly distinctive – even down to the oddly unpronounceable name – then the *Hôtel Ha(a)ïtza* may fit the bill. A 1930s villa given an extensive redesign by the French architect Philippe Starck, Ha(a)ïtza is a marvellously stylish hotel which manages to look both olde-worlde and strikingly modern. There's a great restaurant, a large pool, and views over the dunes and the Atlantic Ocean. €€€€

La Plage 10 av Nelly-Deganne, http://hotelarcachon.com. The slick monochrome facade and identikit balconies of *La Plage* look somewhat incongruous against the fanciful Arcachonaise villas on the same block. Behind the urban frontage, however, the rooms are comfortable and there's private parking, a fitness room and a well-stocked breakfast buffet. Breakfast costs extra. €€€

La Villa du Moulleau 12 av Louis Garros, www.villadumoulleau.com. *La Villa du Moulleau* occupies a typically Arcachon building, with balconies, verandas, and fussy decoration on the roof. The rooms are comfy, the breakfast is good, and the grounds contain a swimming pool perfect for escaping the summer heat. €€

★ **Ville d'hiver** 20 av Victor-Hugo, http://hotelvilledhiver.com. Impressively transformed from a nineteenth-century water plant, this unique hotel offers freestanding blocks of rooms, dotted around a charming garden. Warm wood furnishings, contemporary decor and balconies afford each room its own character and privacy, but best of all is the outdoor swimming pool, housed in the old purification tank. Breakfast costs extra. €€€

EATING

★ **Le Cabane de l'Aiguillon** boulevard Pierre-Loti, http://lacabanedelaiguillon.com. The hut here sells oysters all year round but come in fair weather to enjoy the produce outside, under the leafy pergola and by the water's edge. In addition to oysters, you can also enjoy clams, whelks and prawns, simply accompanied by bread, lemon and white wine. Hard to beat. €

La Cabane du Breton 4 rue du Maréchal de Lattre de Tassigny, www.lacabanedubreton.fr. Cheap, cheerful and very good, this crêperie is a perfect place to grab a light lunch. Sweet and savoury options available. €

Le Cabestan 6bis avenue du Général-de-Gaulle, 05 56 83 18 62. A straight-shooting seafood restaurant with warm service and traditional surroundings, this is the place to tuck into Arcachon's famous oysters. €

Grand Café Victoria-Trattoria 26 boulevard Prom. Veyrier Montagnères, https://grandcafevictoria.fr. Right on the waterfront with views across the beach and out to

sea, Victoria is a popular spot for local seafood as well as perennial crowd-pleasers like pizza and pasta. €€

★ **Pâtisserie Alain Guignard** 11 avenue Notre-Dame-des-Passes. An Arcachon institution with a twenty-year pedigree. Indulge your sweet tooth with fruit crumble, *canelés*, layer cake, chocolate cake, biscuits, fruit tarts, coffee and éclairs. €

La Pizzeria Jehanne 19 rue Jehenne, www.pizzeria-jehenne.com. Good Italian food – primarily pizza and pizza – served up in an atmospheric restaurant with exposed brick walls and a wood-beamed ceiling. Very friendly service too. €€

La Table du Boucher 16 rue du Maréchal-de-Lattre-de-Tassigny. Head to this welcoming local joint if you want a change from fish and seafood – the meat-heavy offerings on the menu are cooked to perfection. The *andouillette* and veal with confit onions are both delicious, but you can't go wrong with steak and chips. €€

16

Cap Ferret

On the opposite side of Arcachon Bay, the tiny town of **CAP FERRET** sits on the tip of a sandy wooded peninsula. It crashed onto the tourist scene in the 1920s, when Jean Cocteau began holidaying here: "We row, we nap, we roll in the sand, we stroll around naked, in a landscape like Texas", he wrote in Letters from Piquey (1923). Polite

THE DUNE DU PYLA

The **Dune du Pyla** (https://ladunedupilat.com) is the largest dune in Europe – a vast white lunar landscape of windswept sand, 100m high, 12km south of Arcachon. It's an arduous climb, so take the steps to the top if you're not up for the challenge, but the adventurous shouldn't miss the long, hair-raising slide down to the sea, over slopes as steep as an Olympic ski-jump. Bus #1 leaves from the *gare SNCF* in Arcachon every hour from July to September – two to seven a day in other months. Three minutes away by car is *Hôtel La Co(o)rniche* (46 bd Louis-Gaume; https://lacoorniche.com); the terrace, with views of the bay and dunes, is the ideal spot for cocktails or a plate of oysters. There are also a number of large and well-equipped campsites in the vicinity.

society wanted to join in, and Cap Ferret quickly became a well-heeled holiday resort. Surrounded by the pine forests of Gascony and the Pays de Buch, the peninsula is full of wooded enclaves, quiet coves and long sandy beaches, and makes a perfect place for enjoying some relaxing beach time or getting active in the water with surfing and stand-up paddleboarding among the many available options.

GETTING AROUND AND INFORMATION   CAP FERRET

Boats Passenger ferries run all year round between Cap Ferret and nearby Arcachon (30min; buy tickets at the jetty; http://bassin-arcachon-info.com). Bikes can be taken on board. Ferries also run to Dune du Pyla and Le Moulleau, and a number of boat cruises and tours are also available.
Bike hire Many hotels offer bike rental, or else Western

Flyer (between the jetty and the Tourist Office; http://westernflyer.fr) rents bikes, electric bikes and scooters.
Tourist office 12 av de l'Océan (http://lege-capferret.com), just down from the jetty. A P'tit train tour runs from outside the tourist office.

ACCOMMODATION

Accommodation in Cap Ferret in high summer is very hard to find and very expensive (even camping!). Book as far ahead as you possibly can. Out of season many places close down for the winter.
Camping Brémontier Le Grand Crohot Océan, http://campingbremontier.fr. 10km north of Cap Ferret in a protected pine forest with a shop and bread delivery, bike rental, a supervised beach and a sailing club. Open May–Sept. €
Chez Annie 7 rue des Roitelets, 05 56 60 66 25. Run by the affable Annie, who speaks very little English but is happy to mime, this is a home away from home, right down to the homemade crêpes and apricot jam at breakfast. The three well-furnished wood cabins are comfortable and spotless, the beach is a short walk away and there's a pretty garden to relax in. €€
Hôtel Côté Sable 37 bd de la Plage, https://hotel-cotesable.com/fr. A luxurious hotel and spa with 15 stylish rooms, a top-notch restaurant, sea views and the opportunity to enjoy trips on the hotel's own boat. Try to nab the room with the freestanding bathtub. €€€
★ **La Maison du Bassin** 5 rue des Pionniers, http://lamaisondubassin.com. Oak floors, plush beds and

chandeliers add a restrained elegance to the small but perfectly formed rooms at this hotel, which has the feel of a bourgeois summer home. The attached restaurant, with its huge terrace hemmed in by vines, is also excellent and the staff are attentive and knowledgeable about the area. Breakfast is extra. €€€
★ **Des Pins** 23 rue des Fauvettes, http://hoteldespins.eu. *Des Pins* feels like a genteel Edwardian boarding house, with fresh, pale rooms off a wood-panelled hall. There are sleeping cabins in the garden and a gypsy caravan. The only downside is bad soundproofing. Breakfast costs extra. €€
Villa Seabird allée des Bambous, https://www.villa-seabird.com. A small B&B on the northern outskirts of Cap Ferret, with friendly owners, comfy rooms and a pleasant garden. A very good budget choice. €
Yamina Lodge 169 av de Bordeaux, http://yamina-lodge.com. Three rooms and a villa in purpose-built, wooden cabins nestled beneath towering pine trees, this is an idyllic spot to unwind. Country-style interiors with wicker furnishings and fine wood floors add to the Zen feel, plus there are roomy terraces, bikes for hire and a romantic jacuzzi. Breakfast costs extra. €€€

EATING

L'Escale 2 avenue Ocean, www.facebook.com/LEscale CapFerret. Right on the waterfront by the pier, ready to draw in those arriving by ferry from Arcachon, *l'Escale* serves up cheerful fish, seafood and meat dishes on its attractive outdoor terrace. The oysters are a good choice. €€
Chez Hortense 26 avenue du Sémaphore, www.facebook.com/chezhortense.capferret. *Chez Hortense* is something of an institution in Cap Ferret, having earned a solid reputation over forty years for its seafood, particularly the mussels.

Happily, it lives up to the hype – but everyone knows it, so make sure you book well in advance. €€€€
Pinasse Café 2bis avenue de l'Océan, http://pinasse-cafe.com. Right next to Cap Ferret's main jetty, where the Arcachon boat disembarks, *Pinasse* is a tourist honeypot, but against all odds it's also an excellent little restaurant, serving an array of fresh seafood. Secure a table on the picturesque terrace and watch as the ships come in, with the waves lapping beneath you. €€

Lacanau and Hourtin

North of Cap Ferret, **Lacanau** and, smaller, **Hourtin** are two other favoured beach getaways for the Bordelais. Unlike Arcachon or Cap Ferret, which are both rather upmarket, Lacanau and Hourtin are favoured more by a younger, surfy crowd and, appropriately, the waves here are often among the best on this part of the coastline. If you're keen to hit the surf then there are numerous summer surf schools all along the beaches in both towns.

Lacanau and Hourtin are both tales of two halves. **Lacanau** town, which is 12km inland of the beach, is a small and quiet place with a slow pace of life year-round with very little to offer visitors and **Hourtin**, which is also 12km from the beach, is similar though even smaller and quieter. Lacanau-Ocean and Hourtin Plage are the purpose-built beach resorts. In-between the towns and the ocean are two lakes, the Étang de Lacanau and the Lac d'Hourtin. Both are massive (the Lac d'Hourtin being the largest of the two), shallow lakes which, in summer, offer warm, calm waters with boating, swimming, kayaking, paddle boarding and more. They're perfect alternatives to the ocean if you're a nervous swimmer or have small kids in tow. Linking town, ocean and lake together are a web of superbly maintained cycle paths. Bikes can be hired in both beach towns.

There's not a lot in the way of hotel-style accommodation in either place, and what there is books up months in advance in summer and is generally poor value for money. There are, however, dozens of campsites ranging from the simple to the highly extravagant. When it comes to eating don't expect anything too memorable. Like almost any beach resort most of the ocean-side restaurants are of the 'churn them in, spit them out' tourist variety. Head inland to Lacanau or Hourtin town to find something a little more local.

Soulac-sur-Mer

Soulac-sur-Mer is the Arcachon you've never heard of. Right at the northern tip of the coastline, where the Garonne spills into the Atlantic, this small town has a very fleeting moment of popularity in the 1920's. During this period some elaborate art-deco style villas and houses were constructed around the town, although today these are massively outnumbered by considerably less attractive new builds. As with Arcachon, there's plenty of open space in the town and shady trees, and the beach itself has a considerably more sheltered aspect than most of Aquitaine beaches. This translates into generally calmer waters (this is especially the case the further north of town you go) and there are even a few semi-natural sea-water swimming pools as well as various World War II bunkers and defensive towers. Continue up the coast north of town for around 9km and you'll reach the very tip of the peninsula, and the Pointe de Grave marked by the Grave lighthouse. It contains a small museum (free) and you can climb to the top for views of the estuary and the ocean.

As with all the beach resorts around Bordeaux there are surf schools around the main town beaches and bicycle rental outlets will allow you to peddle off through the forest to distant horizons (and some year-round quiet beaches).

The town **tourist office** (http://medoc-atlantique.com) is at 68 rue de la Plage. As with anywhere on the coast, accommodation is at a premium in high summer and prices are high.

Les Landes

South of Bordeaux is **LES LANDES**, part of the largest pine forest in Western Europe. Nearly 10,000 square kilometres, parts of it were declared a *parc naturel régional* in 1970. It's a beautiful place, and has become increasingly popular with summer beach visitors. The area is strong on outdoor pursuits with numerous cycle and hiking trails running through the forest and along the coast. Large lakes mean there are also lots of opportunities for kayaking, sailing and fishing; horse riding is also popular. But, above and beyond all else, Les Landes is all about the beach. Kilometres of soft, golden sand unfurl along the coast and most of it is remarkably undeveloped. The reason for this is the surf: huge winter swells destroy anything left on or near the beach. The surfing here is world class, with the town of Hossegor in the south being home to one of the best beach break waves on the planet. Surfers flock to the area from March to November, but in the dead of winter, the place falls quiet as most places close up. Other stunning beaches include Soustons, Messanges and – the most beautiful of all of them – Moliets. The River Adour meanders (and frequently floods) the gentle landscape inland from Hossegor. For large parts of its journey through Les Landes a quiet road doubles as a cycle and walking path along the river, and attractive villages such as Saubusse, Josse and Port-de-Lanne make for good places to enjoy this other face of Les Landes.

Mont de Marsan makes a good base for exploring the inland part of Les Landes. It's the administrative heart of the region, 100km south of Bordeaux, and served by regular trains. **Parc Jean-Rameau**, on the north bank of the river Douze, is the prettiest part of the town. If you're lucky enough to be in the area in mid-July, you can enjoy Les Fêtes Madeleine (http://fetesmadeleine.fr), a week of parades, sports, flamenco and bullfighting.

INFORMATION   LES LANDES

Tourist office 1 place Charles-de-Gaulle, Mont-de-Marsan (http://tourisme-montdemarsan.fr).
Activities The tourist office provides maps of local walking and cycling routes and also organizes a guided tour of Mont-de-Marsan in English (July & Aug, from the office Mon–Sat

10.30am). Another outdoor activity on offer is canoeing on one of the three rivers whose confluence is at the town. For canoe hire try Canoë Loisir (http://canoeloisir.fr) in nearby Roquefort.

ACCOMMODATION

Camping Landes Cigales av de l'Océan, Moliets, www. camping-les-cigales.fr. This campsite within an easy walk of Moliets beach offers tent pitches and chalets. Staff can arrange surfing, bodyboarding and kite-surfing activities. €
Logis Hôtel de l'Océan rue de la Balise, Moliets, www.l-ocean.fr. The rooms are nothing fancy, but they're clean and functional in this hotel just a stone's throw from Moliets beach, making it an ideal place to base yourself to enjoy the sun, sand and surf. There's a good on-site bar-restaurant. €€
Les Prés d'Eugénie Eugénie-les-Bains, http:// michelguerard.com. An idyllic retreat marooned on its own estate, where you'll sleep in a renovated nineteenth-century colonial mansion, surrounded by manicured gardens and vineyards, dine on three-Michelin-starred cuisine, and be

pampered in a luxurious spa – this kind of luxury comes at quite a price, of course. There are also a variety of deals, spa breaks and cooking classes available. €€€€
Le Renaissance 225 av de Villeneuve, Mont de Marsan, http://le-renaissance.com. Comfortable, spotless rooms in this mid-size country hotel 1km from the centre of Mont-de-Marsan, with a swimming pool, restaurant and lovely gardens. Breakfast costs extra. €€
Le Richelieu 3 rue Robert-Wlérick, Mont de Marsan, http://hotel-richelieu-montdemarsan.com. Reliable and friendly hotel, with a decent on-site restaurant, private parking and comfortable, well-equipped rooms right in the centre of Mont de Marsan. Part of the *Citadel* chain, it's smart and functional rather than stylish, but good value. €

EATING

Le Bistrot de Marcel 1 rue Pont du Commerce, Mont de Marsan, http://lebistrotdemarcel.fr. Traditional cuisine sourced from local ingredients and is served in a prime Mont de Marsan location overlooking the Midouze river. Service is leisurely, so make a night of it and order the *menu du sud-ouest*. €€
Brûlerie Montoise 1 rue du 4-septembre, Mont de Marsan, http://bruleriemontoise.fr. The coffee is roasted daily, the teas are plentiful and the cakes are fresh – what more do you need for a sightseeing break in Mont de Marsan? €

La Cagette avenue de l'Océan, Moliets, www.lacagette moliets.com. The menu at this extremely popular restaurant in Moliers is primarily fish-focused, with ceviche and tuna dishes particular highlights. Other strong choices include the Mauritian chicken. Leave room for dessert: the cheesecakes are sublime. €€€
Un Singe en Hiver place de la Bastide, Moliets, 05 58 48 56 74. Decent bar-restaurant in Moliers serving a range of dishes, including tapas, seafood and chicken and chips: there's something for everyone, making it a good family choice. €€

16

A PICNIC WITH FRIENDS ALONG THE EMBANKMENT

Contexts

History

No history of Bordeaux is complete without looking at the wider southwest region and France as a whole. This last point is especially important in a modern, Paris-centric France. Southwest France has always had – and usually prided itself upon having – a good deal of independence from northern France. Its history until the later Middle Ages only sporadically collided with that of the north. The region was subsequently often hostile to creeping integration; and even after full inclusion within the French state, its history has been replete with episodes of resistance, opposition and dissent.

In the seventeenth century, individuals from the south regarded crossing the River Loire as "going to France", and used the term "Frenchmen" to designate those who lived north of that river. This southern sense of otherness has been fully reciprocated. Well into the nineteenth and twentieth centuries, northerners regarded the south as exotically different – and implicitly inferior and less civilised. "The real France," observed the early nineteenth-century writer and historian, Jules Michelet, "is northern France." So strong was this sentiment, that the history of France has invariably been told from a northern, often Parisian perspective, which has discounted or ignored key episodes in the development of Southwest France.

Prehistoric man

Historians' neglect is all the more regrettable in that the Southwest has a particularly rich, diverse and complex heritage – as well as a very ancient one. No other region in France can boast the extraordinary vestiges of discovered in the southwest, which shows a flourishing hunter-gatherer "reindeer culture" in existence as early as circa 15,000 BC, notably in the Dordogne. The region was also – along with neighbouring Provence – the first area in France to welcome farming and pastoral lifestyles from between 6,000 and 4,000 BC onwards.

Roman rule

The city of Bordeaux, which was originally known as Burdigala, was founded around 300BC by Celtic tribes. When in 55–54 BC Julius Caesar drew all of France into the Roman republic, the southern part of Gaul (as he called it) was more ethnically diverse than the north. In 16 AD Emperor Augustus established the new Gallo-Roman province of Aquitania, stretching from Poitiers south to the Pyrenees. Its capital was Burdigala, and regional administrative centres were set up in Vesunna (Périgueux) and Divona Cadurcorum (Cahors), each with its forum, amphitheatre, law courts and temples. During more than three centuries of peace – the Pax Romana – that followed, the Romans built roads, introduced new technologies, traded, planted vineyards and established an urbanized society administered by an educated, Latin-speaking elite.

6,000–4,000 BC	58 BC	416 AD
Farming and pastoral lifestyles are established in Southwest France.	Roman Conquest of Gaul begins with the arrival of Julius Caesar. Last resistance to the invaders is offered by the Gauls at Uxellodunum (at Puy d'Issolud near Vayrac), in Quercy.	Visigoths conquer the Southwest region.

During the Roman period Bordeaux was an important centre for lead and tin mining. Although the Mediterranean coast is better known for its Roman sites, Bordeaux and some neighbouring areas have vestiges of a Roman past. Even more durable than ruins though, has been the linguistic impact of the Romans: as well as being the language of the rulers, Latin penetrated rural areas and eventually fused with the local Celtic dialects to form two broad new language groups: the langue d'Oïl (where "yes" is *oïl* – later, *oui*), spoken north of the Loire, and the langue d'Oc, or Occitan (where "yes" is *oc*), to the south.

By the third century AD, Roman authority was starting to crack. Oppressive aristocratic rule and an economic crisis turned the destitute peasantry into gangs of marauding brigands, who were particularly rampant in the southwest. But more devastating were the incursions across the Rhine by various restless Germanic tribes, starting with the Alemanni and Franks, who pushed down as far as Spain, ravaging farmland and looting towns along the way. Some urban centres in the southwest were hurriedly fortified while the nobles hot-footed it to their country villas, which became increasingly self-sufficient – economically, administratively and militarily.

The crunch came, however, in the fifth century when first the Vandals and then the Visigoths stormed through the region as the Roman Empire crumbled. For nearly a hundred years the Visigoths ruled a huge territory extending across southern France and into Spain, with its capital at Toulouse.

Christianity and independence

The Visigoths' destructive and mercenary temperament did not conduce to sustained rule, and in 507 AD they were driven out of the region by the Franks, a northern tribe who gave their name to modern France. The end of the Visigoths marked the beginning of a long period of relative independence for Aquitaine and the southwest. Although the Frankish king, Clovis, was to found the Merovingian dynasty whose power technically extended to this region, he failed to re-establish the same overarching authority as the Romans had had. The power vacuum had been filled, in part, by representatives of the early Church.

Christianity had arrived from Rome in the early fourth century and was spreading slowly through France, but the invasion of the Vandals and Visigoths had put its advance on hold. It fell to bishop Chronope, active in the region between 506 and 533 AD, to re-establish the faith by a prolific programme of church building. Clovis himself had embraced Christianity around 500 AD and thereafter was happy to devolve a great deal of everyday administration to local bishops.

The Merovingian empire began to disintegrate in the late seventh century, leaving the way clear for their chancellors, the Pepin family, to take control. One of their most dynamic scions, Charles Martel, defeated the Spanish Moors when they swept up through the southwest as far as Poitiers in 732. His grandson, Charlemagne, continued the expansionist policy of the Carolingian dynasty – so called for their fondness for the name Charles, or "Carolus" – to create an empire which eventually stretched from the Baltic to the Pyrenees. Charlemagne and his descendants, however, had no more genuine control over the southwest region than the Merovingians had, preferring, like them, to rule from a distance. In 781 Charlemagne created the quasi-independent

496	732	905
Clovis enlarges the Frankish state and (in 507) defeats the Visigoths near Poitiers.	Charles Martel checks the Arab advance from Spain into the rest of Europe at Poitiers.	Navarre, straddling the Pyrenees, becomes a kingdom under Sancho I.

kingdom of Aquitaine – an area extending from the Loire to the Cévennes and from the Rhône to the Pyrenees and with Bordeaux as its capital. Within the kingdom, the Carolingians delegated administrative power to royally appointed bishops, now joined by a growing number of counts who had been awarded territory in exchange for their loyalty. In theory, the king retained feudal authority, but in reality the bishops and counts did largely as they pleased. The royal position became weaker still in the ninth century, in part due to a long-drawn-out battle of succession following Charlemagne's death in 814, but also thanks to a series of extravagantly destructive raids by the Vikings, who sailed their longboats down from Scandinavia. They had been raiding coastal areas for decades, but in 844 they penetrated deep inland along the Garonne and other rivers, plundering towns and churches as they went.

In the face of these destabilizing invasions the Carolingians were obliged to delegate ever more autonomy to the provincial governors until these eventually grew more powerful than the king. So it was that when Hugues Capet succeeded to the French throne in 987, founding a four-hundred-year dynasty that in theory ruled the whole of France, he in practice had authority only over a small area near Paris. By this point, the local aristocratic families of the southwest were more embroiled in jostling for power with one another than with the king and the counts of Poitou (based at Poitiers) and Toulouse were fighting for control of what was once again the Duchy of Aquitaine. The former emerged victorious, thus creating a vast territory that by the twelfth century reached from the Loire to the Pyrenees. The Poitou counts also ushered in a period of relative peace, rapid economic growth and renewed religious vigour, demonstrated in a wave of church building. To them we owe the lovely Romanesque churches seen throughout the region to this day. At least some of this building activity was spurred and financed by the great procession of pilgrims passing along the various routes to Santiago de Compostela in Spain.

English rule

It was the huge kingdom created by the amalgamation of the territories of the counts of Poitou and the dukes of Aquitaine that indirectly allowed the whole of the southwest including the city of Bordeaux to fall into the hands of the English Crown. The cause of this catastrophe for the French royal family, the Capetian dynasty, was the strong-willed Eleanor of Aquitaine (1122–1204), who inherited the domains of Aquitaine and Poitou in 1137 at the tender age of 15. Fifteen years later, she ditched her first husband, the French king, to marry Henry of Anjou, thereby creating an empire comprising Anjou and Normandy in addition to Eleanor's possessions. This in itself was a disastrous blow to the Capetians, but it was compounded in 1154 when Henry succeeded to the English throne (as Henry II). As a result, almost half of France fell under English rule. Much of it would remain so for the next three hundred years.

For the southwest region itself, however, English rule ushered in a period of peace, stability and impressive economic progress. With the major exception of Richard the Lionheart (Richard Coeur de Lion), Eleanor's third son, who plundered the region ruthlessly, the English overlords proved to be popular. For the most part they ruled from a distance, often preferring to stay put in England, and ensured the loyalty of their southern subjects by granting a large degree of independence to

950	1130
Beginning of the pilgrimage through France to the supposed tomb of St James at present-day Santiago de Compostela, in Spain, where his relics had been discovered around 813.	Aimery Picaud, a monk from Poitou, writes the *Liber Sancti Jacobi*, or *Codex Calixtinus*, the world's first travel guide, for the benefit of pilgrims on the road to Santiago de Compostela.

many of Aquitaine's rapidly growing towns and their local lords. Peasants lived under relatively privileged feudal conditions, helped by the fact that local lords were often in competition for their services. An important factor here was the building of dozens of new towns, the bastides, designed to secure border areas and accommodate the rapidly expanding population. In order to attract peasants to inhabit the new towns and cultivate the surrounding land, feudal lords had to offer enticing terms and considerable freedom.

The region continued to produce wheat and oats, but the real sensation of the era of English rule was the transformation of wine production into a lucrative and international industry. Merchants exporting the beloved claret of the English to London and other British ports grew wealthy, and the proceeds filtered through to the whole region. As English rule was delivered from across the Channel and therefore somewhat removed, it did not mean any perceptible invasion by the English language. On the contrary, independence from northern France allowed local language and culture to flourish, creating perfect conditions for the high-culture phenomenon of the troubadours.

The Hundred Years War

Though the English had lost their possessions north of the Loire by the mid-thirteenth century, they remained a perpetual thorn in the side of the French kings thanks to their grip on Aquitaine. Skirmishes took place throughout the century, followed by various peace treaties. But the spark that ignited the ruinous – and misnamed – Hundred Years War (1337–1453) was a Capetian succession crisis. When the last of the line, Charles IV, died without an heir in 1328, the English king, Edward III, leapt in to claim the throne of France for himself. It went instead to Charles's cousin, Philippe de Valois. Edward acquiesced for a time, but when Philippe began whittling away at English possessions in Aquitaine, Edward renewed his claim and embarked on a war.

The major battles of the war were almost all fought in the northern half of the country, where Edward won an outright victory at Crécy, before his son, the Black Prince, took the French king, Jean le Bon, prisoner at the Battle of Poitiers in 1356 and established a capital at Bordeaux. The resulting treaty appeared to give the English victory, but the French fought back, banishing the English entirely but for a toehold in Bordeaux. In 1415, though, the tables turned again as Henry V inflicted a crushing defeat on the French army, against all odds, at the legendary battle of Agincourt. Once again, France seemed on the verge of unravelling at the seams, until Jeanne d'Arc (Joan of Arc) arrived on the scene. In 1429 she rallied the demoralized French troops, broke the English siege at Orléans and tipped the scales against the invaders. The English were slowly but surely driven back to their southwest heartland until even that was lost at the Battle of Castillon in 1453. Within months, the English surrendered Bordeaux, and their centuries-long adventure in France came to an end. Although Castillon was the only major battle fought in the southwest, the region did not spare itself from bloodshed. The region's powerful families, operating from their fortified bases, sought to take advantage of the general chaos by attacking their neighbours and trying to strengthen their own hands. Many nobles swapped sides repeatedly, fighting under English or French colours as it suited them.

1152	1337–1453	1348
Eleanor of Aquitaine marries Henry Plantagenet. He becomes Henry II of England in 1154. A third of France – including much of the southwest – is ruled by the English crown.	Hundred Years' War.	The Black Death appears on the Mediterranean coast of France and quickly spreads across the country.

ELEANOR OF AQUITAINE

Eleanor of Aquitaine would have been a remarkable woman had she lived at any time in history. Determined and strong-willed, yet also beautiful, cultured and capricious, she dominated the twelfth-century affairs of both England and France. She was born around 1122. At the age of 15, when her father William X of Aquitaine died, she inherited the Duchy of Aquitaine, which extended from the Loire to the Pyrenees. In the same year, 1137, she married Prince Louis, who became King Louis VII of France only a month later. From 1147 to 1149 she accompanied her husband on the Second Crusade to Jerusalem, where she led her own troops into battle, wearing the costume of an Amazonian warrior.

Disagreements in the Holy Land presaged the end of their relationship and although Eleanor bore Louis two daughters, the marriage was annulled in 1152 because of consanguinity. Almost immediately, Eleanor married Henry Plantagenet, Count of Anjou and Duke of Normandy, who succeeded to the English throne in 1154 as Henry II. The union of Eleanor and Henry brought together England, Normandy and the west of France in the same powerful Angevin empire which would survive for the next two hundred years.

Eleanor bore Henry five sons and three daughters. Two of her sons, Richard the Lionheart and John (surnamed Lackland), became kings of England. Her daughters made strategic marriages: Matilda to Henry the Lion, Duke of Saxony and Bavaria; Eleanor to Alfonso VIII, King of Castile; and Joan first to William II of Sicily and then Raymond VI of Toulouse. Because of her dispersed but influential extended family Eleanor has been dubbed "the grandmother of Europe". All the while Eleanor took a hand in administering the kingdom and especially her own lands. At the same time, she was as versed in culture and poetry as she was in politics and military affairs, and was the patron of troubadours, whose art flourished at the court of Poitiers.

Eleanor's life took a new turn in 1173 when her sons Richard and John rebelled against their father. Motivated, it is assumed, by her husband's infidelities, Eleanor gave them her support. The rebellion failed, however, and as a consequence she was imprisoned in England, where she remained until Henry's death in 1189. She then became even more active in affairs of state. Acting as regent she administered Richard the Lionheart's realm while he was away on crusades in the Holy Land (1189–94), keeping it together in defiance of the ambitions of her other son, John, and of the French king, Philip II Augustus. When Richard was later captured by the Duke of Austria, she raised the money for his ransom and went personally to bring him home.

Richard the Lionheart died in 1199 without an heir and John succeeded to the throne of England. By now Eleanor was nearing 80 but she still strove to keep the Plantagenet kingdom intact, journeying to Spain to fetch her granddaughter, Blanche, from the Castilian court so that she could marry her to the son of the king of France. In 1200 she commanded an army which put down a rebellion against John in Anjou. At the end of her life Eleanor retired to a convent at Fontevraud in the Loire, where she died in 1204 and was buried with her husband, Henry. The nuns of Fontevraud described her as a queen "who surpassed almost all the queens of the world". After her death, her ancestral domains continued to be loyal to England, and Aquitaine was only finally acquired by the French crown in the fifteenth century, during the Hundred Years' War.

Most towns and castles were attacked at some point and many changed hands on numerous occasions, either by treaty or force. By the end of the war, farms and villages lay abandoned and roving bands of brigands terrorized the countryside, having

1453	1539	1562
The English are beaten by the French in the last battle of the Hundred Years' War at Castillon-la-Bataille, in Guyenne, near Bordeaux. They abandon all French possessions except Calais.	French is decreed the legal language by the royal edict of Villers-Cotterets, exacerbating the decline of the Occitan language.	The Wars of Religion start between Huguenots (Protestants) and Catholics.

THE TROUBADOURS

Troubadour poetry originated in the Southwest around 1100, and flourished until the early fourteenth century. At its heart lies witty and lyrical inventiveness, expressed in the subtle and nuanced Occitan language.

It developed in princely court culture – its first practitioner was William, Duke of Aquitaine, then resident at Poitiers. But troubadours came to be drawn from every rank of society (including women, or trobairitzes) down to wandering minstrels, known as jugglers (joglars) who mixed poetry and song with other forms of performance including acrobatics.

Troubadour poetry included political satires, odes to nature, and works of spirituality, alongside anti-clerical compositions. Roughly half of what has come down to us, however, concerned *fin'amor* – "perfect love", for which troubadour poetry is most renowned.

The idealised love that troubadours evoked was not without hints of sensual passion, but focused on the champion's quest to win his lady: "my lady tries me and tests me so she can know how I love her", as William of Aquitaine put it.

The prestige of the troubadours helped spread notions of chivalry and courtly love in northern France (notably through the patronage of Eleanor of Aquitaine), Italy, Catalonia, Spain, Portugal, Germany and England.

abandoned all pretence of fighting for one side or the other. The population had been reduced by roughly a half to under twelve million, partly by warfare, but largely through famine and disease; millions died as the bubonic plague repeatedly swept through France during the fourteenth and fifteenth centuries.

Gradually the nightmare ended, though the south now had to kowtow to the hated Northerners. Even so, Louis XI proved to be an astute ruler who allowed some of the privileges granted by the English to remain. Trade, and particularly the wine trade but also, in the case of Bordeaux, a significant trade with the West Indies in sugar and slaves, helped the city and surrounding towns to flourish.

The Wars of Religion

In the early sixteenth century the ideas, art and architecture of the Renaissance began to penetrate France. As elsewhere in Europe, the Renaissance had a profound influence on every aspect of life, engendering a new optimism and spirit of enquiry that appealed in particular to the new class of wealthy merchants. At the same time, increased trade and improved communications, including the invention of the printing press, helped disseminate ideas throughout Europe. Among them came the new Protestant message espoused by Martin Luther and John Calvin that the individual was responsible to God alone and not to the Church.

Such ideas gained widespread adherence throughout France, partly feeding on resentment of Catholic clergy who were often seen as closely linked to the oppressive feudal regime, but mainly because a handful of powerful families converted and, where the feudal overlord led, his subjects were bound to follow. On the national scale, the most significant families to convert were those of the Bourbon-d'Albret royal dynasty.

1594	1598	1659
Henri of Navarre, having converted to Catholicism, is crowned Henri IV of France.	The Edict of Nantes effectively brings the Wars of Religion to an end.	The Treaty of the Pyrenees ends a conflict between France and Spain. The border between the two countries is definitively drawn.

As the Protestant faith took hold and Catholics felt increasingly threatened, the sporadic brutal attempts to stamp out Protestantism, such as a massacre in Cahors in 1560, erupted two years later into a series of bitter civil wars. Interspersed with ineffective truces and accords, the Wars of Religion lasted for the next thirty years.

On the Catholic side, a powerful lobbying group of traditionalists, organized mainly by the de Guise family, led an army against the Huguenots, who were in turn marshalled by Admiral de Coligny. The two armies toured northern France, occasionally clashing directly, but more often capturing and converting towns that had taken one side or the other. The duc de Guise was murdered in 1563, an act for which his allies held Coligny responsible. And in 1572, Coligny was among the victims of the war's bloodiest and most notorious date: the St Bartholomew's Day Massacre, when some three thousand Protestants, gathered in Paris for the wedding of Protestant Henri d'Albret to Marguerite de Valois, the sister of Henry III of France, were slaughtered.

Just as in earlier conflicts, the nationwide dispute was used as a pretext by powerful families in the southwest to consolidate their positions. Once again, private armies roamed the region, vying with each other in their savagery, but with only vaguely religious motives. Before his death, Coligny famously complained of Huguenot generals in the southwest who took no interest in the wider struggle and "refused to fight unless they could turn around and see their own chimney". Some towns were attacked and changed hands repeatedly, either in violence or as a result of various truces, by which they were nominally declared either Catholic or Protestant. In reality, the majority of ordinary people, though cruelly affected by the fighting, saw little impact on their notions of religion, which remained a hotch-potch of rural paganism and local folklore, with only hints of orthodox Christianity, until several centuries later. A twist of fate signalled the beginning of the end of the conflicts, when Henri d'Albret – king of Navarre and leader of the Protestant army – became heir to the French throne when Henry III's son died in 1584. Five years later, Henry III himself was dead, leaving a tricky problem, since a Protestant could not be king. After trying to seize the crown by force, Henri d'Albret eventually abjured his faith and became Henry IV of France. "Paris is worth a Mass," he is reputed to have said.

Once on the throne Henry IV set about reconstructing and reconciling his kingdom. Under the visionary Edict of Nantes of 1598 the Protestants were accorded freedom of conscience, freedom of worship in specified places, the right to attend the same schools and hold the same offices as Catholics, their own courts and the possession of a number of fortresses, including Montauban, as a guarantee against renewed attack.

The stirrings of discontent

Aquitaine had barely drawn breath after the end of the Wars of Religion, when a different type of conflict erupted – this time one whose causes the ordinary peasantry could identify with all too easily. The countryside lay in ruins and the cost of the wars and rebuilding fell squarely on their shoulders. Ruinous taxes, a series of bad harvests, high prices and yet more outbreaks of the plague combined to push them over the edge in the late sixteenth century. There were peasant rebellions in

1681	1685	1789
The Canal du Midi opens, connecting Toulouse (and the Atlantic via the Garonne river system) with the Mediterranean near Béziers.	Louis XIV's Revocation of the Edict of Nantes: Protestant worship in France is prohibited.	The storming of the Bastille in Paris marks the beginning of the French Revolution.

BORDEAUX BOOMS

Although it left most of the lucrative slave trade to Nantes, Bordeaux profited enormously through links with the French sugar-producing colony of Saint-Domingue (present-day Haiti). It was also well placed to pick up on growing European, especially English, demand for wines and *eaux-de-vie*. Quality wine-producers – Lafite, Latour, Margaux and others – and producers of cognac, too, were starting to make a durable impact on European palates. The scale of the wealth displayed in the city of Bordeaux – from lush private residences through to public establishments such as the port facilities and the theatre – left even English tourists gasping in admiration.

Normandy and Brittany, but the worst of the "Croquants'" (yokels') uprisings broke out in the southwest. The first major revolt occurred in the winter of 1593, when a number of towns and castles were attacked. After two years of skirmishes, nobles pulled together an army in 1595 and the rebellion was quickly and savagely put down by the allied forces of the local nobility. The same grievances resurfaced in more uprisings in May 1637, however, no doubt nourished in part by tales of the earlier failed rebellion, passed down by word of mouth from generation to generation. This time, the revolt was altogether more serious. In the face of one tax demand too many, a ten-thousand-strong peasant army tried unsuccessfully to seize Périgueux. Instead, they took Bergerac and then marched on Bordeaux. They were stopped, however, at Ste-Foy-la-Grande and the final showdown took place soon after against 3400 royal troops at La Sauvetat-du-Dropt, south of Bergerac, leaving at least a thousand Croquants dead. The leaders were executed, while the surviving rebels returned to the land.

Thereafter, the long reign of Louis XIV (1643–1715) saw the French Crown and Catholic religion begin to reassert control over the southwest. With the exception of the Frondes (of 1648–52), when aristocrats joined the lower classes in rebelling against royal taxes and when the army had to be brought in to crush demonstrations in Bordeaux, the state successfully reinstated military and feudal control. At the same time, Protestant rights were gradually eroded until in 1685 Louis revoked the Edict of Nantes, forbade Protestant worship and set about trying to eliminate the faith completely. Orders were given for the destruction of Protestant churches and of the castles of its most fervent supporters. Thousands of Protestants fled the southwest for the safety of the Netherlands, Germany and England.

At the same time, France began to establish a colonial empire in North America, Africa, India and the Caribbean, and, as trade from these places started to grow in the early eighteenth century, so Bordeaux and the other Atlantic ports prospered and this became a Golden Age for Bordeaux. The port in Bordeaux became the biggest and most important in France and the second biggest in the world after London. Bordeaux supplied much of Europe with coffee, cocoa, sugar, cotton and indigo. It also became a major slave trading port. It's thought that around 150,000 African slaves were shipped to the New World from the ports of Bordeaux. Around 5000 grandiose new buildings were constructed by the architect Victor Louis and the Bordeaux cityscape took on the look that it largely retains today.

1792	1804	1814
Declaration of the First Republic. Louis XVI is tried and executed the following year.	Napoleon becomes emperor.	Louis XVIII, the younger brother of Louis XVI, enters Southwest France from Spain with the allied armies that have defeated Napoleon.

> ## THE LANGUAGE OF "OC"
>
> North of a line running from the confluence of the Dordogne and Garonne rivers in the west to Grenoble in the east, the word for "yes" was "*oïl*" (modern-day "*oui*"), while to the south it was "*oc*". France could thus be divided into the areas of *langue d'oïl* ("the tongue of *oui*") and *langue d'oc*. The latter term – written "Languedoc" – came to refer to all of the southern region in which the Occitan language (or *patois*, as its detractors would have it) was spoken.
>
> The tongue remained in current use in most of the region well into the nineteenth century. Increasingly successful attempts are currently being made to revive the language and Occitan culture in the modern Southwest.

Revolution

For the majority of people, however, little had changed. The gap between rich and poor grew ever wider as the clergy and aristocracy clung onto their privileges and the peasants were squeezed for higher taxes. Their general misery was exacerbated by a catastrophic harvest in 1788, followed by a particularly severe winter. Bread prices rocketed and on July 14, 1789, a mob stormed the Bastille in Paris, a hated symbol of the oppressive regime. As the Revolution spread, similar insurrections occurred throughout the country, accompanied by widespread peasant attacks on landowners' châteaux and the destruction of tax and rent records. In August the new National Assembly abolished the feudal rights and privileges of the nobility and then went on to nationalize Church lands.

In these early stages the general population of the southwest supported the Revolution. However, as the Parisian revolutionaries grew increasingly radical and proposed ever more centralization of power they found themselves in bitter opposition. Towards the end of 1792, as the First Republic was being declared, they finally lost out to the extremists and in October the following year the Terror was unleashed as mass executions took place throughout France; estimates run to three thousand in Paris and 14,000 in the regions. Though revolutionary bands wrought a fair amount of havoc in the southwest, looting and burning castles and churches, hacking away at coats of arms and religious statuary, on the whole the region escaped fairly lightly; many aristocrats simply fled and their possessions were sold off at knock-down prices.

Among many administrative changes following the Revolution, one of the most significant was the creation of *départements* in 1790 to replace the old provinces. Thus began yet another attempt at national unification, accompanied by efforts to draw the traditionally independent southwest into mainstream France. The campaign continued in the nineteenth century with moves to stamp out Occitan and other regional dialects.

From Napoleon I to the Third Republic

By the end of 1794, more moderate forces were in charge in Paris. However, continuous infighting left the way open for Napoleon Bonaparte, who had made a name for himself as commander of the Revolutionary armies in Italy and

1848–52	1868	1870	1907
The short-lived Second Republic ends with a coup d'état, establishing Louis Napoleon Bonaparte's Second Empire.	Phylloxera destroys vineyards.	Proclamation of the Third Republic, which will survive until 1940.	Wine Growers' Revolt in Bas Languedoc.

Egypt, to seize power in a coup d'état in 1799. Napoleon quickly restored order and continued the process of centralization, replacing the power of local institutions by appointing a *préfet* to each *département* answerable only to the emperor, as Napoleon declared himself in 1804.

Although popular in the southwest at first, it was the burden of the unceasing Napoleonic wars that eventually cost the emperor his support. The economy of Bordeaux in particular, and the southwest in general, was hard hit when Napoleon banned commerce with Britain, to which Britain responded by blockading French ports in 1807. In 1814 the Duke of Wellington marched on Bordeaux. Due to damages made throughout the Spanish Wars Bordeaux was ready to renounce Napoleon and declare loyalty to the Bourbon Monarchy, naming Louis XVIII's grand-nephew as the Duc de Bordeaux. Few tears were shed in the region when Napoleon was finally defeated in 1815. The subsequent restoration of the monarchy, on the other hand, saw opinions divided along predictable lines: the aristocracy and the emerging bourgeoisie (the middle classes) rallied to the king, while the working population supported the uprising in 1848 – a shorter and less virulent reprise of the 1789 Revolution – which ended in the declaration of the Second Republic. During this time Bordeaux prospered and evolved (the Pont de Pierre, the first bridge to cross the Garonne river, was built).

The new government started off well by setting up national workshops to relieve unemployment and extending the vote to all adult males – an unprecedented move for its time. But in elections held later in 1848 the largely conservative vote of the newly enfranchised peasants was sufficient to outweigh the urban, working-class radicals. To everyone's surprise, Louis-Napoleon, nephew of the former emperor, romped home. In spite of his liberal reputation, he restricted the vote again, censored the press and pandered to the Catholic Church. In 1852, following a coup and further street fighting, he had himself proclaimed Emperor Napoléon III.

Like his uncle, Napoléon III pursued an expansionist military policy, both in France's colonial empire and in Europe. And also like his uncle, this brought about his downfall. Napoléon III declared war on Prussia in 1870 and was quickly and roundly defeated by the far superior Prussian army. When Napoléon was taken prisoner the politicians in Paris – Cahors' Léon Gambetta among them – quickly proclaimed the Third Republic. Though it experienced a difficult birth, the Third Republic survived until 1940.

Into the twentieth century

Napoléon was more successful on the economic front, however. From the 1850s on, France experienced rapid industrial growth, while foreign trade trebled. The effect on the southwest, however, was mixed. The towns along the region's great rivers – notably Bordeaux – benefited most from the economic recovery. Although the region had no coal or mineral resources to stimulate large-scale industrialization, industries were established along the navigable rivers – tanneries, paper mills, textiles and glass industries. At the same time, agricultural areas within easy access of the rivers grew wealthy from exporting wheat, wine and tobacco. Many towns were given a facelift as their ramparts were torn down, wide avenues sliced through the cramped medieval

1939	1940
The Spanish Civil War ends with a mass emigration of defeated Republicans over the border into Southwest France. Outbreak of World War II.	On 22 June, an amnesty allows Nazi Germany to occupy northern and western France. The rest of the country is controlled by the Vichy government under Marshal Pétain.

quarters and a start was made on improving sanitation and water supply. Transport was also modernized and the region's first railway, the Bordeaux–Paris line, was completed in 1851.

All this created pockets of economic growth, but the rural areas in between became increasingly marginalized. Local industries dwindled in the face of competition from cheap manufactured goods and imports, while the railways simply provided the means for people to quit the country for the cities. But by far the biggest single crisis to hit the area's rural economy in the late nineteenth century was phylloxera. The parasite, which attacks the roots of vines, wiped out almost one third of the region's vineyards in the 1870s and 1880s. For a while growers tried all sorts of remedies, from flooding the fields to chemical fumigation, before it was discovered that vines in America, where phylloxera originated, were immune and that by grafting French vines onto American root-stock it was possible to produce resistant plants and the vineyards were slowly re-established.

The World Wars

Such problems paled into insignificance, however, when German troops marched into northern France following the outbreak of World War I in 1914. The French government fled south to Bordeaux while thousands of southern men trekked north to lose their lives in the mud and horror of Verdun and the Somme battlefields. By the time the Germans were forced to surrender in 1918, the cost to France was 1.3 million dead, a quarter of whom were under 25 years of age, and three million wounded. Every town and village in the southwest, as elsewhere in France, has its sad war memorial recording the loss of this generation of young men.

In the aftermath of the war, agricultural and industrial production declined and the birth rate plummeted, although this was offset to some extent in the southwest by an influx of land-hungry refugees from Spain in the late nineteenth century and from Italy in the first decades of the twentieth. The French government lurched from crisis to crisis while events across the border in Germany became increasingly menacing.

In April 1940, eight months after the outbreak of World War II, Hitler's western offensive began as he overran Belgium, Denmark and Holland. In June the French government retreated to Bordeaux again and millions of refugees poured south as Paris fell to the Germans. Maréchal Pétain, a conservative 84-year-old veteran of World War I, emerged from retirement to sign an armistice with Hitler and head the collaborationist Vichy government, based in the spa town of Vichy in the northern foothills of the Massif Central. France was now split in two. The Germans occupied the strategic regions north of the Loire and all along the Atlantic coast, including Bordeaux, while Vichy ostensibly governed the "Free Zone" comprising the majority of southern France. The frontier, with its customs points and guardposts, ran from the Pyrenees north through Langon and Castillon-la-Bataille to just south of Tours, and from there cut east to Geneva. Then, in 1942, German troops moved south to occupy the whole of France until they were driven out by Britain, America and their allies after 1944.

Resistance to the German occupation didn't really get going until 1943 when General de Gaulle, exiled leader of the "Free French", sent Jean Moulin to unify the disparate

1946–58	1957	1958	1972
Fourth Republic.	France is one of the original members of the European Economic Community (now the EU).	Fifth Republic is proclaimed.	France's 96 *départements* are grouped into 22 regions, including Aquitaine in the Southwest.

and often ideologically opposed Resistance groups. Moulin was soon captured by the Gestapo and tortured to death by Klaus Barbie – the infamous "Butcher of Lyon", who was convicted as recently as 1987 for his war crimes – but the network Moulin established became increasingly effective. Its members provided information to the Allies and blew up train tracks, bridges and factories. They undertook daring raids into enemy-held towns, but for every action, the Germans hit back with savage reprisals.

Soon afterwards the Germans were being driven out, but the fighting didn't stop there. In the weeks following liberation thousands of collaborators were executed or publicly humiliated – women accused of consorting with the enemy had their heads shaved and were sometimes paraded naked through the streets. Not surprisingly, the issue of collaboration left deep scars in rural communities throughout the region. During the following decades, Bordeaux underwent extensive redevelopment. The university and big new hospitals were built as were more bridges spanning the river and the city once again began to prosper. In 1995 Alain Juppé became Mayor of Bordeaux. He launched an ambitious plan to renovate and clean many of the historic buildings, introduce a public tram system, and transform the old town into a pedestrian area.

Into the millennium

The millennium sees the same issues that have dominated the last fifty years in the region remaining paramount. One of the main themes impacting the southwest, as in much of rural France, is that of depopulation as people flock to Bordeaux and other cities in search of greater opportunities. That said, over the past few years as fast internet and homeworking has become more common (not to mention the Covid-19 pandemic leading people to reassess their priorities) there has started to be a reversal of this rural-urban migration.

Agriculture remains the backbone of the region's economy, notably wine production but also poultry, maize, fruit, tobacco, fishing and forestry. Despite this, agricultural production is in slow decline as the younger generation gives up the battle to make a living through farming.

Besides agriculture and industry, tourism plays an increasingly important role in the regional economy. In recent years an enormous effort has gone into improving facilities, marketing the region and launching some show-stopping tourism projects, most notably the Cité du Vin and the surrounding dockland rejuvenation in Bordeaux.

Across France, however, the economy continues to be hampered by the seemingly perpetual stand-off between advocates of economic reform to liberalize markets and stimulate growth, and uncompromising defenders of the "French Model", with generous social allowances and high job security. Almost every section of society seems to have seen this debate come its way in recent years: from teachers to car manufacturers, employees in all industries have taken action to block any reforms which might erode their privileges. In the 2007 presidential election, it seemed as though momentum was swinging behind the arguments of the economic reformers, as former interior minister Nicolas Sarkozy, a member of the centre-right UMP party, was elected president having campaigned for a hard-line "rupture" with the French Model. In power, however, he only fitfully pursued a free-market agenda.

1990	2002	2007
Opening of high-speed Paris–Bordeaux rail link, the *train à grande vitesse* (TGV).	France adopts the euro.	In the presidential election, eleven of the eighteen départements of the Southwest back the losing candidate, socialist Ségolène Royal, against the winner Nicolas Sarkozy.

By 2012 the power pendulum had swung the other way, with the Socialists once again claiming massive victories in the polls and painting the southwest a sea of red. François Hollande was elected president, having promised to beat the recession by taxing wealthier citizens and larger corporations while separating risky investment banking enterprises from retail. He also promised to lower the retirement age from 62 to 60 and create 60,000 new teaching posts. All that renovation work that had taken place in Bordeaux over the previous decade or so paid off in 2007 when the city was given UNESCO World Heritage status on account of its well preserved historic central core and its long role as a place of cultural exchange.

2015 terrorist attacks and a political revolution

This was a particularly traumatic year for France, following a number of devastating terrorist incidents in the capital (although none in the southwest). In January, the Paris office of the satirical magazine *Charlie Hebdo* was attacked leaving twelve people (including eight staff members) dead, though this wasn't the first time the publication had been targeted by extremists; on this occasion a branch of Al Qaeda claimed responsibility. Then, in November a series of coordinated attacks across the capital left 130 dead, 90 of whom lost their lives at the Bataclan theatre whilst attending a concert – these were the deadliest attacks in western Europe since the Madrid train bombings in 2004.

It wasn't all bad news though and in 2015 Bordeaux was awarded 'Best European Destination' and is now one of the most visited cities in France. In the 2017 presidential elections, former Minister of Economy, Emmanuel Macron – who had founded the centrist/liberal leaning La République En Marche! party just a year earlier and was just 39 – triumphed handsomely in a second round run off against Marine Le Pen's National Front who managed to increase their vote share (from 2012) to 21 percent in the first round. Bordeaux and all of the southwest voted overwhelmingly for Macron. The honeymoon period for Macron didn't last long though, as France's youngest president since Napoleon continues to power on with his controversial programme of domestic reform. Whilst there was some brief respite in the form of the national football team's glorious World Cup victory in Moscow in July 2018 (the second in its history), further trouble lay ahead as the year drew to a close with the so-called gilets jaunes (Yellow Vests), a grassroots citizen's protest movement that was initially borne out of Macron's decision to raise taxes on fuel; this soon escalated into a wider anti-government movement, the result of which was some of the worst civil disorder France had witnessed for years.

France was hard hit by the Covid-19 pandemic and extremely strict lockdowns and curfews were imposed at various times throughout 2020–21. As in most countries the pandemic restrictions had a very severe economic impact.

The Presidential elections of April 2022 are a re-run of those of 2017 with Macron standing against Le Penn. Macron again won but with a reduced majority. Bordeaux and much of the rest of the southwest voted in favour of Macron. It should be said though that for many people, Macron, whose popularity had declined enormously over the five proceeding years, was considered the better of two bad choices. This time there was no honeymoon period for the president and in European elections in

2012	2015	2017
François Hollande defeats Sarkozy in closely fought presidential election	Series of Islamist terrorist shootings occur in different parts of France (though not the southwest).	Emmanuel Macron is elected French president.

2024 his party received a battering. Within hours of these results being announced and for reasons that remain baffling to many French (including, it's said, members of his own party), Macron called snap parliamentary elections. His party was soundly beaten into third place with the winners being an alliance of left-wing parties. However, no one party could claim a majority and a political deadlock ensued. Between January 2024 and December 2024, the country had four different Prime Ministers, a collapse of government and a rejected budget. Many voters held Macron personally responsible for the worst political crisis in decades. The next Presidential elections are due in 2027.

2018	2020-21	2024
France wins the World Cup. The anti-government movement *"gilets jaunes"* causes ongoing civil disorder.	The Covid-19 pandemic hits France hard. Extreme lockdowns and social restrictions imposed.	After his party receives a trouncing in European elections, President Macron calls a parliamentary election. No party wins a majority, the government collapses and France sees four PMs in a year.

Books

There are very few books in English dedicated only to Bordeaux or even just southwest France. However, there are a great many titles on France as a whole and which often include sections on the southwest or are otherwise relevant to the area. The most highly recommended books in this selection are marked by a ★ symbol.

HISTORY

GENERAL

Colin Jones *The Cambridge Illustrated History of France*. A political and social history of France from prehistoric times to the mid-1990s, concentrating on issues of regionalism, gender, race and class. Good illustrations and a friendly, non-academic writing style.

★ **Graham Robb** *The Discovery of France*. Captivating, brilliant study of France which makes a superb antidote to the usual narratives of kings and state affairs. With affection and insight, and in fine prose, Robb describes a France of vast wastes inhabited by "faceless millions" speaking mutually unintelligible dialects, and reveals how this France was gradually discovered and, inevitably, "civilized".

Robert Tombs & Isabelle Tombs *That Sweet Enemy: The British and the French from the Sun King to the Present*. A fascinating, original and mammoth study of a strangely intimate relationship. The authors are a French woman and her English husband, and they engage in lively debate between themselves. Covers society, culture and personalities, as well as politics.

THE MIDDLE AGES AND RENAISSANCE

Natalie Zemon Davis *The Return of Martin Guerre*. A vivid account of peasant life in the sixteenth century and a perplexing and titillating hoax in the Pyrenean village of Artigat.

★ **J.H. Huizinga** *The Waning of the Middle Ages*. Primarily a study of the culture of the Burgundian and French courts – but a masterpiece that goes far beyond this, building up meticulous detail to re-create the whole life and mentality of the fourteenth and fifteenth centuries.

R.J. Knecht *The French Renaissance Court*. The definitive work by a genuine authority. Not exactly a racy read, but successfully mixes high politics with sharp detail on life at court, backed up by plentiful illustrations.

Marion Meade *Eleanor of Aquitaine*. Highly accessible biography of one of the key characters in twelfth-century Europe. The author fleshes out the documented events until they read more like a historical novel.

Marina Warner *Joan of Arc*. Brilliantly places France's patron saint and national heroine within historical, spiritual and intellectual traditions.

★ **Alison Weir** *Eleanor of Aquitaine: By the wrath of God, Queen of England*. A magnificent medieval pot pourri of romantic events that vividly chronicles the extraordinary life of this fascinating woman. Contains some interesting photographs, including one of the effigy on Eleanor's tomb at Fontevraud abbey, the only verifiable image of her still in existence.

EIGHTEENTH AND NINETEENTH CENTURIES

Vincent Cronin *Napoleon*. An enthusiastic and engagingly written biography of France's emperor.

Christopher Hibbert *The French Revolution*. Well-paced and entertaining narrative treatment by a master historian.

★ **Lucy Moore** *Liberty: The Lives and Times of Six Women in Revolutionary France*. This original book follows the lives of six influential – and very different women – through the Revolution, taking in everything from sexual scandal to revolutionary radicalism.

Ruth Scurr *Fatal Purity: Robespierre and the French Revolution*. This myth-busting biography of the "remarkably odd" figure of the man they called The Incorruptible, and who went on to orchestrate the notorious Terror, ends up being one of the best books on the Revolution in general.

TWENTIETH CENTURY

Marc Bloch *Strange Defeat*. Moving personal study of the reasons for France's defeat and subsequent caving-in to fascism. Found among the papers of this Sorbonne historian after his death at the hands of the Gestapo in 1942.

Carmen Callil *Bad Faith: A Forgotten History of Family and Fatherland*. This quietly angry biography of the loathsome Louis Darquier, the Vichy state's Commissioner for Jewish Affairs, reveals the banality of viciousness in wartime France.

Jonathan Fenby *The General: Charles de Gaulle and the France he Saved*. This monumental but utterly readable biography does not always get under the famously private president's skin, but does show how de Gaulle not only shaped but embodied the ideals and ambitions of the postwar nation – or a certain, proudly, idealistically reactionary segment of it, at least.

Ian Ousby *Occupation: The Ordeal of France 1940–1944*.

Revisionist 1997 account which shows how relatively late resistance was, how widespread collaboration was, and why.
Robert Pike *Defying Vichy: Resistance in the Heart of South-West France*. Well-researched and fascinating look at the wartime resistance in the southwest of France.

Anne-Marie Walters *Moondrop to Gascony*. An absorbing and spine-tingling account of the real life of a secret agent in World War II; written in the immediate aftermath of the war, it reveals the naked courage of the French Resistance.

SOCIETY AND POLITICS

Julian Barnes *Something to Declare*. This journalistically highbrow collection of 18 essays on French culture – films, music, the Tour de France, and, of course, Flaubert – wears its French-style intellectualism on its sleeve, but succeeds in getting under the skin anyway.

Mary Blume *A French Affair: The Paris Beat 1965–1998*. Incisive and witty observations on contemporary French life by the *International Herald Tribune* reporter who was stationed there for three decades.

Jonathan Fenby *On the Brink*. While the country isn't perhaps quite as endangered as the title suggests, this provocative book takes a long, hard look at the problems facing contemporary France, from unemployment to corruption in its self-serving, self-selecting ruling class.

★ **Mark Girouard** *Life in the French Country House*. Girouard meticulously re-creates the social and domestic life that went on within the walls of French châteaux, starting with the great halls of early castles and ending with the commercial marriage venues of the twentieth century.

Tim Moore *French Revolutions: Cycling the Tour de France*. A whimsical bicycle journey along the route of the Tour by

a genuinely hilarious writer. Lots of witty asides on Tour history and French culture.

Charles Timoney *Pardon My French: Unleash Your Inner Gaul*. Incisive and often very droll dissection of contemporary culture through the words and phrases that the French use all the time. Looks and maybe sounds like a gift book, but it's rather brilliant.

Gillian Tindall *Célestine: Voices from a French Village*. Intrigued by some nineteenth-century love letters left behind in the house she bought in the Berry region, Tindall researches the history of the village back to the 1840s. A brilliant, warm-hearted piece of social history.

Lucy Wadham *The Secret Life of France*. Funny and perceptive insider view of the French, written by an expat who married one of them. Particularly good on women and female culture, and generally more intelligent than most in this genre.

Theodore Zeldin *The French*. A wise and original book that attempts to describe a country through the prism of the author's intensely personal conversations with a fascinating range of French people. Chapter titles include "How to be chic" and "How to appreciate a grandmother".

ART, ARCHITECTURE AND POETRY

André Chastel *French Art*. Authoritative, three-volume study by one of France's leading art historians. Discusses individual works of art in some detail – from architecture to tapestry, as well as painting – in an attempt to locate the Frenchness of French art. With glossy photographs and serious-minded but readable text.

★ **David Cairns** *Berlioz: The Making of an Artist 1803–1832*. The multiple-award-winning first volume of Cairns' two-part biography is more than just a life of the passionate French composer, it's an extraordinary evocation of post-Napoleonic France and its burgeoning Romantic culture.

Stephen Romer (editor) *20th-Century French Poems*. A collection of around 150 French poems spanning the whole of the century. Although there's no French text, many of the translations are works of art in themselves, consummately rendered by the likes of Samuel Beckett, T.S. Eliot and Paul Auster.

Rolf Toman (editor) *Romanesque: Architecture, Sculpture, Painting*. Huge, sumptuously illustrated volume of essays on every aspect of the genre across Europe, with one chapter specifically devoted to France.

GUIDES

Glynn Christian *Edible France*. A guide to food rather than restaurants: regional produce, local specialities, markets and best shops for buying goodies to bring back home. Dated, but still reliable for the provinces, if not Paris.

Philippe Dubois *Where to Watch Birds in France*. Maps, advice on when to go, habitat information, species' lists – everything you need.

David Hampshire *Living and Working in France*. An invaluable guide for anyone considering residence or work in France; packed with ideas and advice on job hunting, bureaucracy, tax, health and so on.

Rod Phillips *The Wines of South-West France*. Written by a true expert, this is a comprehensive guide to the rich wine culture of southwest France.

Jeanne Strang *Goose Fat and Garlic, Country Recipes from South-West France*. A huge store of traditional gastronomy from the old southwest. Strang lived and worked in the area for more than forty years.

Jeanne Strang *Magrets & Mushrooms: More Country Recipes from South-West France*. Who wouldn't want to recreate the fabulous food of the southwest when they return home? This well-regarded book shows you how.

French

French can be a deceptively familiar language because of the number of words and structures it shares with English. Despite this, it's far from easy, though the bare essentials are not difficult to master and can make all the difference. Even just saying "Bonjour Madame/Monsieur" and then gesticulating will often get you a smile and helpful service. People working in tourist offices, hotels and so on almost always speak English and tend to use it when you're struggling to speak French.

Pronunciation

One easy rule to remember is that **consonants** at the ends of words are usually silent: the most obvious example is Paris, pronounced "Paree", while the phrase *pas plus tard* (not later) sounds something like "pa-plu-tarr". The exception is when the following word begins with a vowel, in which case you generally run the two together: *pas après* (not after) becomes "pazaprey". Otherwise, consonants are much the same as in English, except that: *ch* is always "sh", *c* is "s", *h* is silent, *th* is the same as "t", and *r* is growled (or rolled). And to complicate things a little, *ll* after *i* usually sounds like the "y" in yes – though there are exceptions, including common words like *ville* (city), and *mille* (thousand). And *w* is "v", except when it's in a borrowed English word, like *le whisky* or *un weekend*.

Vowels are the hardest sounds to get exactly right, but they rarely differ enough from English to make comprehension a problem. The most obvious differences are that *au* sounds like the "o" in "over"; *aujourd'hui* (today) is thus pronounced "oh-jor-dwi". Another one to listen out for is *oi*, which sounds like "wa"; *toi* (to you) thus sounds like "twa". Lastly, adding "m" or "n" to a vowel, as in *en* or *un*, adds a nasal sound, as if you said just the vowel with a cold.

PHRASEBOOKS AND COURSES

Rough Guide French Phrasebook Mini dictionary-style phrasebook with both English–French and French–English sections, along with cultural tips, a menu reader and downloadable scenarios read by native speakers.

Breakthrough French One of the best teach-yourself courses, with three levels to choose from. Each comes with a book and CD-ROM.

The Complete Merde! The Real French You Were Never Taught at School More than just a collection of swearwords, this book is a passkey into everyday French, and a window into French culture.

Oxford Essential French Dictionary Very up-to-date French–English and English–French dictionary, with help on pronunciation and verbs, and links to free online products.

Michel Thomas A fast-paced and effective audio course that promises "No books. No writing. No memorizing", with an emphasis on spoken French, rather than conjugating verbs and sentence construction http://michelthomas.com.

Basic words and phrases

French nouns are divided into masculine and feminine. This causes difficulties with adjectives, whose endings have to change to suit the nouns they qualify – you can talk about *un château blanc* (a white castle), for example, but *une tour blanche* (a white tower). If you're not sure, stick to the simpler masculine form – as used in this glossary.

ESSENTIALS

hello (morning or afternoon) bonjour	**good night** bonne nuit
hello (evening) bonsoir	**goodbye** au revoir

thank you merci
please s'il vous plaît
sorry pardon/Je m'excuse
excuse me pardon
yes oui
no non
OK/agreed d'accord
help! au secours!
here ici
there là
this one ceci
that one celà
open ouvert
closed fermé
big grand
small petit

more plus
less moins
a little un peu
a lot beaucoup
inexpensive pas cher/bon marché
expensive cher
good bon
bad mauvais
hot chaud
cold froid
with avec
without sans
entrance entrée
exit sortie
man un homme
woman une femme (pronounced "fam")

NUMBERS

1 un
2 deux
3 trois
4 quatre
5 cinq
6 six
7 sept
8 huit
9 neuf
10 dix
11 onze
12 douze
13 treize
14 quatorze
15 quinze
16 seize
17 dix-sept
18 dix-huit
19 dix-neuf
20 vingt

21 vingt-et-un
22 vingt-deux
30 trente
40 quarante
50 cinquante
60 soixante
70 soixante-dix
75 soixante-quinze
80 quatre-vingts
90 quatre-vingt-dix
95 quatre-vingt-quinze
100 cent
101 cent-et-un
200 deux cents
300 trois cents
500 cinq cents
1000 mille
2000 deux mille
5000 cinq mille
1,000,000 un million

TIME

today aujourd'hui
yesterday hier
tomorrow demain
in the morning le matin
in the afternoon l'après-midi
in the evening le soir

now maintenant
later plus tard
at one o'clock à une heure
at three o'clock à trois heures
at ten thirty à dix heures et demie
at midday à midi

DAYS AND DATES

January janvier
February février
March mars
April avril
May mai
June juin

July juillet
August août
September septembre
October octobre
November novembre
December décembre

Sunday dimanche
Monday lundi
Tuesday mardi
Wednesday mercredi
Thursday jeudi
Friday vendredi

Saturday samedi
August 1 le premier août
March 2 le deux mars
July 14 le quatorze juillet
November 23 le vingt-trois novembre
2025 deux mille vingt-cinq

TALKING TO PEOPLE

When addressing people a simple *bonjour* is not enough; you should always use *Monsieur* for a man, *Madame* for a woman, *Mademoiselle* for a young woman or girl. This has its uses when you've forgotten someone's name or want to attract someone's attention. "Bonjour" can be used well into the afternoon, and people may start saying "bonsoir" surprisingly early in the evening, or as a way of saying goodbye.
Do you speak English? Parlez-vous anglais?
How do you say it in French? Comment ça se dit en français?
What's your name? Comment vous appelez-vous?
My name is … Je m'appelle …
I'm … Je suis …
… English … anglais[e]
… Irish … irlandais[e]
… Scottish … écossais[e]
… Welsh … gallois[e]

… American … américain[e]
… Australian …australien[ne]
… Canadian … canadien[ne]
… a New Zealander … néo-zélandais[e]
… South African … sud-africain[e]
I understand Je comprends
I don't understand Je ne comprends pas
Could you speak more slowly? S'il vous plaît, parlez moins vite
How are you? Comment allez-vous?/ Ça va?
Fine, thanks Très bien, merci
I don't know Je ne sais pas
Let's go Allons-y
See you tomorrow À demain
See you soon À bientôt
Leave me alone (aggressive) Laissez-moi tranquille
Please help me Aidez-moi, s'il vous plaît

FINDING THE WAY

bus autobus/bus/car
bus station gare routière
bus stop arrêt
car voiture
train/taxi/ferry train/taxi/bac or ferry
boat bâteau
plane avion
shuttle navette
train station gare (SNCF)
platform quai
What time does it leave? Il part à quelle heure?
What time does it arrive? Il arrive à quelle heure?
a ticket to … un billet pour …
single ticket aller simple
return ticket aller retour
validate/stamp your ticket compostez votre billet
valid for valable pour
ticket office vente de billets
how many kilometres? combien de kilomètres?
how many hours? combien d'heures?
hitchhiking autostop
on foot à pied
Where are you going? Vous allez où?
I'm going to … Je vais à …

I want to get off at … Je voudrais descendre à …
the road to … la route pour …
near près/pas loin
far loin
left à gauche
right à droite
straight on tout droit
on the other side of à l'autre côté de
on the corner of à l'angle de
next to à côté de
behind derrière
in front of devant
before avant
after après
under sous
to cross traverser
bridge pont
town centre centre ville
all through roads (road sign) toutes directions
other destinations (road sign) autres directions
upper town ville haute/haute ville
lower town ville basse/basse ville
old town vieille ville

QUESTIONS AND REQUESTS

The simplest way of asking a question is to start with *s'il vous plaît* (please), then name the thing you want in an interrogative tone of voice. For example:

Where is there a bakery? S'il vous plaît, où est la boulangerie?

Which way is it to the Eiffel Tower? S'il vous plaît, la route pour la Tour Eiffel?

Can we have a room for two? S'il vous plaît, une chambre pour deux?

Can I have a kilo of oranges? S'il vous plaît, un kilo d'oranges?

QUESTION WORDS

where? où?
how? comment?
how many/how much? combien?
when? quand?

why? pourquoi?
at what time? à quelle heure?
what is/which is? quel est?

ACCOMMODATION

a room for one/two persons une chambre pour une/deux personne(s)
a double bed un grand lit/ un lit matrimonial
a room with two single beds/twin une chambre à deux lits
a room with a shower une chambre avec douche
a room with a bath une chambre avec salle de bain
for one/two/three nights pour une/deux/trois nuits
Can I see it? Je peux la voir?
a room on the courtyard une chambre sur la cour
a room over the street une chambre sur la rue
first floor premier étage
second floor deuxième étage
with a view avec vue
key clé
to iron repasser
do laundry faire la lessive
sheets draps

blankets couvertures
quiet calme
noisy bruyant
hot water eau chaude
cold water eau froide
Is breakfast included? Est-ce que le petit-déjeuner est compris?
I would like breakfast Je voudrais prendre le petit-déjeuner
I don't want breakfast Je ne veux pas le petit-déjeuner
bed and breakfast chambres d'hôtes
Can we camp here? On peut camper ici?
campsite camping/terrain de camping
tent tente
tent space emplacement
hostel foyer
youth hostel auberge de jeunesse

DRIVING

service station garage
service service
to park the car garer la voiture
car park un parking
no parking défense de stationner/ stationnement interdit
petrol/gas station station d'essence
fuel essence
unleaded sans plomb
leaded super
diesel gazole

oil huile
air line ligne à air
put air in the tyres gonfler les pneus
battery batterie
the battery is dead la batterie est morte
plug (for appliance) prise
to break down tomber en panne
petrol can bidon
insurance assurance
green card carte verte
traffic lights feux rouges

HEALTH MATTERS

doctor médecin
I don't feel well Je ne me sens pas bien
medicines médicaments
prescription ordonnance
I feel sick Je suis malade
I have a headache J'ai mal à la tête
stomach ache mal à l'estomac
period règles

SIGN LANGUAGE

Défense de … It is forbidden to …
Fermé closed
Ouvert open
Rez-de-chaussée (RC) ground floor
Sortie exit

pain douleur
it hurts ça fait mal
chemist/pharmacist pharmacie
hospital hôpital

condom préservatif
morning-after pill/emergency contraceptive pilule du lendemain
I'm allergic to … Je suis allergique à …

OTHER NEEDS

bakery boulangerie
food shop alimentation
delicatessen charcuterie, traiteur
cake shop pâtisserie
cheese shop fromagerie
supermarket supermarché
to eat manger
to drink boire
tasting, eg wine dégustation, tasting
camping gas camping gaz

tobacconist tabac
stamps timbres
bank banque
money argent
toilets toilettes
police police
telephone téléphone
cinema cinéma
theatre théâtre
to reserve/book réserver

RESTAURANT PHRASES

I'd like to reserve a table for two people, at eight thirty Je voudrais réserver une table pour deux personnes à vingt heures trente
I'm having the €30 set menu Je prendrai le menu à trente euros

Waiter! (never "garçon") Monsieur/Madame!/ s'il vous plaît!
the bill/check please l'addition, s'il vous plaît

Food and dishes

BASIC TERMS

l'addition bill/check
beurre butter
bio or biologique organic
bouteille bottle
carafe d'eau jug of water
la carte the menu
chauffé heated
couteau knife
cru raw
cuillère spoon
cuit cooked
emballé wrapped
à emporter takeaway
entrée starter
formule lunchtime set menu
fourchette fork
fumé smoked
gazeuse fizzy
lait milk
le menu set menu
moutarde mustard
oeuf egg
offert free
pain bread
pimenté spicy
plat main course

poivre pepper
salé salted/savoury
sel salt
sucre sugar
sucré sweet
table table
verre glass
vinaigre vinegar

SNACKS

un sandwich/ une baguette a sandwich
…jambon beurre with ham and butter
…au fromage with cheese, no butter
…mixte with ham and cheese
…au pâté (de campagne) with pâté (country-style)
croque monsieur grilled cheese and ham sandwich
panini toasted Italian sandwich
tartine buttered bread or open sandwich, often with jam
oeufs eggs **au plat** fried **à la coque** boiled **durs** hard-boiled
…brouillés scrambled
…nature plain
…aux fines herbes with herbs
…au fromage with cheese
omelette omelette

salade de tomates tomato salad
salade verte green salad

PASTA (PÂTES), PANCAKES (CRÊPES), TARTES AND COUSCOUS

nouilles noodles
pâtes fraîches fresh pasta
crêpe au sucre/ aux oeufs pancake with sugar/ eggs
galette buckwheat pancake
pissaladière tart of fried onions with anchovies and black olives
tarte flambée thin pizza-like pastry topped with onion, cream and bacon
couscous steamed semolina grains, usually served with meat or veg, chickpea stew and chilli sauce
couscous royal couscous with spicy merguez sausage, chicken and beef or lamb kebabs

SOUPS (SOUPES)

bisque shellfish soup
bouillabaisse soup with five fish
bouillon broth or stock
bourride thick fish soup
consommé clear soup
garbure potato, cabbage and meat soup
pistou parmesan, basil and garlic paste added to soup
potage thick vegetable soup
potée auvergnate cabbage and meat soup
rouille red pepper, garlic and saffron mayonnaise served with fish soup
soupe à l'oignon onion soup with a rich cheese topping
velouté thick soup, usually fish or poultry

STARTERS (HORS D'OEUVRES)

assiette de charcuterie plate of cold meats
assiette composée mixed salad plate, usually cold meat and veg
crudités dressed raw vegetables
hors d'oeuvres combination of the above often with smoked or marinated fish

FISH (POISSON), SEAFOOD (FRUITS DE MER) AND SHELLFISH (CRUSTACÉS OR COQUILLAGES)

anchois anchovies
anguilles eels
barbue brill
baudroie monkfish or anglerfish
bigorneau periwinkle
brème bream
cabillaud cod
calmar squid
carrelet plaice

claire type of oyster
colin hake
congre conger eel
coques cockles
coquilles St-Jacques scallops
crabe crab
crevettes grises shrimp
crevettes roses prawns
daurade sea bream
éperlan smelt or whitebait
escargots snails
flétan halibut
friture assorted fried fish, often like whitebait
gambas king prawns
hareng herring
homard lobster
huîtres oysters
langouste spiny lobster
langoustines saltwater crayfish (scampi)
limande lemon sole
lotte de mer monkfish
loup de mer sea bass
maquereau mackerel
merlan whiting
moules (marinières) mussels (with shallots in white wine sauce)
oursin sea urchin
palourdes clams
poissons de roche fish from shoreline rocks
praires small clams
raie skate
rouget red mullet
saumon salmon
sole sole
thon tuna
truite trout
turbot turbot
violet sea squirt

FISH DISHES AND TERMS

aïoli garlic mayonnaise
anchoïade anchovy paste or sauce
arête fish bone
assiette de pêcheur assorted fish
beignet fritter
darne fillet or steak
la douzaine a dozen
frit fried
friture deep-fried small fish
fumé smoked
fumet fish stock
gigot de mer large fish baked whole
grillé grilled
hollandaise butter and vinegar sauce

à la meunière in a butter, lemon and parsley sauce
mousse/mousseline mousse
pané breaded
poutargue mullet roe paste
quenelles light dumplings

MEAT (VIANDE) AND POULTRY (VOLAILLE)

agneau (de pré-salé) lamb (grazed on salt marshes)
andouille cold pork and tripe sausage
andouillette hot, cooked tripe sausage
bavette flank-like steak
boeuf beef
boudin blanc sausage of white meats
boudin noir black pudding
caille quail
canard duck
caneton duckling
contrefilet sirloin roast
coquelet cockerel
la cuisson? how would sir/ madam like his/her steak done?
...bleu almost raw
...saignant rare
...à point medium rare
...bien cuit well done
...très bien cuit ruined
dinde/dindon turkey
entrecôte rib steak
faux filet sirloin steak
foie liver
foie gras (duck/goose) liver
gibier game
gigot (d'agneau) leg (of lamb)
grenouille (cuisses de) frogs' (legs)
langue tongue
lapin/lapereau rabbit/young rabbit
lard/lardons bacon/diced bacon
lièvre hare
merguez spicy, red sausage
mouton mutton
museau de veau calf's muzzle
oie goose
onglet tasty, flank-like steak
os bone
poitrine breast
porc pork
poulet chicken
poussin baby chicken
rillettes pork mashed with lard and liver
ris sweetbreads
rognons kidneys
rognons blancs testicles
sanglier wild boar
steak steak

tête de veau calf's head (in jelly)
tournedos thick slices of fillet
tripes tripe
tripoux mutton tripe
veau veal
venaison venison

MEAT AND POULTRY DISHES AND TERMS

aïado roast shoulder of lamb stuffed with garlic and other ingredients
aile wing
blanquette, daube, types of stew **estouffade, hochepôt, navarin, ragoût**
blanquette de veau veal in cream and mushroom sauce
boeuf bourguignon beef stew with Burgundy, onions and mushrooms
brochette kebab
carré best end of neck, chop or cutlet
cassoulet casserole of beans, sausages and duck/goose
choucroute sauerkraut with peppercorns, sausages, pork and ham
civet game stew
confit meat preserve
coq au vin chicken slow-cooked with wine, onions and mushrooms
côte chop, cutlet or rib
cuisse thigh or leg
en croûte in pastry
épaule shoulder
farci stuffed
au feu de bois cooked over wood fire
au four baked
garni with vegetables
gésier gizzard
grillade grilled meat
grillé grilled
hâchis chopped meat or mince hamburger
magret de canard duck breast
marmite casserole
médaillon round piece
mijoté stewed
pavé thick slice
pieds et paques mutton or pork tripe and trotters
poêlé pan-fried
poulet de Bresse chicken from Bresse
râble saddle
rôti roast
sauté lightly fried in butter
steak au poivre (vert/rouge) steak in a black peppercorn sauce (green/red peppercorn)
steak tartare raw chopped beef, topped with a raw egg yolk

tagine North African casserole
viennoise fried in egg and bread crumbs

GARNISHES AND SAUCES

américaine sauce of white wine, cognac and tomato
auvergnate with cabbage, sausage and bacon
béarnaise sauce of egg yolks, white wine, shallots and
  vinegar
beurre blanc sauce of white wine and shallots, with
  butter
bonne femme with mushroom, bacon, potato and
  onions
bordelaise in a red wine, shallot and bone-marrow
  sauce
boulangère baked with potatoes and onions
bourgeoise with carrots, onions, bacon, celery and
  braised lettuce
chasseur sauce of white wine, mushrooms and shallots
châtelaine with artichoke hearts and chestnut purée
diable strong mustard seasoning
façon in the style of …
forestière with bacon and mushroom
fricassée rich, creamy sauce
mornay cheese sauce
pays d'auge cream and cider
périgourdine sauce with foie gras and possibly truffles
piquante with gherkins or capers, vinegar and shallots
provençale sauce of tomatoes, garlic, olive oil and
  herbs
savoyarde with gruyère cheese

VEGETABLES (LÉGUMES), GRAINS (FÉCULENTS), HERBS (HERBES) AND SPICES (ÉPICES)

ail garlic
anis aniseed
artichaut artichoke
asperge asparagus
avocat avocado
basilic basil
betterave beetroot
blette/bette Swiss chard
cannelle cinnamon
capre caper
cardon cardoon
carotte carrot
céleri celery
champignons, cèpes, mushrooms **ceps, girolles,**
  chanterelles, pleurotes
chou (rouge) (red) cabbage
choufleur cauliflower
concombre cucumber
cornichon gherkin
échalotes shallots

endive chicory
épinards spinach
estragon tarragon
fenouil fennel
fèves broad beans
flageolets flageolet beans
gingembre ginger
haricots beans
...verts green beans
...rouges kidney beans
laurier bay leaf
lentilles lentils
maïs maize (corn)
menthe mint
moutarde mustard
oignon onion
panais parsnip
persil parsley
petits pois peas
piment rouge/vert red/green chilli pepper
pois chiche chickpeas
pois mange-tout mange-tout
pignons pine nuts
poireau leek
poivron (vert, rouge) sweet pepper (green, red)
pommes de terre potatoes
primeurs spring vegetables
radis radish
riz rice
safran saffron
sarrasin buckwheat
thym thyme
tomate tomato
truffes truffles

VEGETABLE DISHES AND TERMS

à l'anglaise boiled
beignet fritter
duxelles fried mushrooms and shallots with cream
farci stuffed
feuille leaf
fines herbes mixture of tarragon, parsley and chives
gratiné browned with cheese or butter
à la grecque cooked in oil and lemon
jardinière with mixed diced vegetables
mousseline mashed potato with cream and eggs
à la parisienne sautéed potatoes, with white wine and
  shallot sauce
parmentier with potatoes
petits farcis stuffed tomatoes, aubergines, courgettes
  and peppers
râpée grated or shredded
à la vapeur steamed
en verdure garnished with green vegetables

FRUIT (FRUIT) AND NUTS (NOIX)

abricot apricot
amande almond
ananas pineapple
banane banana
brugnon, nectarine nectarine
cacahouète peanut
cassis blackcurrant
cerise cherry
citron lemon
citron vert lime
datte date
figue fig
fraise (des bois) strawberry (wild)
framboise raspberry
fruit de la passion passion fruit
grenade pomegranate
groseille redcurrant
mangue mango
marron chestnut (also **châtaigne**)
melon melon
mirabelle small yellow plum
myrtille bilberry
noisette hazelnut
noix walnuts; nuts
noix de cajou cashew nut
orange orange
pamplemousse grapefruit
pastèque watermelon
pêche peach
pistache pistachio
poire pear
pomme apple
prune plum
pruneau prune
raisin grape
reine-claude greengage

FRUIT DISHES AND TERMS

agrumes citrus fruits
beignet fritter
compôte stewed fruit
coulis sauce of puréed fruit
crème de marrons chestnut purée
flambé set aflame in alcohol
frappé iced

DESSERTS (DESSERTS), PASTRIES (GÂTEAUX/VIENNOISERIES) AND CHEESES (FROMAGES)

brebis sheep's milk cheese
bombe moulded ice-cream dessert
brioche sweet breakfast roll
charlotte custard and fruit in a lining of almond biscuits or sponge
chèvre goat's cheese
clafoutis almond and cherry desert
crème Chantilly vanilla-flavoured and sweetened whipped cream
crème fraîche sour cream
crème pâtissière thick, eggy pastry-filling
crêpe suzette thin pancake with orange juice and liqueur
fromage blanc cream cheese
gaufre waffle
glace ice cream
Île flottante/oeufs à la neige whipped egg-white floating on custard
macaron macaroon
madeleine small sponge cake
marrons Mont Blanc chestnut purée and cream on a rum-soaked sponge cake
palmier caramelized puff pastry
parfait frozen mousse, sometimes ice cream
petit-suisse a smooth mixture of cream and curds
petits fours bite-sized cakes/ pastries
plâteau de fromages cheeseboard
poires belle hélène pears and ice cream in chocolate sauce
tarte tatin upside-down apple tart
yaourt/yogourt yoghurt

Glossary of architectural terms

These are either terms you'll come across throughout this book, or while travelling around.

abbaye abbey

ambulatory passage round the outer edge of the choir of a church

apse semicircular termination at the east end of a church

Baroque mainly seventeenth-century style of art and architecture, distinguished by ornate classicism

basse ville/ville basse lower town

bastide walled town

capital carved top of a column

Carolingian dynasty (and art, sculpture etc) named after Charlemagne; mid-eighth to early tenth centuries

château mansion, country house, castle

château fort castle

chevet east end of a church

choir the eastern part of a church between the altar and nave, used by the choir and clergy

classical architectural style incorporating Greek and Roman elements: pillars, domes, colonnades, etc, at its height in France in the seventeenth century and revived, as Neoclassical, in the nineteenth century

clerestory upper storey of a church, incorporating the windows

cloître cloister

donjon castle keep

église church

flamboyant florid, late (c.1450–1540) form of Gothic

Gallo-Roman from the Roman era in France

Gothic late medieval architectural style characterized by pointed arches, verticality and light

haute ville/ville haute upper town

hôtel (particulier) mansion or townhouse

Merovingian dynasty ruling France and parts of Germany (and associated art etc) from sixth to mid-eighth centuries

narthex entrance hall of church

nave main body of a church

porte gateway

Renaissance classically influenced art/architectural style imported from Italy to France in the early sixteenth century

retable altarpiece

Roman Romanesque (easily confused with Romain, which means Roman)

Romanesque early medieval architecture distinguished by squat, rounded forms and naive sculpture, called Norman in Britain

stucco plaster used to embellish ceilings etc

tour tower

transepts transverse arms of a church

tympanum sculpted panel above a church door

voussoir wedge-shaped stones used in an arch or vault

Small print and index

ABOUT THE AUTHORS

Stuart Butler is a guidebook author, writer and award-winning photographer who has written multiple guidebooks on France. He also writes about Spain, East Africa (where he is the tourism manager of a wildlife conservancy), the Himalayas and South Asia. He lives with his wife and children in the far southwest of France and when not working can be found surfing on the beautiful beaches of Les Landes or hiking in the gorgeous Pyrenees.

Owen Morton is never happier than when exploring new places, with a particular fondness for wandering the former Soviet world and the Middle East. He is the author of numerous guidebooks, including The Rough Guide to Georgia, Armenia and Azerbaijan, The Pocket Rough Guide to Pembrokeshire and The Pocket Rough Guide to Orkney, as well as updates to guides to other destinations ranging from Jordan to the Philippines. His favourite animal is the wonderfully expressive and permanently furious manul. Follow him on Instagram at @ owenmortonmanul.

A ROUGH GUIDE TO ROUGH GUIDES

Published in 1982, the first Rough Guide – to Greece – was a student scheme that became a publishing phenomenon. Mark Ellingham, a recent graduate in English from Bristol University, had been travelling in Greece the previous summer and couldn't find the right guidebook. With a small group of friends he wrote his own guide, combining a contemporary, journalistic style with a thoroughly practical approach to travellers' needs.

The immediate success of the book spawned a series that rapidly covered dozens of destinations. And, in addition to impecunious backpackers, Rough Guides soon acquired a much broader readership that relished the guides' wit and inquisitiveness as much as their enthusiastic, critical approach and value-for-money ethos. These days, Rough Guides include recommendations from budget to luxury and cover more than 120 destinations around the globe, from Amsterdam to Zanzibar, all regularly updated by our team of roaming writers.

Browse all our latest guides, read inspirational features and book your trip at **roughguides.com**.

Rough Guide credits

Editor: Kate Drynan
Cartography: Carte
Picture Editor: Piotr Kala
Picture Manager: Tom Smyth
Layout: Pradeep Thapliyal
Publishing Technology Manager: Rebeka Davies
Production Operations Manager: Katie Bennett
Head of Publishing: Sarah Clark

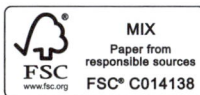

MIX
Paper from
responsible sources
FSC
www.fsc.org
FSC® C014138

Publishing information

First edition 2025

Distribution

UK, Ireland and Europe
Apa Publications (UK) Ltd; mail@roughguides.com
United States and Canada
Two Rivers; ips@ingramcontent.com
Australia and New Zealand
Woodslane; info@woodslane.com.au
Worldwide
Apa Publications (UK) Ltd; mail@roughguides.com

Special Sales, Content Licensing and CoPublishing
Rough Guides can be purchased in bulk quantities
at discounted prices. We can create special editions,
personalized jackets and corporate imprints tailored to
your needs. mail@roughguides.com.

roughguides.com

EU Representative
LOGOS EUROPE, 9 rue Nicolas Poussin, 17000,
LA ROCHELLE, France; Contact@logoseurope.eu;
+33 (0) 667937378

Printed by Finidr in Czech Republic

ISBN: 9781835292266

This book was produced using **Typefi** automated
publishing software.

A catalogue record for this book is available from the
British Library.

Help us update

We've gone to a lot of effort to ensure that this edition of
The Rough Guide to Bordeaux is accurate and up-to-
date. However, things change – places get "discovered",
transport routes are altered, restaurants and hotels raise
prices or lower standards, and businesses cease trading. If
you feel we've got it wrong or left something out, we'd like
to know, and if you can direct us to the web address, so
much the better.

Please send your comments with the subject line
"**Rough Guide Bordeaux Update**" to mail@roughguides.
com. We'll send a copy of the next edition (or any other
Rough Guide if you prefer) for the very best emails.

Acknowledgements

Many thanks to the Région Nouvelle Aquitaine Regional Tourism Board, Aurélie Lascourreges and Vera Louro at Cité du
Vin, Karen Bon at Dordogne Valley, Katia Veyret at Saral Tourisme, and to all the team in-house and out who helped to put
this first edition together.

Photo credits
(Key: T-top; C-centre; B-bottom; L-left; R-right)

All images **Shutterstock**

Cover: The Grosse Cloche **Shutterstock**

Index

YOUR TAILOR-MADE TRIP
STARTS HERE

Tailor-made trips and unique adventures crafted by local experts

Rough Guides has been inspiring travellers with lively and thought-provoking guidebooks for more than 35 years. Now we're linking you up with selected local experts to craft your dream trip. They will put together your perfect itinerary and book it at local rates.

Don't follow the crowd – find your own path.

HOW ROUGHGUIDES.COM/TRIPS WORKS

STEP 1
Pick your dream destination, tell us what you want and submit an enquiry.

STEP 2
Fill in a short form to tell your local expert about your dream trip and preferences.

STEP 3
Our local expert will craft your tailor-made itinerary. You'll be able to tweak and refine it until you're completely satisfied.

STEP 4
Book online with ease, pack your bags and enjoy the trip! Our local expert will be on hand 24/7 while you're on the road.

BENEFITS OF PLANNING AND BOOKING AT ROUGHGUIDES.COM/TRIPS

PLAN YOUR ADVENTURE WITH LOCAL EXPERTS

Rough Guides' English-speaking local experts are hand-picked, based on their experience in the travel industry and their impeccable standards of customer service.

SAVE TIME AND GET ACCESS TO LOCAL KNOWLEDGE

When a local expert plans your trip, you save time and money when you book, even during high season. You won't be charged for using a credit card either.

MAKE TRAVEL A BREEZE: BOOK WITH PEACE OF MIND

Enjoy stress-free travel when you use Rough Guides' secure online booking platform. All bookings come with a money-back guarantee.

WHAT DO OTHER TRAVELLERS THINK ABOUT ROUGH GUIDES TRIPS?

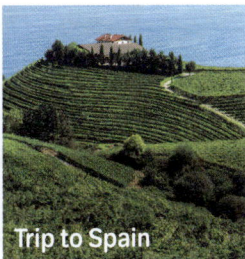

Trip to Spain

This Spain tour company did a fantastic job to make our dream trip perfect. We gave them our travel budget, told them where we would like to go, and they did all of the planning. Our drivers and tour guides were always on time and very knowledgable. The hotel accommodations were better than we would have found on our own. Only one time did we end up in a location that we had not intended to be in. We called the 24 hour phone number, and they immediately fixed the situation.

Don A, USA ★★★★★

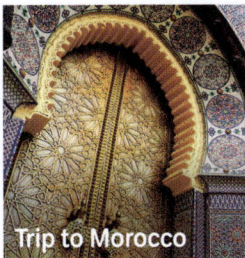

Trip to Morocco

Our trip was fantastic! Transportation, accommodations, guides – all were well chosen! The hotels were well situated, well appointed and had helpful, friendly staff. All of the guides we had were very knowledgeable, patient, and flexible with our varied interests in the different sites. We particularly enjoyed the side trip to Tangier! Well done! The itinerary you arranged for us allowed maximum coverage of the country with time in each city for seeing the important places.

Sharon, USA ★★★★★

Map symbols

The symbols below are used on maps throughout the book

– – –	Chapter division boundary	✉	Post office	⌒	Sand dune
	Motorway	ⓘ	Tourist office	🗼	Lighthouse
	Major road	⊙	Statue		Beach
	Minor road	✸	Viewpoint	♣	Vineyard
	Pedestrian road	∴	Archaeological site		Building
	Railway	P	Parking	→	Church/cathedral
	Ferry route	✚	Hospital		Market
–Ⓐ–	Tram	✡	Synagogue		Christian cemetery
	Hiking trail	♜	Chateau		Park
✈	Airport	♜	Fort		

Listings key

- ■ Accommodation
- ● Eating
- ■ Drinking/nightlife
- ● Shopping

City plan

The **city plan** on the pages that follow is divided as shown:

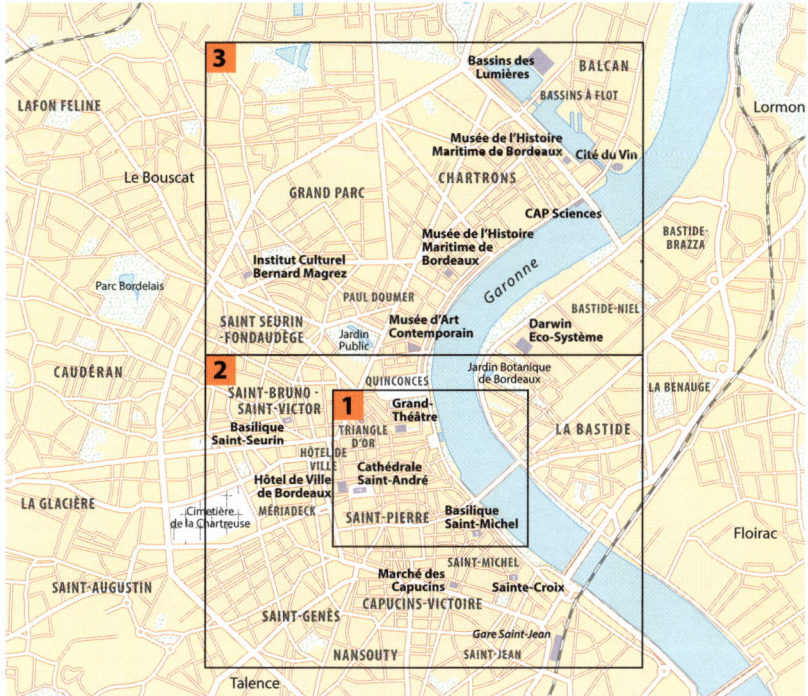

LAFON FELINE

3

Bassins des
Lumières

BALCAN

BASSINS À FLOT

Lormon

Le Bouscat

GRAND PARC

Musée de l'Histoire
Maritime de Bordeaux

Cité du Vin

CHARTRONS

CAP Sciences

BASTIDE-
BRAZZA

Musée de l'Histoire
Maritime de
Bordeaux

Institut Culturel
Bernard Magrez

Garonne

Parc Bordelais

PAUL DOUMER

BASTIDE-NIEL

SAINT-SEURIN
-FONDAUDÈGE

Jardin
Public

Musée d'Art
Contemporain

Darwin
Eco-Système

CAUDÉRAN

2

Jardin Botanique
de Bordeaux

QUINCONCES

LA BENAUGE

SAINT-BRUNO -
SAINT-VICTOR

1

Grand-
Théâtre

LA BASTIDE

Basilique
Saint-Seurin

TRIANGLE
D'OR

HÔTEL DE
VILLE

Cathédrale
Saint-André

LA GLACIÈRE

Hôtel de Ville
de Bordeaux

MÉRIADECK

Cimetière
de la Chartreuse

SAINT-PIERRE

Basilique
Saint-Michel

Floirac

SAINT-AUGUSTIN

Marché des
Capucins

SAINT-MICHEL

Sainte-Croix

SAINT-GENÈS

CAPUCINS-VICTOIRE

Gare Saint-Jean

NANSOUTY

SAINT-JEAN

Talence

1

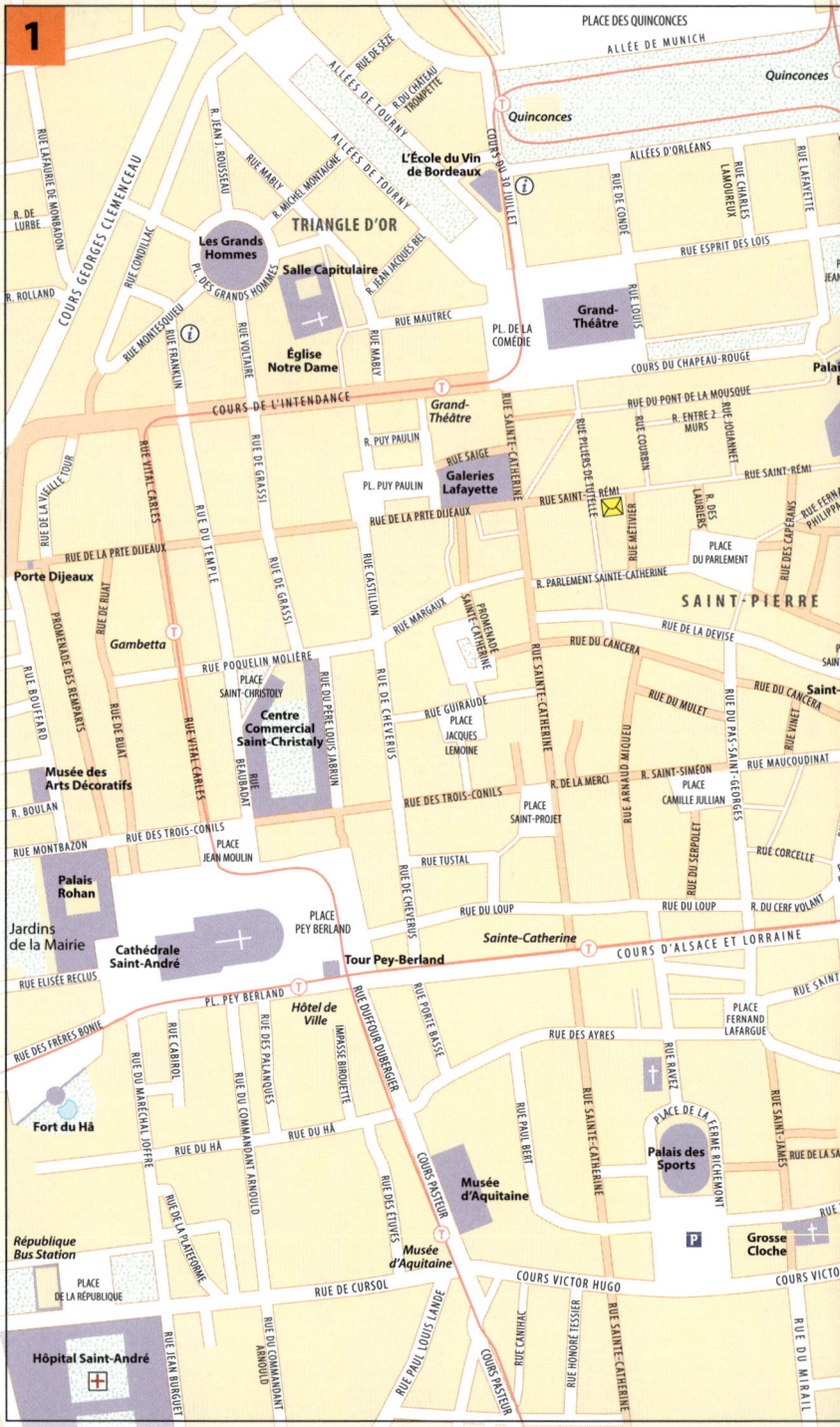

PLACE DES QUINCONCES

ALLÉE DE MUNICH

Quinconces

RUE DE SÈZE

ALLÉES DE TOURNY

R. DU CHATEAU TROMPETTE

Quinconces

COURS DU 30 JUILLET

ALLÉES D'ORLÉANS

RUE DE CONDÉ

RUE CHARLES LAMOUREUX

RUE LAFAYETTE

RUE JEAN J. ROUSSEAU

RUE MARLY

ALLÉES DE TOURNY

L'École du Vin de Bordeaux (i)

RUE ESPRIT DES LOIS

RUE LAFAYETTE

R. DE LURBE

RUE LAFAURIE DE MONBADON

COURS GEORGES CLEMENCEAU

R. MICHEL MONTAIGNE

TRIANGLE D'OR

RUE CONDILLAC

Les Grands Hommes

Salle Capitulaire

PL. DES GRANDS HOMMES

R. JEAN JACQUES BEL

Grand-Théâtre

COURS DU CHAPEAU-ROUGE

JEAN

R. ROLLAND

RUE MONTESQUIEU

RUE VOLTAIRE

RUE MAUTREC

PL. DE LA COMÉDIE

RUE LOUIS

Palai E

RUE FRANKLIN (i)

Église Notre Dame

RUE MARLY

RUE DU PONT DE LA MOUSQUE

R. ENTRE 2 MURS

RUE JOUANNET

COURS DE L'INTENDANCE

Grand-Théâtre (T)

RUE SAINTE-CATHERINE

RUE PILIERS DE TUTELLE

R. COURBIN

RUE SAINT-RÉMI

RUE DE LA VIEILLE TOUR

RUE VITAL CARLES

R. PUY PAULIN

RUE DE GRASSI

RUE SAIGE

PL. PUY PAULIN

Galeries Lafayette

RUE SAINT-

RÉMI

RUE FERNA

PHILIPPA

RUE DE LA PRTE DIJEAUX

R. DES LAURIERS

RUE DES CAPERANS

RUE DE RUAT

RUE DE LA PRTE DIJEAUX

RUE DU TEMPLE

RUE CASTILLON

RUE DE GRASSI

PLACE DU PARLEMENT

Porte Dijeaux

R. PARLEMENT SAINTE-CATHERINE

PROMENADE DES REMPARTS

Gambetta (T)

RUE MARGAUX

PROMENADE SAINTE-CATHERINE

SAINT-PIERRE

RUE DE LA DEVISE

P SAIN

RUE POQUELIN MOLIÈRE

PLACE SAINT-CHRISTOLY

RUE DE CHEVERUS

RUE SAINTE-CATHERINE

RUE DU CANCERA

RUE DU MULET

RUE DU CANCERA

Saint

RUE BOUFFARD

RUE DE RUAT

RUE VITAL CARLES

RUE DU PÈRE LOUIS JABRUN

Centre Commercial Saint-Christaly

RUE GUIRAUDE

PLACE JACQUES LEMOINE

RUE DU PAS-SAINT-GEORGES

RUE VINET

RUE ARNAUD MIQUEU

RUE MAUCOUDINAT

Musée des Arts Décoratifs

RUE BEAUBADAT

R. DE LA MERCI

R. SAINT-SIMÉON

PLACE CAMILLE JULLIAN

R. BOULAN

RUE DES TROIS-CONILS

RUE DES TROIS-CONILS

PLACE SAINT-PROJET

RUE DU SERPOLET

RUÉ CORCELLE

RUE MONTBAZON

PLACE JEAN MOULIN

RUE TUSTAL

Palais Rohan

RUE DE CHEVERUS

RUE DU LOUP

RUE DU LOUP

R. DU CERF VOLANT

Jardins de la Mairie

PLACE PEY BERLAND

Cathédrale Saint-André

Sainte-Catherine (T)

COURS D'ALSACE ET LORRAINE

RUE ÉLISÉE RECLUS

Tour Pey-Berland

RUE SAINT

PL. PEY BERLAND

Hôtel de Ville

RUE DUFFOUR DUBERGIER

RUE PORTE BASSE

PLACE FERNAND LAFARGUE

RUE DES FRERES BONIE

RUE CABIROL

RUE DU MARÉCHAL JOFFRE

RUE DES PALANQUES

IMPASSE BIROUETTE

RUE DES AYRES

RUE RAVEZ

RUE SAINTE-CATHERINE

RUE SAINT-JAMES

Fort du Hâ

RUE DU COMMANDANT ARNOULD

RUE DU HÂ

RUE PAUL BERT

PLACE DE LA FERME RICHEMONT

RUE DE LA SA

RUE DU HÂ

RUE DE LA PLATEFORME

Palais des Sports

RUE

République Bus Station

RUE PASTEUR

RUE DES ÉTUVES

Musée d'Aquitaine

P

Grosse Cloche

PLACE DE LA RÉPUBLIQUE

Musée d'Aquitaine (T)

COURS VICTOR HUGO

COURS VICTO

RUE DE CURSOL

RUE PAUL LOUIS LANDE

RUE CANIHAC

RUE HONORÉ TESSIER

RUE SAINTE-CATHERINE

RUE DU MIRAIL

Hôpital Saint-André ✚

RUE JEAN BURGUET

RUE DU COMMANDANT ARNOULD

COURS PASTEUR

Parc aux
Angéliques

e Vert
uais

*Quinconces
(Jean-Jaurès)*

Parc fleuri
du Miroir
d'eau

LA BASTIDE

RUE NUYENS

RÈS L'AUTRE QUAI

ALLÉE JEAN GIONO

RUE JEAN-PAUL ALAUX

RUE LÉONCE MOTELAY

R. NUYENS

QUAI DES QUEYRIES

RUE LOUIS
EMIÉ

ALLÉE DU PARIS-ORLÉANS

**Cinéma
Megarama**

ALLÉE SERR

RUE HONORÉ
PICON

ALLÉE SERR

RUE FOURTEAU

QUAI DES QUEYRIES

RUE SEM

*Stalingrad
(Parlier)*

**Miroir
d'eau**

OURSE

**National
uanes**

Ⓣ

QUAI DE LA DOUANE

Place de la Bourse

*Embarcadère
des Quinconces*

Jardins des
Lumières

PASSERELLE GARONNE

Ga r o n n e

PLACE
DE STALINGRAD

Stalingrad

Ⓐ Ⓣ

DES AIDES

RUE DU CHAI DES FARINES

*Ponton
d'honneur*

PARVIS MAISON
ÉCOCITOYENNE

RUE DU QUAI
BOURGOGNE

PLACE
DU PALAIS

**Porte
Cailhau**

QUAI RICHELIEU

QUAI RICHELIEU

PONT DE PIERRE

*Place du
Palais*

Ⓣ

R. DE LA PRÉE
SAINT-JEAN

RUE DE LA HALLE

RUE AUSONE

IMP. FAURE

RUE DU MUGUET

RUE DE LA ROUSSELLE

RUE NEUVE

RUE DU PUITS DESCAZEAUX

RUE DU SOLEIL

RUE RENIÈRE

IMP. DE LA FONT BOUQUIÈRE

Porte de Bourgogne

Ⓣ

**Porte de
Bourgogne**

QUAI DES SALINIÈRES

COURS VICTOR HUGO

RUE GENSAN

RUE DES PONTETS

RUE DE LA TOUR DU PIN

RUE DE LA FUSTERIE

QUAI DES SALINIÈRES

Ⓟ

QUAI DE LA GRAVE

R. DE L'OBSERVANCE

RUE PILET

RUE DABADIE

RUE MAUBEC

RUE DES FAURES

RUE GABILLON

RUE DES MENUTS

RUE SAINT-FRANÇOIS

SAINT-MICHEL

RUE DES FAURES

PL. DUBURG

QUAI DE LA MONNAIE

Saint-Michel

Ⓣ

RUE CARPENTEYRE

**Flèche
Saint-Michel**

PL. CANTELOUP

✝

R. DASVIN

**Basilique
Saint-Michel**

RUE DES ALLAMANDIERS

N

0		200

metres

Palais Gallien

Jardin Public

Jardin

Monume
aux Girondi

Quin

L'Éco
de Bo

**SAINT SEURIN-
FONDAUDEGE**

Fondaudège Museum

PL. TOURNY

TRIANGLE D'O

Les Grands
Hommes

Salle Capitulaire

Gran
Théât

Basilique St-Seurin

Site Archéologique
de St-Seurin

**Porte
Dijeaux**

Gambetta

Grand

Jardin
Georges
Mandel

Piscine Judaïque

Cimetière
Protestant

**Centre
Commercial
Saint-Christaly**

HÔTEL DE VILLE

Musée des
Arts Décoratifs

Musée de
l'illusion

MÉRIADECK
Mériadeck
Shopping Mall

**Palais
Rohan**

**Monuments
aux Morts**

**Église
Saint-Bruno**

Saint-Bruno -
Hôtel de Région

Mériadeck

Musée des
Beaux-Arts

Jardins
de la Mairie

Cathédrale
Saint-André

Tour Pey-Berland

Hôtel de
Ville

ESPLANADE
CHARLES DE GAULLE

Bordeaux
Métropole

Mus
d'Ac

Cimetière
de la Chartreuse

Fort
du Hâ

Palais de Justice

Musée
d'Aquitaine

Hôtel de Police

Library
Mériadeck

République
Bus Station

Patinoire de
Mériadeck

PLACE DE LA
RÉPUBLIQUE

Gra
Synagog

**SAINT-BRUNO
-SAINT-VICTOR**

Hôpital
Saint-André

Église
Sainte-Eulalie

SAINT-GENÈS

Saint-Nicolas

Saint

Chapelle
des Dames
de la Foi

Bergonie

Saint

N

0			400

metres

Parc aux Angéliques

Archives de Bordeaux

RUE RAYMOND LAVIGNE
RUE REIGNIER
RUE HORTENSE
RUE DE LA ROTONDE

Quinconces

PL. DE MUNICH

Jardin Botanique de Bordeaux

LA BASTIDE

CONCES
ES

ALLÉE JEAN GIONO

AVENUE ABADIE

AVENUE THIERS

Espace Vert des Quais

QUAI LOUIS XVIII

D'ORLÉANS

RUE NOYENS
RES L'AUTRE QUAI

ALLÉE JEAN GIONO

Quinconces (Jean-Jaurès)

QUAI DES QUEYRIES

R. JEAN-PAUL ALAUX

RUE LÉONCE MOTELAY

RUE NOYENS

Sainte-Marie de la Bastide

AVENUE THIERS

RUE PAUL CAMELLE
RUE DE NUITS
RUE DE DIJON

Parc fleuri du Miroir d'eau

QUAI DE LA DOUANE

QUAI MARECHAL LHUITY

Miroir d'eau

Stalingrad (Parlier)

ALLÉE DU PARC-ORLÉANS

ALLÉE SERR

R. SAINTE-MARIE

R. DUBESSAN

Jardin Botanique

RUE PAUL CHABRELY

Maison Cantonale

RUE DE CHATEAUNEUF

Palais de la Bourse

PLACE DE LA BOURSE

Cinéma Megarama

ALLÉE SERR

RUE JARDEL

AVENUE THIERS

Musée national des Douanes

SAINT-PIERRE

Embarcadère des Quinconces

Place de la Bourse

Jardins des Lumières

QUAI DES QUEYRIES

RUE SEM

R. HONORÉ

R. FOURTEAU PICON

PLACE DE STALINGRAD

Stalingrad

RUE CAVIMONT

RUE MONTMEJEAN

RUE DE LA BENAUGE

RUE PROMIS

Ponton d'honneur

PARVIS MAISON ÉCOCITOYENNE

RUE SEM

RUE HENRI DUNANT

RUE DE CÉNAC

SAINT-PIERRE

R. MAUCOU-DINAT

Porte Cailhau

PL. DU PALAIS

RUE SEM

RUE DE LA SAUVE

SENTE DE LA FREGATE

RUE RENÉ BUITHAUD

Benauge

QUAI RICHELIEU

Place du Palais

Porte de Bourgogne

P

QUAI DESCHAMPS

RUE DES OSIERS

Porte de Bourgogne

QUAI DES SALINIERS

Parc des Berges

RUE DE LA GARONNE

Marché Neuf

QUAI DESCHAMPS

COURS VICTOR HUGO

QUAI DES SALINIERS

QUAI DE LA GRAVE

Garonne

SAINT-MICHEL

Marché Royal

Basilique Saint-Michel

P

QUAI DE LA MONNAIE

Saint-Michel

Flèche de la Basilique

PL. CANTELOUP

R.G. PHILIPPE

QUAI DE LA MONNAIE

R. CARPENTEYRE

Conservatoire de Bordeaux - Jacques Thibaud

Saint-Croix

BD DES FRÈRES MOGA

Musée d'Ethnographie

Théâtre National de Bordeaux en Aquitaine

PL. PIERRE RENAUDEL

Église Sainte-Croix

QUAI DE PALUDATE

PONT SAINT-JEAN

CAPUCINS - VICTOIRE

RUE ÉLIE GINTRAC

COURS DE LA MARNE

PLACE DES CAPUCINS

Marché des Capucins

RUE DES DOUVES

RUE JULES GUESDE

R.E. LAPARRA

R. DU MOUTON

Château Descas

RUE JEAN DESCAS

BOULEVARD DES FRÈRES MOGA

RUE DE TAUZIA

PLACE ANDRÉ MEUNIER

Tauzia

BELCIER

QUAI DE PALUDATE

COURS DE LA MARNE

SAINT-JEAN

Saint-Jean Train Station

RUE DE SAGET

RUE DE BAC NINH
PONT EN U
R. CAMBON

Gare Saint-Jean

Gare Saint-Jean Bus Station

RUE MORION

RUE LAFITEAU

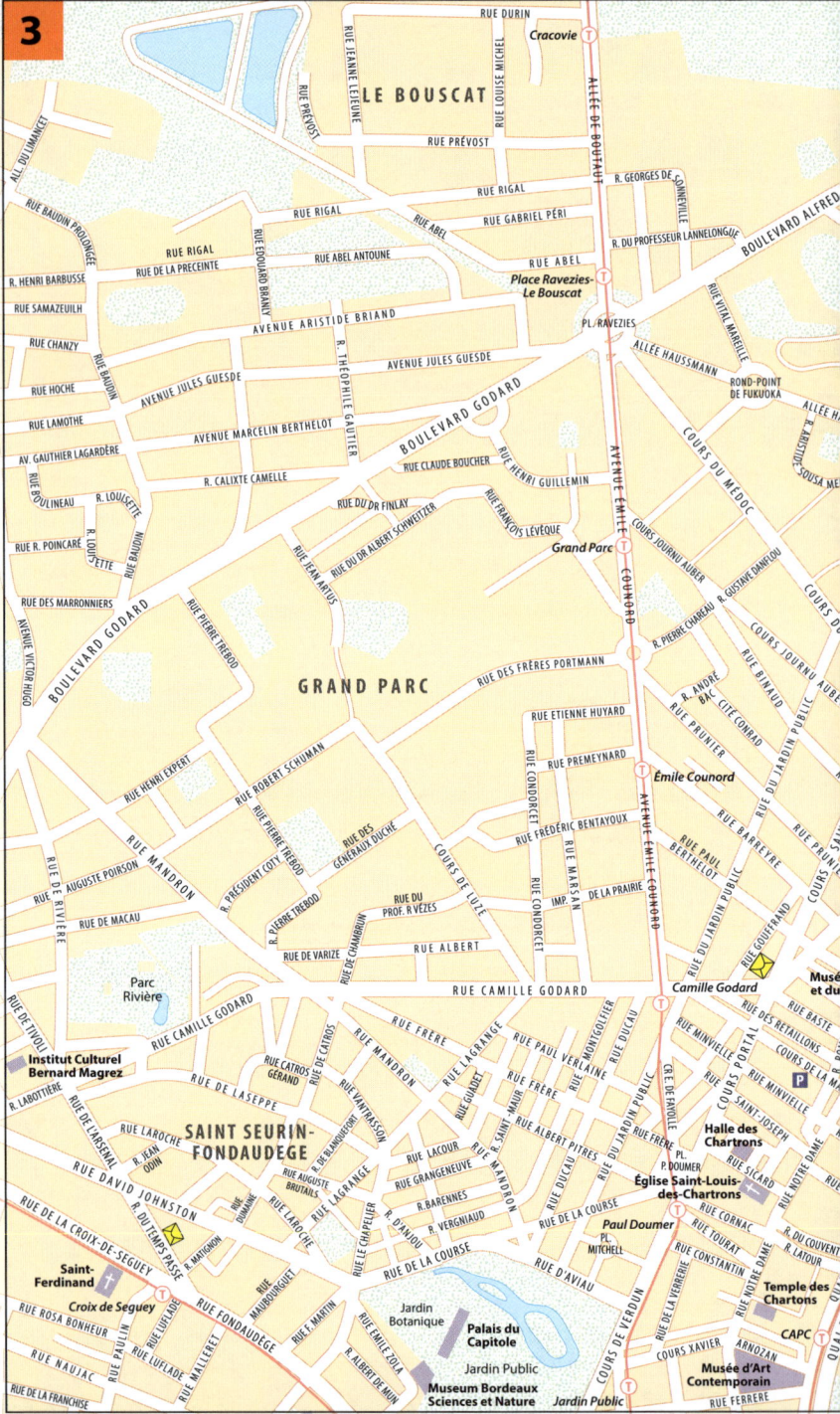

3

RUE DURIN

Cracovie

LE BOUSCAT

RUE JEANNE LEFEBVRE

RUE PRÉVOST

RUE LOUISE MICHEL

ALLÉE DE BOUTAUT

RUE PRÉVOST

RUE RIGAL

R. GEORGES DE SONNEVILLE

RUE RIGAL

RUE ABEL

RUE GABRIEL PÉRI

R. DU PROFESSEUR LANNELONGUE

BOULEVARD ALFRED

ALL. DU LIMANCET

RUE BAUDIN PROLONGÉE

RUE RIGAL

RUE RIGAL

RUE ÉDOUARD BRANLY

RUE ABEL ANTOUNE

RUE ABEL

Place Ravezies-Le Bouscat

RUE VITAL MAREILLE

R. HENRI BARBUSSE

RUE DE LA PRECEINTE

PL. RAVEZIES

RUE SAMAZEUILH

AVENUE ARISTIDE BRIAND

ALLÉE HAUSSMANN

RUE CHANZY

R. THÉOPHILE GAUTIER

AVENUE JULES GUESDE

ROND-POINT DE FUKUOKA

ALLÉE H

RUE HOCHE

RUE BAUDIN

AVENUE JULES GUESDE

BOULEVARD GODARD

COURS DU MÉDOC

RUE LAMOTHE

COURS DE L

AV. GAUTHIER LAGARDÈRE

AVENUE MARCELIN BERTHELOT

RUE HENRI GUILLEMIN

-SOUSA ME

RUE BOULINEAU

R. CALIXTE CAMELLE

RUE CLAUDE BOUCHER

AVENUE ÉMILE COUNORD

R. LOUISETTE

RUE DU DR FINLAY

RUE FRANÇOIS LÉVÊQUE

COURS JOURNU AUBER

RUE R. POINCARÉ

R. LOUISETTE

RUE BAUDIN

RUE JEAN ARTUS

RUE DU DR ALBERT SCHWEITZER

Grand Parc

R. PIERRE CHAMEAU

RUE GUSTAVE DAMELOU

COURS D

RUE DES MARRONNIERS

BOULEVARD GODARD

RUE PIERRE TRÉBOD

RUE DES FRÈRES PORTMANN

R. ANDRÉ BAC CITÉ CONRAD

COURS JOURNU AUBER

AVENUE VICTOR HUGO

RUE ÉTIENNE HUYARD

RUE BIMAUD

RUE DU JARDIN PUBLIC

GRAND PARC

RUE PREMEYNARD

RUE PRUNIER

RUE CONDORCET

Émile Counord

RUE HENRI EXPERT

RUE ROBERT SCHUMAN

RUE FRÉDÉRIC BENTAYOUX

RUE BARREYRE

RUE PAUL BERTHELOT

RUE PRUNIE

RUE PIERRE TRÉBOD

RUE DES GÉNÉRAUX DUCHÉ

RUE MARSAN

RUE D' AUGUSTE POIRSON

RUE MANDRON

RUE PRÉSIDENT COTY

COURS DE LUZE

IMP. DE LA PRAIRIE

COURS S

RUE DE RIVIÈRE

R. PIERRE TRÉBOD

RUE DU PROF. R. VÉZES

RUE CONDORCET

AVENUE ÉMILE COUNORD

RUE DE MACAU

RUE DE CHAMBRUN

RUE GOUFFRAND

Musé et du

RUE ALBERT

RUE DE VARIZE

RUE DU JARDIN PUBLIC

RUE DES RETAILLONS

RUE BASTE

Parc Rivière

RUE CAMILLE GODARD

RUE CAMILLE GODARD

Camille Godard

RUE MINVIELLE

COURS PORTAL

COURS DE LA M

RUE DE TIVOLI

Institut Culturel Bernard Magrez

RUE CATROS GÉRAND

RUE DE CATROS

RUE MANDRON

RUE FRÈRE

RUE PAUL VERLAINE

RUE MONTGOLFIER

RUE DUCAU

RUE MINVIELLE

P

R. LABOTTIÈRE

RUE DE LASEPPE

RUE VANTRASSON

RUE LAGRANGE

RUE FRÈRE

CITÉ DE FAYOLE

RUE SAINT-JOSEPH

RUE DE L'ARSENAL

RUE LAROCHE

RUE DE BLANQUEFORT

RUE GUADET

RUE R. SAINT-MAUR

RUE DU JARDIN PUBLIC

RUE FRÈRE

Halle des Chartrons

RUE NOTRE DAME

SAINT SEURIN-FONDAUDÈGE

R. JEAN ODIN

RUE AUGUSTE BRUTAILS

RUE LACOUR

RUE ALBERT PITRES

RUE MANDRON

PL. P. DOUMER

RUE SICARD

RUE DAVID JOHNSTON

RUE LAGRANGE

RUE LAROCHE

RUE GRANGENEUVE

RUE DUCAU

Église Saint-Louis-des-Chartrons

RUE CORNAC

R. DIMANIE

RUE LE CHAPELIER

R. BARENNES

R. D'ANJOU

RUE VERGNIAUD

RUE DE LA COURSE

Paul Doumer

RUE TOURAT

R. DU COUVENT

R. LATOUR

RUE DE LA CROIX-DE-SEGUEY

R. DU TEMPS PASSÉ

PL. MITCHELL

RUE CONSTANTIN

Temple des Chartrons

Saint-Ferdinand

R. MATIGNON

RUE MAUBOURGUET

RUE DE LA COURSE

RUE D'AVIAU

RUE DE LA VERRERIE

Croix de Seguey

RUE FONDAUDÈGE

RUE T. MARTIN

RUE DE VERDUN

CAPC

RUE ROSA BONHEUR

RUE PAULIN

RUE LUFLADE

RUE MALLERET

RUE ÉMILE ZOLA

Jardin Botanique

Palais du Capitole

Jardin Public

Musée d'Art Contemporain

RUE NAUJAC

R. ALBERT DE MUN

COURS XAVIER

ARNOZAN

RUE DE LA FRANCHISE

Museum Bordeaux Sciences et Nature

Jardin Public

RUE FERRERE

BACALAN

CITÉ DUTREY
New York
R. CHARLEVOIX DE VILLERS

PL. ADOLPHE BUSCAILLET

Église Saint Rémi

BOULEVARD ALFRED DANEY

P

Bassins des Lumières

RUE DE NEW YORK

RUE PROFESSEUR VILLEMIN

RUE CHARLEVOIX DE VILLERS

COURS DUPRÉ SAINT-MAUR

RUE LUCIE AUBRAC

RUE BLANQUI

RUE POURMANN

RUE ACHARD

QUAI VIRGINIE HERIOT

RUE LUCIEN FAURE

Bassins à Flot n° 2

QUAI HENRI BRUNET

QUAI HUBERT PROM

RUE DANIEL IFFLA OSIRIS

RUE DELBOS

RUE DELBOS

Musée Mer Marine

RUE DES ÉTRANGERS

R. DE OUAGADOUGOU

Rue Achard

PL. PIERRE CÉTOIS

BASSINS À FLOT

AN HAMEAU

COURS LOUIS TARGUE

COURS DU RACCORDEMENT

RUE BOILEAU

R. ARMAND DULAMON

RUE BOURBON

RUE MARCEL PAGNOL

RUE LUCIEN FAURE

QUAI LAWTON

Bassins à Flot n° 1

RUE DES ÉTRANGERS

RUE BLANQUI

RUE DE GIRONDE

Les Vivres de l'Art

P

PL. VICTOR RAULIN

CITÉ CHANTECRIT

Parc Chante-Grillon

PL. LEWIS BROWN

COURS EDOUARD VAILLANT

R. DU COMMANDANT HAUTREUX

RUE DE LA FAÏENCERIE

RUE CHARLES DURAND

Musée de l'Histoire Maritime de Bordeaux

The Spaceship

Vertigina

Les Halles de Bacalan

QUAI DU MAROC

QUAI ARMAND LALANDE

QUAI DU SÉNÉGAL

Cité du Vin

AN-LOUIS

RUE DE LEYBARDIE

RUE LUCIEN FAURE

RUE BOURBON

RUE LUCIEN FAURE

QUAI DE BACALAN

QUAI DE BACALAN

La Cité du Vin

CHARTRONS

COURS BALGUERIE STUTTENBERG

R. VEILLARD

R. DURET

RUE JOSÉPHINE

RUE DELORD

RUE CHANTECRIT

RUE DUPATY

COURS EDOUARD VAILLANT

RUE DELORD

RUE BOURBON

RUE DUPATY

CAP Sciences

P

PONT JACQUES CHABAN DELMAS

E STUTTENBERG

PL. SAINT-MARTIAL

RUE SURSON

RUE LOMBARD

RUE MAURICE

RUE CHARLES PUVO

Église Saint-Martial

COURS DU MÉDOC

RUE DENISE

Les Hangars

QUAI DE BACALAN

QUAI DE BACALAN

RUE POYENNE

R. DARBON

PL. PAUL ET JEAN-PAUL AVISSEAU

P

P

QUAI DES CHARTRONS

QUAI DES CHARTRONS

Cours du Médoc

Les Hangars (Médoc)

Garonne

PEYRE

Chartrons

Bastide Darwin

QUAI DE BRAZZA

QUAI DE BRAZZA

RUE RENE CHAR

RUE DU COMMANDANT COUSTEAU

RUE JOSEPH BONNET

BASTIDE-BRAZZA

PARC D'ACTIVITÉS DES QUEYRIES

P

RUE DU MARÉCHAL NIEL

RUE BOUTHIER

N

Darwin Eco-Système

RUE HORTENSE

BASTIDE-NIEL

0 ——————— 400
metres

BORDEAUX TRAMS

- Line A
- Line B
- Line C
- Line D

Carré des Jalles
La Boëtie
Germignan
Chai
Cantinolle
Les Sources
Eysines-Centre
Picot
Simone Veil
Hippodrome
Champ de Courses-Treulon
Sainte Germaine
Les Écus
Mairie du Bouscat
Calypso

Gare de Banquefort
Frankton
Gare de Bruges
Ausone
La Vache
Cracovie
Place Ravezies–Le Bouscat
Grand Parc
Émile Counord
Camille Godard
Paul Doumer

Parc des Expositions-
Stade Matmut-Atlantique
Palais des Congrès
Quarante Journaux
Berges du Lac
Les Aubiers

Berges de la Garonne
Cleveau
La Gardette-
Bassens-
Carbon Blanc
Carriet
Mairie de Lormont
Brandenburg
New York
Rue Achard
La Cité du Vin
Les Hangars
Cours du Médoc
Chartrons
Lauriers
Bois Fleuri
Iris
Buttinière
Carnot
Cenon Gare
Jean Jaurès
Galin

Le Hailland-Rostan
Les Pins
Hôtel de Ville Mérignac
Frères Robinson
Pin Galant
Mérignac Centre
Lycées de Mérignac

Courbet
Barriere du Médoc
Croix-de-Seguey
Fondaudège Museum

Jardin
Public
CAPC
Palmer
Thiers-Benauge
Pelletan
Jardin Botanique
La Morlette

Aéroport de Bordeaux-
Mérignac
Lindbergh
Gadera
Parc Chemin-Long
Mérignac
Soleil
St-Bruno-Hôtel de Région
Quatre
Chemins
Pierre
Mendès-France
Alfred de Vigny

Quinconces
Palais de Justice
Mériadeck
Gambetta
Grand
Théâtre
Place de
la Bourse
Stalingrad
Jean Zay
La Marègue

Fontaine d'Arlac
Peychotte
Stade Chaban-Delmas
Hôtel Pellegrin
Saint-Augustin
François Mitterand
Hôtel de Ville
Musée
d'Aquitaine
Hôtel de Police
Victoire
Saint-Nicolas
Bergonié

Sainte-Catherine
Place du Palais
Porte de Bourgogne
Saint-Michel
Sainte-Croix
Tauzia
Gare Saint-Jean
Belcier

Floirac-
Dravemont

Carle Vernet
Terres Neuves
La Belle Rose
Stage Musard
Calais Centujean

Barrière-Saint-Genès
Roustaing
Forum
Peixotto
Béthanie
Arts et Métiers
François Bordes

Montaigne Montesquieu
Doyen Brus
UNITEC
Saige

Pessac Centre
Camponac
Médiathèque

Gare de Bègles
Parc de Mussonville
Lycée Václav Havel
Villenave d'Ornon
Pont de la Maye

Bougnard
Châtaigneraie
Cap Métiers
Hôpital Haut-Léveque
Gare Pessac Alouette
France Alouette

Villenave Pyrénées